SCIENCE AND TECHNOLOGY
OF OIL SHALE

edited by

T. F. Yen

Associate Professor of Chemical Engineering
Environmental Engineering Sciences
and Medicine (Biochemistry)
University of Southern California, Los Angeles

ANN ARBOR SCIENCE
PUBLISHERS INC
P.O. BOX 1425 • ANN ARBOR, MICH. 48106

FOREWORD

Dr. Yen is to be congratulated on revealing so much information on the important subject, oil shale. His is the first comprehensive discussion since 1925 of the potential value and the problems—technical, economic and environmental—connected with the commercial development of our large resources of oil shale.

The 1925 ACS Monograph #25, *Shale Oil*, authored by Professor Ralph H. McKee and several others I knew in the Chemical Engineering Department at Columbia University, served a very useful purpose at the time but is long out of date. In this volume Dr. Yen has contributed a great deal from his own important studies on oil shale at the University of Southern California and in addition has presented the current research of authorities in related disciplines.

It is a pleasure for me to write this foreword to a modern book on oil shale at a time when all energy sources are so vitally important.

Robert Evans Vivian
Dean-Emeritus, School of Engineering
Emeritus Professor of Chemical Engineering
Vivian Hall of Engineering
University of Southern California
Los Angeles, California

March 1976

PREFACE

The most abundant organic matter on earth is known as kerogen. It is found in various concentrations in mineral matrices such as sedimentary rock or marlstone. These mineral systems, in a materials science sense, form a composite termed *oil shale* due to its ability to yield oil from the kerogen portion upon heating. Presently there are vast amounts of oil shale deposits throughout our globe.

The United States has a very extensive oil shale reserve. Even excluding the vast marine shale deposits of Alaska and the southeastern United States, the reserves of the Green River Formation of Colorado, Utah and Wyoming alone are equivalent to an oil resource of at least two trillion barrels. Nevertheless, the science and technology of oil shale have been neglected due to the availability of petroleum and the ease of its refining.

Oil shale could prove to be an alternate route in supplementing our current short supply of petroleum. This book marks the first systematic monograph on this topic published in the United States within the last five decades. Hopefully, the contents will stimulate future workers to revive this forgotten but greatly needed field of energy sources.

The editor is grateful for the patience and cooperation of the many oil shale experts who contributed to this volume. Furthermore, two major companies in the oil shale industry have unveiled their processes in this book. The only governmental research center on oil shale also contributed three important papers. The editor extends his thanks to the publisher for providing the color illustrations located in the front of the book. He further wishes to acknowledge the assistance of many of his students and associates, and particularly the clerical assistance of Donna Jue, Judy Dang, and Barbara James.

T. F. Yen

Los Angeles, California January, 1976

CONTENTS

v

Chapter

OIL SHALES OF UNITED STATES–A REVIEW

T. F. Yen

Division of Petroleum and Chemical Engineering
University of Southern California
Los Angeles, California

About 90% of the earth's continental area is covered with a veneer of sedimentary rocks. As the continental U.S. contains no extensive shield areas, its sedimentary cover is somewhat more extensive than the global average. Slightly more than 5% of the sedimentary rocks in the U.S. are shales containing organics equal to or greater than 5%.

Oil shale is commonly defined as organic-rich shale that can yield substantial quantities of oil when subjected to destructive distillation by low confining pressure in a closed retort system. The oil shale deposit which yields at least 10 gallons (3.8 wt %) of oil per short ton of shale by such extraction method is considered the lowest boundary of oil shale. For the upper boundary, certain Australian shale reaches 90+%. The quality of oil shale can be graded as lean or rich depending on the oil yield. Some typical, well-known oil shales are listed in Table 1.1.[1,2]

Other definitions of oil shale, depending on sources, uses, or physical and chemical properties of the shale, can be found elsewhere.[3-6] One such definition is to further limit the minimum ash content to 33% of the oil-yielding shales. According to this definition, any fossil fuel source material which contains less than 33% ash does not belong to oil shale, such as coal or tar sands in general. The definition used by the present author is quite broad: any organic-rich shale, whether yielding oil or gas upon heating, can be classified as oil shale.

In the past, oil shale of U.S. has usually referred to the shale of Green River Formation. Consequently, all official reports and estimates[7-9] are

Table 1.1   Composition and Oil Yield of Some Oil Shales

Location of Sample	% Org. C	% S	% N	% Ash	Oil Yield (gal/ton)
Kiligwa River, Alaska[1]	53.9	1.5	0.30	34.1	139
Piceance Creek, Colorado[1]	12.4	0.63	0.41	65.7	28
Elko, Nevada[2]	8.6	1.1	0.48	81.6	8.4
Dunnet, Scotland[1]	12.3	0.73	0.46	77.8	22
Ione, California[2]	62.9	2.1	0.42	23	52
Sao Paulo, Brazil[1]	12.8	0.84	0.41	75.0	18
Puertollano, Spain[1]	26.0	1.7	0.55	62.8	47
Shale City, Oregon[1]	25.8	2.2	0.51	48.3	48
Coolaway Mt., Australia[1]	81.4	0.49	0.83	4.4	200
Soldiers Summit, Utah[2]	13.5	0.28	0.39	66.1	17
Ermelo, South South Africa[1]	52.2	0.74	0.84	33.6	100
New Glasgow, Canada	7.92	0.70	0.54	84.0	9.4

based on a single formation only. The reason, of course, is that only the Green River Shale is being thoroughly studied. Only recently, due to the energy shortage of 1973, one is awakened to the alternative sources of energy—the diluted sources of kerogen, bitumen and hydrocarbons.[10,11] Such an amount is vast when compared with the concentrated fossil fuels such as petroleum and coal deposits (Figure 1.1).

The objective of this chapter is to call attention to all scientists and engineers directly involved in supply/demand estimates and projections or in the survey of domestic reserves of fossil fuels. The present figures may be underestimated and as new technology is developed, based on scientific discoveries, future projection undoubtedly could be made more accurately for the use of oil shale and shale oil (Table 1.2).

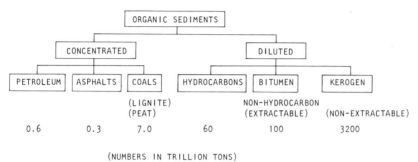

Figure 1.1   Classification of organic sediments.   The abundance of various fossil fuels in the ecosystem is present in trillion tons.

Table 1.2   Supply Estimates of Shale Oil of 1985 (in Q)[a]

Agency	Dates	Supply
Federal Energy Administraiton Project Independence	November, 1974	2.1[b]
Ford Foundation	September, 1974	1[c]
National Petroleum Council	December, 1972	1.5
National Petroleum Council	August, 1974	0.2
National Academy of Engineering	May, 1974	1
Joint Committee on Atomic Energy	May, 1974	0.2
Institute of Gas Technology	December, 1973	2.1
Commerce Technical Advisory Board	February, 1975	0.5

[a]The total energy demand for 1985 is 108 Q (3.1% growth) or 125 Q (4.3% growth). Total domestic supply is approximate as 94Q still require 14Q (based on 3.1% growth) for imports.   Domestic oil supply is about 25Q and synthetic oil supply is 0.3Q in 1985.

[b]Based on $11 oil acc. supply.

[c]Based on growth for technical fix.

[d]This value is for Case I;   for Case II and III, 0.8Q and for Case IV 0.2Q.

POTENTIAL AND DISTRIBUTION OF OIL SHALES

It is not generally realized that extraction and upgrading of the organic components of oil shales other than Green River Formation will yield oil and gas. Even for the Green River Formation in Colorado, Utah and Wyoming, the deposits of the known resources are estimated to contain 1.9-2.0 trillion bbl of crude oil equivalence (See Table 1.3 for shale of 10 gal/ton or higher). Within the 600 billion bbl of oil equivalence of high-grade shale (25-100 gal/ton), an 80 billion bbl of oil equivalence can be readily recovered using current technology (Figure 1.2). This alone would replace the domestic supply of oil for 20 years.

Table 1.3   Shale Oil Resource of Green River Formation
(in billions of barrels of oil equivalence)

	25-100[a]	10-25	5-10
Known Resources	600[b]	1400	2000
Possible Extension	600	1400	2000
Undiscovered and Unappraised	–	–	–
Total	1200	2800	4000
Grand Total[c]			8000

[a]Grades of shale based on oil equivalence of gal/ton.
[b]The known resource can be further related to different usages in Figure 1.2.
[c]Equivalent to 45,000 Q.

Numerous organic-rich shale deposits from widely different geologic ages occur throughout the U.S. They range in age from Precambrian to tertiary and may be grouped as follows, in order of increasing age:

1. Pleiocene and Miocene and Sisquoc and Monterey Formations of diatomaceous shales of California.
2. Eocene shales of the Green River Formation of the tri-states.
3. Jurassic and Triassic marine shales of northern Alaska.
4. Permian shales of the Phosphoria Formation of southern Montana
5. Pennsylvania Cannel-Shale deposits of the eastern United States.
6. Devonian and Mississippian shales of the central and eastern United States (Chattanooga shale).

7. Ordovician Black shales of the Appalachian Basin (Maquoketa Shale and Utica Shale).

8. Nonesuch shales of Precambrian Age in Michigan and Wisconsin.

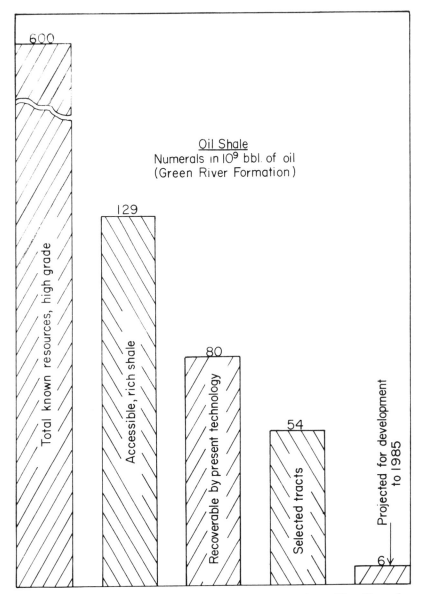

Figure 1.2   Total known high-grade oil shale resources of Green River Formation and the projected amount for development (expressed in billion bbl of oil).

These domestic sources are roughly located in the map of Figure 1.3. In many cases, only a rough guess of the location is available. From Table 1.4 it is obvious that the U.S. oil shale source is huge. It is estimated that potential resource from shales other than the Green River Formation may yield on the order of 130 trillion barrels of oil. Evidently reserves of this general magnitude represent a portable liquid fuel supply for over 200 years (projected oil for the year of 1985 is 4.3 billion bbl).

CURRENT RECOVERY TECHNOLOGY

Extraction of oil from shale in the last five decades in the U.S. was limited to the Green River Formation; however, small-scale recovery has been experimented with in Nevada, California, and Kentucky. The following is a survey of recovery processes; namely mining, retorting, and upgrading. Regarding retorting, current thinking is that only the *in situ* method will be practical for the future.[13]

A room-and-pillar method is believed to be the most practical underground mining system. Since large reserves are available, the underground mining is confined to the 30-90-foot thickness of 30 gal/ton and richer oil shale situated in the Mahogany zone of the Parachute Creek member of the Green River Formation. An underground room-and-pillar mine can be entered through an adit, shaft, or incline, depending upon the location of the oil zone relative to the surface, topography, disposal site, underground water, rock mechanics and other considerations. Materials, handling systems, economics and other parameters will depend upon the type of mine entry utilized. The recovery of oil shale from the room-and-pillar operation will depend upon the overburden; for example, if an oil zone is not encumbered by more than 1500 ft of overburden, then the room heights from 30-60 ft can be constructed and 65-75% oil shale recovery can be achieved.

Applications of surface mining techniques such as open pit and strip mining may be useful in the Green River, Washakie, Piceance and Uinta Basins and other areas containing significant shale oil deposits.

Surface mining techniques have been successfully employed in coal mines and ores of other resource recovery industries. Generally, in the areas of oil shale deposits, both overburden and oil shale will require drilling and blasting and use of large "jumbo" rotary drills. Large shovels, draglines and trucks will be required to move the blasted material to the disposed area or to primary crushers from which ores or wastes would be conveyed to either a dump or a processing area. The advantages of surface mining are the relative safety aspects and the capability for recovering nearly all of the oil shale in a given zone. Major disadvantages are the overburden limitation and the large amount of surface area disturbance.

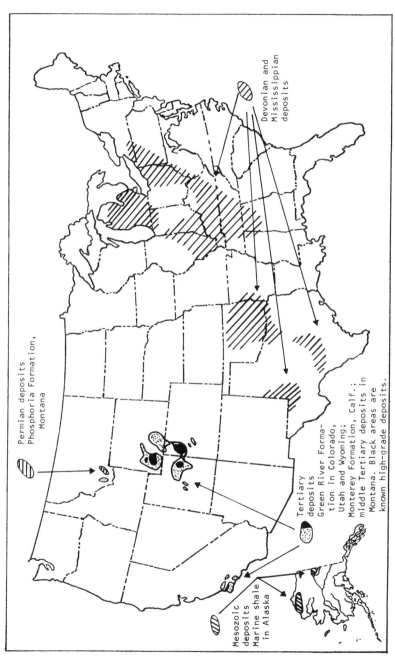

Figure 1.3 Location of U.S. oil shale deposits and types.

Table 1.4   Oil Shale Resources of U.S. (in billion bbl)

Deposits	Oil Equivalent		
	25-100[a]	10-25	5-10
Green River Formation	1,200	2,800	4,000
Devonian and Mississippian Shale	–	1,000	2,000
Alaskan Marine Shale	250	200	large
Shale associated with coal	60	250	210
Other shales	500	22,000	134,000
Ordovician Black Shale			
Permiam Phosphoria Formation			
Monterey Shale			
Cretaceous Shale beds			
Nonesuch Shale, etc.			

[a]Oil yields in gal/ton.[12]

RETORTING TECHNOLOGY

The oil retorting processes can be classified as either *ex situ* (or surface, off the sites) and *in situ* (or subsurface, within the existing formation). Each process has its advantages and disadvantages. These have been stated in a recent Congressional Hearing on Oil Shale Technology.[13] The following is a summary:

Ex situ recovery

Advantages

1. Recovery efficiency has been demonstrated to be high; (up to 80-90% of the organic content of the retorted shale).
2. Adequate control of process variables is possible.

Disadvantages:

1. Operation cost is high (oil shale must be mined, transported and crushed).
2. Spent shale disposal and land revegetation problems have not been solved.
3. Pollution control is difficult (required for mining, transportation and crushing).
4. Limited only to the rich shale resources accessible for mining.

In situ recovery

Advantages

1. Environmentally desirable because all operations are conducted through well bores. Neither mining nor spent shale disposal is required.
2. Oil can be recovered from deep deposits of oil shale formation.
3. It can extract oil from leaner shale, *e.g.*, deposits containing less than 15 gal/ton.
4. More economic due to elimination or reduction of cost in mining, transportation and crushing.

Disadvantages

1. Process control is difficult due to insufficient permeability and communication within the shale formation.
2. Recovery efficiency is generally lower.
3. Possible contamination of subsurface water.

To compare the advantages versus disadvantages, the *in situ* methods for production of oil from shales optimize recovery economy while minimizing environmental impact. Consequently, considerable emphasis has been placed on *in situ* processes.

Ex Situ Processes

These are processes in which shale rock is mined (surface or underground), crushed, then conveyed to a retorter, where it is subjected to temperatures ranging from 500-550°C in which the chemical bonds linking the organic compounds to the remainder of the rock matrix are broken. The liberated compounds, in the gaseous state, are collected, condensed, and upgraded into a liquid product that is roughly equivalent to a crude oil. This oil is shipped by pipeline to a refinery, where it is refined into the final product.

The first major experimental retort was built 25 years ago and operated by the Bureau of Mines, in Rifle, Colorado. This retort was capable of processing six tons of shale rock daily. Since that time, many private firms have become interested in oil shale extraction and have developed alternate retorting systems. Among these are the Union Oil, Cameron and Jones, TOSCO, NTU and Lurgi-Rohrgas processes. These systems have several limiting factors in common. Among these factors are:

1. Each system requires the use of energy. For every barrel of oil produced, the retorting phase alone will require net energy roughly equivalent to 3/25 of a barrel. In equivalent terms, for each barrel of energy produced, about 12% of a barrel will be needed to supply the energy for the process.

2. Current retorting methods are very inefficient with respect to liberating the organic material found in oil shale. State-of-the-art technology at best can remove 70% of the organic material contained in shale rock. The remaining 30% is connected to the inorganic matrix and is not available as an energy source.

3. The retorting processes result in a large volume of expended shale that must be disposed of. A 100,000 bbl/day plant would require the daily disposal of 4,000 tons of shale rock. Not only must this amount of material be moved and stored, but means must be taken to insure that the mineral contained in the disposed materials cannot get into the ground water and/or the local streams flowing in the area.

A few processes have been exhaustively studied. While they have some basic similarities, each process has a nature inherently its own.

Union Oil

The Union Oil process is one in which the heat needed for retorting is provided by combustion of coke inside the retort. The shale which is fed in the base is pushed up by means of a specially developed pump. The resulting oil is siphoned out at the bottom of the retort.

Cameron and Jones

This process injects heat via an external source. The shale is fed in at the top of the retort and the spent shale removed at the base. Recycled gas heated in a furnace is used as the heat source for the process. All heat utilized in the process comes solely from external sources. The Petrosix process uses this configuration.

TOSCO–II

This process also generates heat at an external source. Ceramic balls that are externally heated and continuously recycled are used to supply the heat for the retort. The shale rock and the balls are fed into a drum structure where the retorting process takes place. The resulting spent shale and oil vapors are removed and the balls sent back to the heater for reheating.

NTU

This process is the model used to design the Garrett Process. It was developed by U.S. Bureau of Mines during the late 1940s. Laramie Energy Research Center is operating a 150-ton batch unit at their Laramie, Wyoming facilities. The NTU system uses air and recycled gas to provide

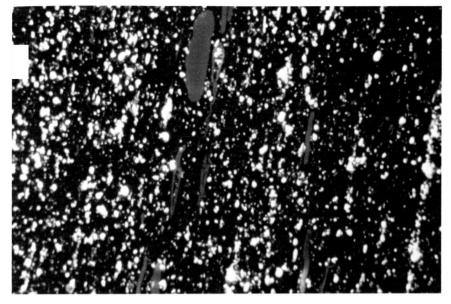

Plate 1. Chattanooga Shale, Vertical (3.5X obj.)
(See pp. 13-14)

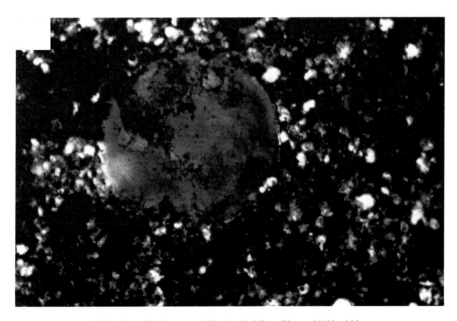

Plate 2. Chattanooga Shale, Bedding Plane (10X obj.)
(See pp. 13-14)

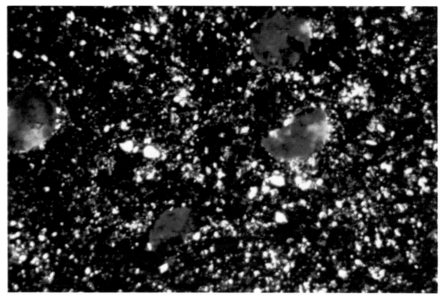

Plate 3.   Chattanooga Shale, Bedding Plane (3.5X obj.)
(See pp. 13-14)

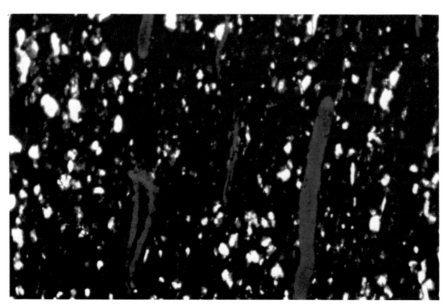

Plate 4.   Chattanooga Shale, Vertical (10X obj.)
(See pp. 13-14)

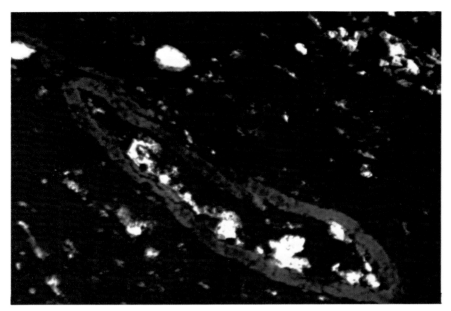

Plate 5.   Chattanooga Shale, Vertical (25X obj.)
(See pp. 13-14)

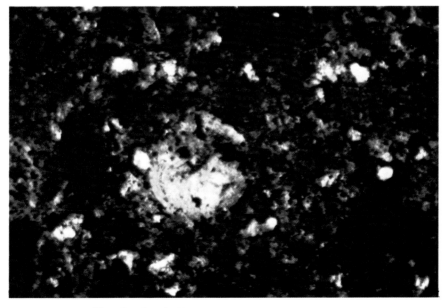

Plate 6.   Appalachian Shale, Bedding Plane (10X obj.)
(See p. 14)

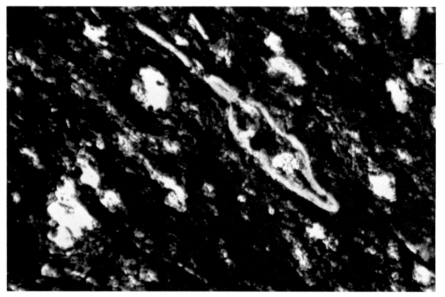

Plate 7.   Appalachian Shale, Vertical (25X obj.)
(See p. 14)

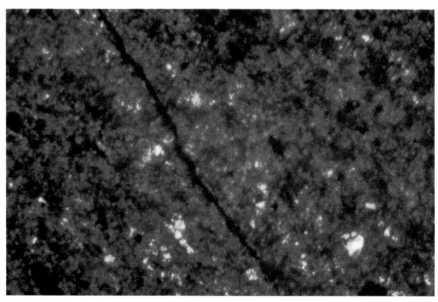

Plate 8.   Green River Oil Shale (100X)
(See p. 14)

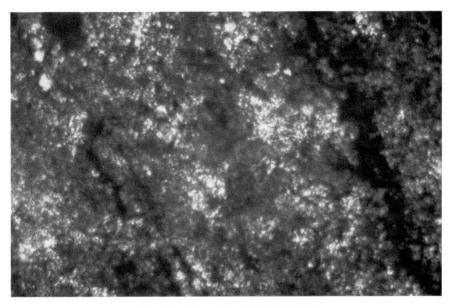

Plate 9.   Green River Oil Shale (250X)
(See p. 14)

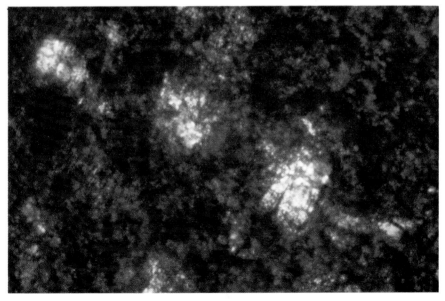

Plate 10.   Green River Oil Shale (500X)
(See p. 14)

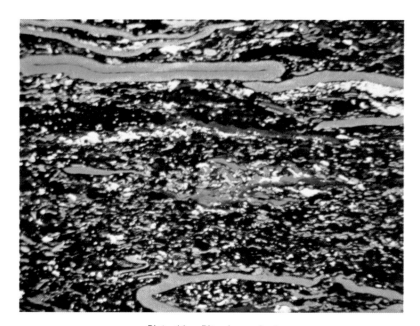

Plate 11. Bituminous Coal
Yellow bands are exinite.
(See p. 15)

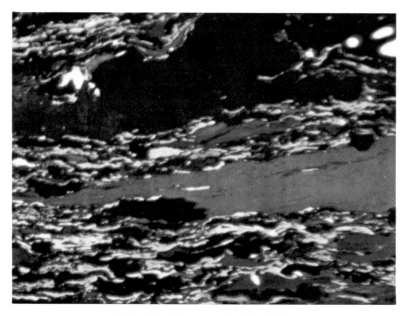

Plate 12. Bituminous Coal Resinite
(See p. 15)

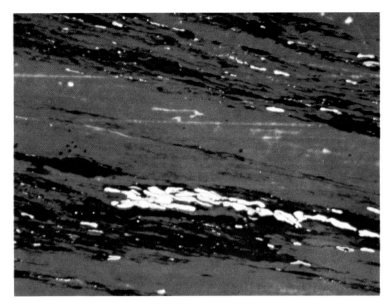

Plate 13.   Vitrinite
(See p. 15)

Plate 14.   Leached Shale Showing the Leaching Front Movement

The yellowish background indicates the presence of carbonates. The black background indicates that carbonate materials have been removed.

(See p. 26)

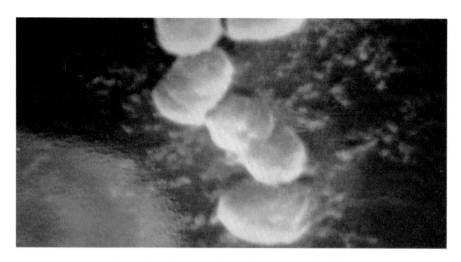

Plate 15. *Thiobacillus thiooxidans* (20 KX)
(See p. 158)

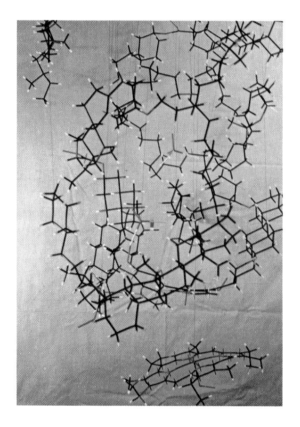

Plate 16. Hypothetical
Kerogen Structure
(See pp. 181 and 203)

the heat required to retort the shale. Maximum temperature in the retort chamber approaches $1600°F$ and the processes recover about 62% of the shale oil based on the Fischer assay. Heating value of the produced gas is very low due to dilution by circulating air.

Lurgi-Rohrgas

This process also uses an external source to supply heat. In this case, solid material (such as sand) is heated and fed into the retort with the shale rock. Spent shale and the solids are removed and separated. The solids are then reheated and continuously recycled.

Properties of the shale oil derived from each of the processes are quite different. Data of a number of the processes are listed in Table 1.5.

Table 1.5   Properties of Crude Shale Oils for *ex situ* Process

Process	NTU	Gas Combustion	TOSCO II	Union	Petrosix[a]
Gravity, API	25.2	19.7	28	20.7	19.6
Sulfur, %	0.76	0.74	0.8	0.77	1.06
Nitrogen, %	1.77	2.18	1.70	2.01	0.86
Pour Point °F	70	80	75	90	25
Viscosity, SUS 100	79	256	120	223	102
% of Fischer Assay	62	85	106	86	—

[a]Shale processed from Irati Formation in Brazil.

In Situ Processes

A recent review of the literature indicates that all *in situ* oil shale processes can be classified into the following categories:

   I. Subsurface chimney
     A. Hot gases
     B. Hot fluids
     C. Chemical extraction
  II. Natural fractures
     A. Unmodified
     B. Enlargement by leaching
 III. Physical induction–no subsurface voids

The above classification is based on the geometry of subsurface retort, and the methods used to degrade and extract exposed kerogens and bitumens. A detailed list with complete references can be found in Table 1.6.

Table 1.6   Classification of *In Situ* Production Methods

Method	Company Name	Reference
I. Subsurface Chimney A. Hot gases	Phillips Petroleum	U.S. 3,490,529[16] U.S. 3,548,938[17] U.S. 3,618,633[18]
	Atlantic Richfield McDonnell Douglas Continental Oil Mobil Oil	U.S. 3,586,377[19] U.S. 3,596,993[20] U.S. 3,480,082[21] U.S. 3,542,131[22]
B. Hot fluids	Shell Oil	U.S. 3,759,328[23] U.S. 3,572,838[24] U.S. 3,565,171[25] U.S. 3,593,789[15]
	Cities Service Oil Garrett Corp.	U.S. 3,601,193[26] U.S. 3,661,423[27]
C. Chemical extraction	Shell Oil	U.S. 3,593,790[14] U.S. 3,666,014[28]
II. Natural fractures A. Unmodified	Shell Oil	U.S. 3,501,201[29] U.S. 3,500,913[30] U.S. 3,513,913[31] U.S. 3,513,914[32]
	Marathon Oil Resources R & D	U.S. 3,730,270[33] S. African 6,908,904[34]
B. Enlarged by leaching	Shell Oil	U.S. 3,481,398[35] U.S. 3,759,328[23] U.S. 3,759,574[36]
III. Physical induction no subsurface voids	Woods R & D Corp.	Neth. Appl. 6,905,815[37]

Most techniques presently patented utilize a subsurface chimney formed either by explosive fracture of country rock or by chemical spalling of rock from the sides of boreholes until a subsurface retort is formed. Subsequent treatment of rubblized material consists of pyrolysis using external heating sources—either hot gases or hot pyrolytic fluids, or combustion of organics initiated by addition of an internal ignition material. Two methods suggest chemical extraction of kerogen from rubblized chimney material with a phenolic Bronsted acid or an unspecified solvent.[2,14]

A number of methods have been proposed that make use of natural fractures and zones of soluble minerals that can be opened and enlarged by solution, eliminating the need for an explosively generated chimney. In these methods, gas pressure and aggressive aqueous fluids are used to expose internal surfaces for secondary pyrolytic extraction of oil precursors. One proposal is to use ultrasonic destruction of mineral matrix and breakdown of kerogen to produce shale oil along natural fractures.[15]

A unique solution to kerogen exposure and application of heat for pyrolysis has been proposed by the Woods Research and Development Company.[37] They plan to use lasers to simultaneously generate voids for oil collection and heat for pyrolytic destruction of contained organics.

All methods examined in the literature require generation of a greater degree of porosity and permeability than is initially present in the rock. Matrix breakdown is usually accomplished thermally, though those processes which do not require a subsurface chimney may include a limited amount of chemical destruction of mineral and organic matrices prior to retorting.

PETROGRAPHIC ANALYSIS OF THIN SECTION CHATTANOOGA SHALE (DEVONIAN SHALE)

Chattanooga Shale is a fine-grained, finely laminated, indurated shale with microlaminae parallel to bedding planes (Plate 1). The long axes of discernible individual crystals are aligned parallel to these laminae, while irregular masses of pyrite and organic debris appear to be flattened along lamination planes. Anhedral crystals of quartz and irregular masses of pyrite constitute the differentiable mineral grains, while the high birefringence characteristic of carbonate minerals is conspicuous by its absence (% $CaCO_3$ = 1.44).

Organic material occurs as a translucent brown material permeating and tinting the entire rock. This material can be observed as coatings on larger mineral grains, and almost certainly occurs as coatings on smaller grains as well (Plates 1-5). Black, string-like concentrations (Plate 5) occur parallel to laminae, and may represent an edge view of the organic coatings, or the concentration of organic material along bedding planes.

Numerous circular (mean diameter = 0.30 mm), reddish-brown, organic masses (Plates 2 and 3) are visible in sections cut parallel to laminae. Masses of the same material are compressed in sections cut perpendicular to bedding planes (Plates 1,4,5), suggesting that they are flattened spheres, most probably spore-like bodies. Frequently, flattening has been incomplete, and part of the internal sphere area has been preserved, either as a black axial line or partial filling (Plates 4 and 5).

APPALACHIAN SHALE (ORDOVICIAN SHALE)

Appalachian Black Shale is a fine-grained, microlaminated rock similar to the previously described Chattanooga Shale (Plates 6 and 7). A few anhedral grains of quartz and pyrite are readily visible, with the pyrite accumulation spread out along laminae. Carbonate minerals are, again, conspicuous by their absence (% $CaCO_3$=0.79).

The organic components of this rock are of three types. As previously described, there is a pervasive translucent brown material throughout the rock, probably representing organic coatings of mineral grains. In addition, two types of flattened organic spheres (mean diameter = 0.11 mm) occur throughout the rock. These two types of spore-like bodies differ in that one is bright yellow (Plate 7) while the other is reddish-brown, similar to those found in the Chattanooga Shale (Plate 5). The two types occur together throughout the rock, and show no recognizable trend toward spatial segregation.

GREEN RIVER OIL SHALE (EOCENE SHALE)

A thin section of Green River shows distinct banding of deep dark brown organics and fine detrital particles in a light-colored crystalline matrix (Plate 8). The matrix is composed of polymineralogic crystal aggregates, and small simple crystals that, when large enough to be identified, are generally quartz or dolomite (Plate 9). This crystalline matrix permeates the entire rock, superimposing a granular texture over distinct dark and light bands.

Clays and associated organics appear to be localized in small blob-like aggregates[20] which string out to form dark laminae. These organo-clay concentrates vary from broad diffuse dark brown bands to narrow opaque strings, but are always parallel to the varved textural grains (Plate 10). There is no evidence of clays or organics in light-colored bands. The clays and organics are intimately associated.

COMPARISON WITH COAL PETROGRAPHY

Since the yellow and red bodies observed are similar to those of coals, thin sections of a highly volatile bituminous coal were used for comparison. The vertical section of exinite, especially for the spores, is yellow (Plate 11). These yellow bodies are admixed with brownish-red resinold matters, such as resinite (Plate 12). In special cases, the vitrinite (Plate 13) is overwhelmingly red. It is possible that the red bodies may indicate high aromatic moieties of the organics in the kerogen component.

Both Paleozoic shales are surprisingly similar, composed primarily of silicate minerals and pyrite, eliminating the potential for matrix modification by techniques developed for the finer-grained, carbonate-rich, tertiary Green River oil shale. The presence of spore-like bodies in both Paleozoic shales is a second similarity that further separates them from Green River shales which have none. This indicates that the kerogen of the nonmarine Green River shales has a different source than that organic in the marine Appalachian and Chattanooga shales, and may, therefore, differ significantly in composition. Even within the Paleozoic shales, there is morphological difference. It can be concluded that both aging and the environment of deposits influences the composition greatly. Among U.S. shales, there is a great variation in structure and composition. The recovery scheme depends on the composition of shale.

ACKNOWLEDGMENT

The support of A.G.A. GR 48-12 is appreciated.

REFERENCES

1. Robinson, W. E. and G. U. Dinneen. "Constitutional Aspects of Oil Shale Kerogen," *Proc. 7th World Petroleum Congress* 3, 669 (1967).
2. McKee, R. H. "Shale Oil," Chemical Catalog Co. (1925).
3. Yen, T. F. in *Analytical Chemistry Pertaining to Oil Shale and Shale Oil*, S. Siggia and P. C. Uden, Eds. (University of Massachusetts, 1975), pp. 59-79.
4. Yen, T. F. and G. V. Chilingar. "Introduction to Oil Shale," in *Oil Shales* (New York: American Elsevier Publishing Co., 1975), pp. 1-12.
5. Jaffe, F. C. "Oil Shale, Nomenclature, Uses, Reserves and Production," Colorado School of Mines, *Mineral Industries Bull.* 5(2), 11 (1962).
6. Prien, C. H. "Oil Shale and Shale Oil," in *Oil Shale and Cannel Coal* (London: Institute Petroleum, 1951), Vol. 2, pp. 76-111.
7. McLean, J. G. and W. B. Davis. "Guide to National Petroleum Council, Report on United States Energy Outlook" (1972).

8. Dent, F. B. and B. Ancker-Johnson. "Commerce Technical Advisory Board's Recommendation for a National Energy Program," U.S. Department of Commerce (1975).

9. Dole, H. M. and G. P. Morrell. "U.S. Energy—A Summary Review," U.S. Department of Interior (1972).

10. Yen, T. F. "Structural Aspects of Organic Components in Oil Shale," in *Oil Shales* (New York: American Elsevier Publishing Co., 1975), Chapter 7.

11. Yen, T. F. "Genesis and Degradation of Petroleum Hydrocarbons in Marine Environment," *ACS Symp. Series* No. 18, 231-266 (1975).

12. Duncan, D. C. and V. E. Swanson. "Organic-Rich Shales of the United States and World Land Areas," *Geol. Survey Circ. No. 523* (1965).

13. Hearing before the Subcommittee on Energy, 93rd Congress on H.R. 9693, "Oil Shale Technology" (1974).

14. Herce, J. A. "Method for Producing Shale Oil from an Oil Shale Formation," U.S. 3,593,790 (Shell Oil Co.).

15. Prats, M. "Method for Producing Shale Oil from an Oil Shale Formation," U.S. 3,593,789 (Shell Oil Co.).

16. Parker, H. W. "Production of Oil from a Nuclear Chimney in an Oil Shale by *In Situ* Combustion," U.S. 3,490,529 (Phillips Petroleum Co.).

17. Parker, H. W. "*In Situ* Method of Producing Oil from Oil Shale," U.S. 3,548,938 (Phillips Petroleum Co.).

18. Needham, R. B. "Shale Oil Recovery," U.S. 3,618,663 (Phillips Petroleum Co.).

19. Ellington, R. T. "Method of Retorting Oil Shale *In Situ*," U.S. 3,586,377 (Atlantic Richfield Co.).

20. Busey, H. M. "Method of Extracting Oil and By-Products from Oil Shale," U.S. 3,596,993 (McDonnell Douglas Corp.).

21. Gilliland, H. E. "*In Situ* Retorting of Oil Shale Using CO_2 as Heat Carrier," U.S. 3,480,082 (Continental Oil Co.).

22. Walton, D. K. and M. S. Slusser. "Method of Recoverying Hydrocarbons from Oil Shale," U.S. Pat. 3,542,131 (Mobil Oil Corp.).

23. Ueber, R. C., P. Van Meurs, and J. R. Brew. "Laterally Expanding Oil Shale Permeabilization," U.S. 3,759,328 (Shell Oil Co.).

24. Templeton, C. C. "Recovery of Aluminum Compounds and Oil from Oil Shale," U.S. 3,572,838 (Shell Oil Co.).

25. Closmann, P. J. "Method for Producing Shale Oil from a Subterranean Oil Shale Formation," U.S. 3,565,171 (Shell Oil Co.).

26. Grady, G. O. "*In Situ* Retorting of Oil Shale," U.S. 3,601,193 (Cities Service Oil Co.).

27. Garret, D. E. "*In Situ* Process for Recovery of Carbonaceous Materials from Subterraneous Deposits," U.S. Pat. 3,661,423 (Occidental Pet. Corp.) (1972).

28. Beard, T. N. "Recovery of Shale Oil," U.S. 3,666,014 (Shell Oil Co.).

29. Closmann, P. J. and R. P. Nordgren. "Method of Producing Shale Oil from a Subterranean Oil Shale Formation," U.S. 3,501,201 (Shell Oil Co.).

30. Nordgren, R. P. and P. J. Closmann. "Method of Recovering Liquefiable Components from a Subterranean Earth Formation," U.S. 3,500,913 (Shell Oil Co.).
31. Bruist, E. H. "Oil Recovery from Oil Shales by Transverse Combustion," U.S. 3,513,913 (Shell Oil Co.).
32. Vogel, J. V. "Method for Producing Oil Shale from an Oil Shale Formation," U.S. Pat. 3,513,914 (Shell Oil Co.).
33. Allred, V. D. "Shale Oil Recovery from Fractured Oil Shale," U.S. 3,730,270 (Marathon Oil Co.).
34. Felix, D. T., A. H. Pelifsky, and G. N. Herbert. "Use of Sonic Energy for Rupturing Molecular Bonds in Shale Oil Recovery," S. African 69,08,905 (Resources Research and Development Corp.).
35. Prats, M. "Permeabilizing by Acidizing Oil Shale Tuffaceous Streaks in and Oil Recovery Therefrom," U.S. 3,481,398 (Shell Oil Co.).
36. Beard, T. N. "Methods of Producing Hydrocarbons from an Oil Shale Formation (Shell Chem. Co.) 1973.
37. "Procedure for *In Situ* Recovery of Minerals and Derivatives Thereof with the Aid of Laser Beams," Neth. Appl. 6,905,815 (Woods R. & D. Co.).

2

MODIFICATION OF THE MINERAL MATRIX
OF GREEN RIVER OIL SHALE BY BIOLEACHING

W. C. Meyer and T. F. Yen

University of Southern California
Los Angeles, California 90007

INTRODUCTION

Bioleaching, utilizing a sulfuric acid medium generated by the sulfur oxidizing capabilities of *Thiobacillus* spp., has proved to be useful in releasing hydrocarbons from petroliferous rocks from the Mahogany Ledge of the Green River formation. The purpose of this chapter is to investigate the texture and mineralogy of the Green River shale to ascertain the nature of kerogen entrapment and the physical effects of bioleaching. Such an understanding should facilitate the development of a method to increase the effectiveness of bioleaching in releasing kerogens for commercial extraction.

SHALE DESCRIPTION

Samples chosen for this study are from the organic-rich Mahogany Ledge of the Green River formation. These rocks are lacustrine, highly indurated, fine-grained, varved, calcareous sedimentary rocks varying in color from tan to black depending on organic content. Rocks of this type are technically marl, but in this chapter will be called shale in convention with common usage.

Varves in the Green River shale consist of carbonate summer laminae, and fine grained winter laminae composed of clay and organic components. Thin sections of the shale show distinct banding of dark components enclosed in a light-colored matrix composed of polymineralogic crystal aggregates and small single crystals, superimposing a granular texture over the entire rock (Figure 2.1).

Clays and associated organics appear to be localized in small blob-like aggregates (~20μ) which string out to form the dark winter laminae. These organo-clay concentrations vary from diffuse dark brown bands to narrow opaque strings, but are always parallel to the varved textural grain. Light-colored bands appear to be composed entirely of small matrix crystals and a few relatively coarse possibly detrital grains, with little evidence of clays or organics. The clays and visible organics are intimately associated, either because they were deposited simultaneously, or have become linked by processes of chem-absorbtion. It would seem reasonable that the first step in liberating adsorbed or mechanically trapped kerogens would be the disaggregation of the crystalline matrix.

The texture of the studied samples suggests two events—deposition of varved lake sediments, followed by diagenetic dolomitization. This would explain why granular mineral matrix is superimposed over the entire rock, filling interstices and decreasing porosity and permeability to effectively zero.

A second interpretation (suggested by Chilingar) holds that this texture may result from penecontemporaneous precipitation of carbonate with deposition. Compaction of primary sediment would result in an upward squeezing of interstitial waters that would become saturated in available salts during migration, causing precipitation and enrichment of dolomite near the top of the deposit.

Better control over geographic and stratigraphic position of samples is required to evaluate the validity of this proposal. Carbonate enrichment near the top of the deposit would support an interpretation of penecontemporaneous deposition. If, however, mineral distribution within the sediment column is found to be homogeneous, secondary deposition by percolating groundwater would be the reasonable mechanism. Without better sample coverage, it will not be possible to decide on the best explanation.

MINERAL COMPOSITION

X-Ray analysis of the studied samples were made using a Norelco diffractometer using CuKα radiation with a nickel filter, 0.006 in. slit at 40 kv and 20 MA. Disordered powder mounts were used for whole-rock mineral analyses. Separate preparations were made for analysis of clay mineralogy using the method devised by Jackson.[1] The indurated nature of the shale made complete disaggregation impossible, but digestion of

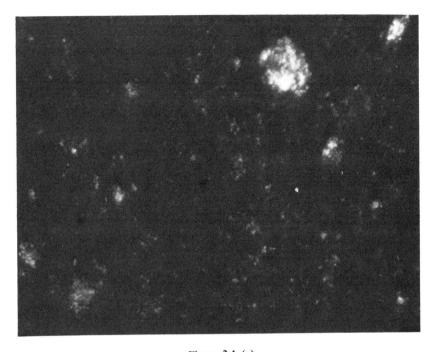

Figure 2.1 (a)

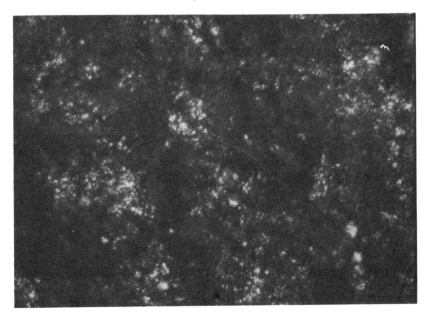

Figure 2.1 (b)

50 g of crushed shale in warm sodium-acetate solution (part of Jackson's method) released enough carbonate-free clay to analyze with no difficulty.

To separate different clay species, clay mounts were treated according to the method proposed by Carrol[2] to promote shifts in position of diagnostic X-ray peaks. This treatment includes dessication, glycolation, and heating to 350°C and 550°C respectively.

Whole rock mineral content can be divided into major and minor constituents based on relative peak intensities (Table 2.1). The shale contains too many mineral species to be easily matched by addition of necessary comparative internal standards; therefore quantitative determinations of mineral abundances were not made.

Table 2.1   Whole Rock Mineralogy

Major	Minor
Quartz SiO_2	Analcite $NaAlSi_2O \cdot H_2O$
Dolomite $CaMg(CO_3)_2$	Montmorillonite $Al_4(Si_4O_{10})_2(OH)_4$
Calcite $CaCO_3$	Orthoclase $KAlSi_3O_8$
	Plagioclase $Na(Ca)Al_{0-2}Si_{2-3}O_8$
	Pyrite FeS_2

Clay Mineralogy
Montmorillonite $Al_4(Si_4O_{10})_2(OH)_4$
Illite $K_{0-2}Al_4(Si_{8-6}Al_{0-2})O_{20}(OH)_4$

Quartz and dolomite were found to be the predominant minerals in these samples. Calcite is also present, probably representing residual primary carbonate that has not undergone diagenesis. Dolomite and calcite appear to form the granular matrix observed in thin section. Feldspar, including both plagioclase and orthoclase, occur primarily as detrital grains making up part of the primary sediment.

Analcite, abundant here and in some other members of the Green River Formation, is thought to have formed authigenically shortly after deposition of the primary sediment.[3] It is possible that some of the plagioclase content of the shale may have been formed by reaction of analcite and quartz.[4] The temperature required for this conversion is about 190°C, somewhat higher than would be expected in these deposits, but in the presence of concentrated brine conversion temperature would be lowered.[3]

Pyrite probably formed in the sediment before or during lithification, when organic-rich bottom sediments provided a reducing environment favorable to formation of this mineral.

A peak of 18.8 Å in the clay and whole-rock mounts that suggests montmorillonite, reported from Green River samples by previous investigators,[3] is the dominant clay group in the studied samples. This peak occurs at somewhat higher Ångström values than is normal for montmorillonite, but the presence of residual organics often causes abberation in X-ray patterns, perhaps explaining the observed shift.[5]

Montmorillonite is a poorly crystallized mineral and often is not detectable by X-ray unless present in excess of 15% of the sample.[2] Therefore, the presence of a montmorillonite peak in the whole-rock pattern suggests this mineral may be present in significant quantities. Water is readily absorbed into the montmorillonite structure causing swelling. If the quartz and carbonate are removed from the shale, the expansive forces of swelling montmorillonite might be useful in disaggregation of the residual fraction.

Illite is the second abundant clay mineral, and could represent primary clays, degraded mica, or potassium-enriched primary clays of other species. Garrels and Mackenzie show that, through time, most clay species will alter to montmorillonite, illite, or chlorite.[6] The age of the Green River formation (Eocene) would be more than sufficient for alteration of primary clays.

It is not possible to determine accurately what percentage of the shale is clay, without data on the whole-rock distribution of elemental oxides. A process of elimination by comparison with mineralogy would reveal how much of these elements is contained in clays but, as yet, the appropriate analyses have not been performed.

To see what effect bioleaching has on mineralogy, the X-ray pattern of raw shale was compared to that of a sample that had undergone a 38.4% weight loss during bioleaching. The mineral compositions of both samples are identical; however, peak intensities of carbonate minerals are strongly reduced suggesting they have been dissolved and partially removed (Figure 2.2). Peak size is not linearly related to the amount of mineral present, so a quantitative estimate of carbonate removal is not indicated by comparing peak heights.

To quantify the amount of carbonate removed by bioleaching, whole-rock weight percentages of organic carbon, carbonate ion, and mineral carbonate were determined on duplicate one-half gram samples (270 mesh) using the Leco gasometric analyzer.[7] Calculation of mineral carbonate

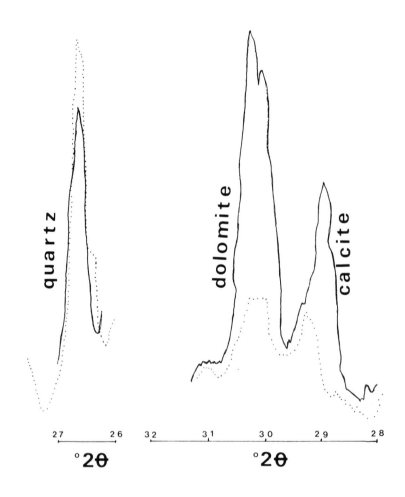

———— WHOLE ROCK (untreated)

········ WHOLE ROCK (bioleached)

quartz

dolomite

calcite

27　　26　　32　　　31　　　30　　　29　　　28

°2θ　　　　　　　°2θ

Figure 2.2

uses a constant derived from the relative weight of calcium and carbonate ion in calcite. Since it was not possible to evaluate quantitatively the ratio of calcite to dolomite in the carbonate fraction, the calcite constant was used for calculated weight percentages. This will yield weight percentages slightly lighter than actual values. Organic carbon was sufficiently abundant to necessitate halving the normal sample weight (0.25 g) for analysis.

Carbon and carbonate data are expressed as weight percent. Raw shale proved to be about 33% mineral carbonate by weight and 10% carbon contained in organic compounds (Table 2.2). Assuming an average hydrocarbon chain of C_{16} in the Green River material, the added hydrogen would bring the total weight of organic constituents to approximately 11%.

Table 2.2   Weight Percent Carbon Components of Raw Shale Carbonate Carbon
(Replicates from same sample)

Sample	Sample Weight (g)	(%) Carbonate Carbon	(%) Carbonate Ion	(%) Mineral Carbonate
1	0.5050	3.70	18.50	30.83
2	0.4950	4.86	24.29	40.47
3	0.4995	3.10	15.49	25.80
4	0.5005	4.41	22.09	36.80
Mean		4.02	20.09	33.47

Whole-Rock   4.02% Carbon (in CO_3)
20.09% CO_3
33.47% Mineral Carbonate

Total Carbon (Replicates from same sample)

Sample	Sample Weight (g)	(%) Carbon
5	0.2500	13.32
6	0.2492	14.06
Mean		13.69

Organic carbon = Total Carbon – Carbonate Carbon
Organic carbon = 13.69% – 4.02% = 9.67%

To ascertain how much carbonate is removed by bioleaching, samples of crushed (16 mesh) bioleached material were analyzed for residual carbonate (Table 2.3). The sample used for this experiment had lost 36.5% of its weight during leaching, and it was found to have approximately 2.3% residual mineral carbonate, indicating that bioleaching is quite effective (See Plate 14, Chapter 1).

Table 2.3   Weight Percent Residual Carbonate in Bioleached Shale (36.5% weight loss) Carbonate Carbon (Replicates from same sample)

Sample	Sample Weight (g)	(%) Carbonate Carbon	(%) Carbonate Ion	(%) Mineral Carbonate
1	0.5000	0.29	1.40	2.47
2	0.4993	0.25	1.29	2.16
Mean		0.27	1.35	2.31

Residual Carbonate Minerals = 2.31%

Electron microprobe analysis of the studied samples (Table 2.4) revealed that with the exception of calcium and magnesium the distribution and concentration of elements chosen for analysis coincided with expectations based on X-ray determined mineralogy. Calcium concentration (10.8%) when compared to magnesium (2.6%) yields a ratio (Ca/Mg = 4.2) much higher than would be expected if carbonate were predominantly dolomite (Ca/Mg = 1). Unless there is some undiscovered source of calcium, this suggests that calcite might be more common in Green River oil shale than expected.

Table 2.4   Microprobe Analysis of Green River Oil Shale

Element	Mean wt %	Maximum wt %	Minimum wt %
Calcium	10.8	21.6	0.9
Magnesium	2.6	5.1	1.0
Aluminum	1.6	4.8	0.3
Silicon	6.8	16.8	2.7
Iron	1.0	0.4	2.4
Uranium*	0.75	0.83	0.65

*The amount of this element is questionable due to lack of a serial of standards. Qualitatively its presence is quite certain.

VISIBLE EFFECTS OF BIOLEACHING

Scanning electron micrographs were taken of shale samples treated for various periods of time to see the effects of bioleaching. Samples were cut to convenient size and polished to a flat surface with #600 grit prior to treatment. Control samples of polished unleached shale (Figure 2.3a) and unleached fractured rock surface (Figure 2.3b) were photographed to ascertain if any material was being removed by crystal plucking during polishing. Neither control showed evidence of pitting due to mechanical processes, so it seems safe to conclude that pitting observed in treated samples is due to chemical action.

Shale bioleached for two days (Figure 2.3c) shows a pitted, spongy-appearing surface texture caused by solution of mineral material. Bioleaching for one week (Figure 2.3d) caused no apparent increase in the number of pits per unit area, but an increase in pit size was noted. Two weeks exposure to bioleaching (Figure 2.3e) medium seemed to further increase pit size but did not result in formation of additional pits.

To quantify the effects of bioleaching, photomicrographs of shale samples bioleached for varying times were used to count and measure the cross-sectional dimensions of solution pits as an indication of the amount

Figure 2.3a

Figure 2.3b

Figure 2.3c

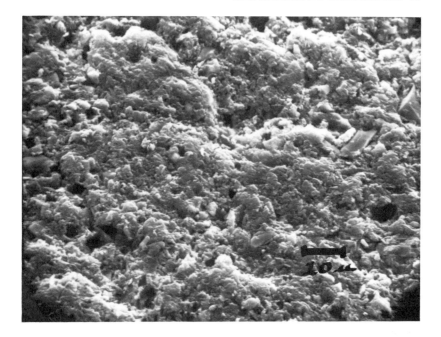

Figure 2.3d

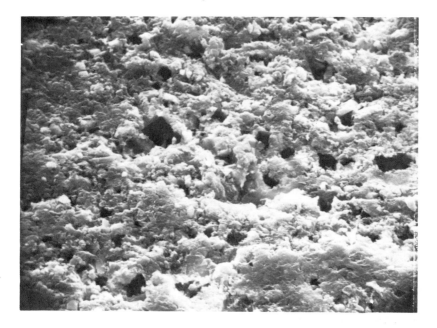

Figure 2.3e

of material removed by solution.   These data (Table 2.5) show that solution pits form rapidly after exposure to the leaching medium.   The number of pits on each sample ranged from 29 to 33, independent of time.   Average pit size (calculated as surface area using the two extreme diameters for each pit) did vary directly with time, increasing from a minimum of 24.8 μ^2 after two days, to a maximum of 54.3 μ^2 after two weeks, indicating that the volume of carbonate removed is a function of time exposed to the bioleaching medium.

Table 2.5   Surface Area Affected by Solution

Photo	Total Number Pits	Area 5 Largest Pits (μ^2)	Total Area 5 Largest Pits (μ^2)	Mean Pit Area 5 Largest Pits (μ^2)
Polished, unleached	0	0	0	0
Polished, leached 2 days	33	35 25 24 20 20	124	24.8
Polished, leached 1 week	29	40 35 30 30 24	159	31.8
Polished, leached 2 weeks	32	96 55 49 36 30	266	54.3

Paired microphotographs of the same area (Figure 2.4) can be used as a stereo-pair if they are taken at slightly different tilt angles.   Figure 2.4 shows a stereo-pair of a solution pit in a shale sample bioleached for two weeks.   Using an equation modified from that devised for interpretation of aerial photographs, these photographs can be used to determine pit depth.

Figure 2.4

Depth (D) is a function of parallax (P)—the difference in distance between the same two points on a stereo-pair magnification (M), and the difference in the tilt at which the photographs were taken (Θ).

$$D = P/2M \sin \Theta/2$$

Using this formula, the relief between points A and B on the stereo-pair in Figure 2.3 is:

$$P = AB-A'B' = 0.053''$$

$$M = 5,000x$$

$$\Theta = 7°$$

$$D = 0.053''/2(5000)(0.061) = (0.053''/0.061 \times 10^4)(2.54 \times 10^4/1'') = 2.2\mu$$

The irregular bottom of this pit is a typical effect of solution. The shelf-like false bottom and the small penetration of the true bottom indicate that continued solution would result in further deepening. This fact, coupled with the observed lateral enlargement with time should result in vertical and lateral interconnection of soluble sites causing an increase in porosity and permeability. This will prove to be an important mechanism to facilitate exposure of fresh surface to the leaching medium and form conducts for the migration of liberated hydrocarbons.

BENEFITS OF BIOLEACHING

Application of bioleaching techniques has many advantages over presently employed retorting technology. Using explosives or compressed air, it is possible to fracture the shale while still in the ground, providing a reservoir that could be filled with water and inoculated with acid-forming bacteria which is necessary to dissolve much of the mineral matrix. Such treatment would expose kerogen for extraction and would eliminate the need for mining, crushing, transportation, and elimination of waste material.

If *in situ* production does not prove practical, pretreatment of shale by bioleaching will eliminate about 40% of the mineral matrix, reducing shipping costs a similar amount. In addition, the remaining shale will be enriched in organic material making recovery more economical, since shale that will release 25 gallons of oil per ton of rock by retorting alone, will provide 40 gallons of oil if pretreated by bioleaching.

CONCLUSIONS

Kerogens in the Green River shale are trapped in an inorganic mineral matrix composed primarily of quartz and carbonate minerals (dolomite and calcite). Liberation of hydrocarbons will depend upon the degree to which this matrix can be disaggregated, exposing kerogen for extraction. Thin sections show organic components within this rock are associated with the clay fraction, possibly through a process of chemical adsorbtion. Expansive properties of montmorillonite, the dominant clay component, may be useful in final disaggregation of the shale, after removal of mineral matrix.

Bioleaching removes carbonate minerals from the shale, eliminating matrix material, and thereby developing porosity and permeability that are effectively nil for untreated shale. This brings more rock surface into contact with the leaching medium, increasing solution of matrix and enlarging pathways for migration of liberated hydrocarbons. Carbonate removal during bioleaching proceeds rapidly upon exposure to the leaching medium, and continues as a function of time.

ACKNOWLEDGMENT

This work is supported by NSF Grant No. GI-35683.

REFERENCES

1. Jackson, M. L. *Soil Chemical Analyses—Advanced Course* (Madison: M. L. Jackson, 1956), pp. 31-59.
2. Carroll, D. "Clay Minerals: A Guide to Their X-Ray Identification," Geol. Soc. Amer., Spec. Pub., No. 126 (1970), pp. 1-80.
3. Bradley, W. H. and H. P. Eugster. "Geochemistry and Paleolimnology of the Trona Deposits and Associated Authigenic Minerals of the Green River Formation of Wyoming," U.S.G.S., Prof. Paper 496-B (1969), pp. 1-71.
4. Campbell, A. S. and W. S. Fyfe. "Analcine-Albite Equilibrium," *Am. J. Sci.* **263**, 807 (1965).
5. Seyfried, William. Personal communication (1973).
6. Garrels, R. M. and F. T. Mackenzie. *Evolution of Sedimentary Rocks* (New York: W. W. Norton, Inc., 1971), p. 235.
7. Kolpack, R. L. and A. S. Bell. "Gasometric Determination of Carbon in Sediments by Hydroxide Absorbtion," *J. Sed. Pet.* **38**, 617 (1968).
8. Chilingar, G. V. Personal communication (1972).

3

PULSED NMR EXAMINATION OF OIL SHALES—
ESTIMATION OF POTENTIAL OIL YIELDS

F. P. Miknis, A. W. Decora and G. L. Cook

U. S. Energy Research
and Development Administration
Laramie Energy Research Center
Laramie, Wyoming 82070

INTRODUCTION

For the past four years the Laramie Energy Research Center has been investigating the application of nuclear magnetic resonance (NMR) as a method of rapidly and reliably predicting potential oil yields of oil shales. With the present interest in the government's oil-shale test-lease program, the need for a rapid and reliable oil-shale assay method is more urgent. The potential of wide-line NMR for this purpose has already been demonstrated by Decora, McDonald and Cook.[1] Another type of NMR, pulsed or transient NMR, is being explored as a method for rapidly providing this information. The pulsed NMR method is more rapid than the wide-line NMR method because no time is spent sweeping the field or frequency to record the signal. Other advantages of pulsed NMR over wide-line NMR are the elimination of line-broadening effects, no need for signal integration, greater sensitivity in a given measuring time, and ease of spectrometer operation. In addition, direct measurements of the spin-spin, T_2, and spin-lattice, T_1, relaxation times by pulsed NMR can provide other useful information about oil shales.

In this chapter we present the results of some pulsed NMR assays on oil-shale samples. Two groups of oil-shale samples from two different cores were analyzed by pulsed NMR in a routine assay-type operation.

Statistical analyses are presented to show that the NMR data linearly correlate with the Fischer assay oil-yield data.

EXPERIMENTAL PROCEDURES

Oil Shales Studied

Two oil-shale cores were studied. The first came from a proposed test-lease core and had been recently Fischer assayed. A total of 141 samples, designated as Group I samples, were selected from this core to represent the entire depth (1,300 to 2,700 ft) and oil-yield ranges (0-70 gal/ton) of the cored interval.

The second core was cut below the B groove of the Mahogany zone. The total length of the core was 1100 ft and the oil-yield range was 0-60 gal/ton. The first 300 samples from this core, designated as Group II samples, were analyzed by pulsed NMR parallel with the Fischer assay-oil-yield determination on the same core sections.

Sample Preparation

To prepare Group I samples for the first study, the sample remaining after Fischer assay was riffled to reduce the sample size to about 75-100 g. This sample was then crushed to a fine powder on a disc grinder, and a representative portion (0.5 g) of the powdered sample was taken for the NMR measurements.

Group II samples for the second study were of the same particle size (8 mesh) as was used in the Fischer assay method. No further crushing was done to the samples prior to the NMR measurements. The samples were, however, riffled to a smaller sample size from which a representative portion (2.5-4.5 g) was taken for the NMR measurements. The riffling of these samples was an attempt to minimize errors in the NMR method that could arise from nonrepresentative sampling.

Instrumentation

Pulsed NMR measurements on the Group I samples were made on a Bruker 322S variable frequency pulsed spectrometer housed at the Marathon Oil Co. Research Center in Denver, Colorado. These measurements of the free induction decay (FID) amplitude following a $90°$ pulse were made at a resonant frequency of 60 mHz a pulse length of 2.5 μsec, a pulse repetition rate of 1 sec and using diode detection. About 30 FID amplitude measurements (requiring about 30 sec) were made for each oil-shale sample, and the average values of these measurements were used to determine the relationship with Fischer assay oil yields by regression analyses. The FID amplitudes were corrected to unit sample weight prior to the regression analyses.

FID amplitudes for the Group II shales were measured on a similar instrument housed at the Laramie Energy Research Center. A resonant frequency of 20 mHz, a pulse length of 6 μsec, a pulse repetition rate of 1 sec, and phase sensitive detection were used for these measurements. Because the Group II samples were coarser than the Group I samples, a larger sample tube (15 mm diameter) was used. As was done for the Group I samples, about 30 FID amplitude measurements were made for each Group II sample, from which an average value was obtained and corrected to unit weight prior to the regression analyses.

Linear Regression Analyses

Linear first-order regression analyses were first performed on the FID amplitudes and Fischer assay oil yields for standard samples chosen from both groups. There were 30 standard samples chosen from Group I and 36 from Group II. Based on the slopes and intercepts of the best least-squares data fits, oil yields were calculated for the remaining samples in both groups. Regression analyses were then performed on the oil yields calculated from NMR measurements and oil yields determined by Fischer assay. The index of determination (square of the correlation coefficient, r) is the parameter we use to judge the "goodness of fit" in the regression analyses. A value of 1.00 for this parameter implies a perfect fit of data points to a straight line.

THEORETICAL CONSIDERATIONS

The basis for the pulsed NMR assay method lies in the assumption that the organic hydrogen content of an oil shale is relatable to the shale's potential oil yield. The FID amplitude, following a $90°$ pulse, is proportional to the total number of resonant nuclei in the sample, just as is the area under the absorption curve in wide-line NMR. Because the resonant nuclei in this case are protons, the FID amplitude is proportional to the hydrogen content of the oil shale.

The basic NMR measurement is shown in Figure 3.1(a). A sample introduced into a magnetic field, H_0, achieves a net magnetization, M, proportional to the amount of hydrogen in the sample. If an rf pulse, H_1, is applied at right angles to H_0, M can be rotated from its equilibrium position and begins to precess about H_1. If the intensity and duration of H_1 are properly chosen, M can be rotated into the xy plane at which time H_1 is turned off. The condition for a $90°$ rotation is

$$\pi/2 \; = \; \gamma \, H_1 \, \tau_p \tag{3.1}$$

where γ is the magnetogyric ratio of the proton, H_1 is the strength of the pulse, and τ_p is the pulse duration. Following the termination of H_1, the individual magnetic moments begin to interact with each other and lose phase coherence as in Figure 3.1(b). The net result is that the signal intensity decreases to zero in a characteristic time, T_2, the spin-spin relaxation time.

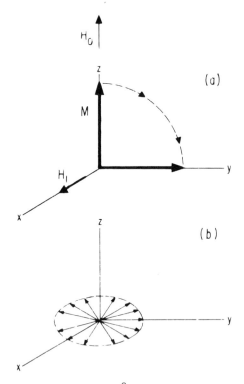

Figure 3.1 A $90°$ pulse sequence.

In the pulsed NMR assay method, measurements are made on M, immediately after the $90°$ pulse, to obtain the maximum signal from all the protons in the sample. These measurements may include signal contributions from inorganic protons (such as adsorbed water, mineral hydrogen, and tightly bound hydroxyl groups) as well as the organic protons in the oil shale. To improve precision of the method, effort is made to distinguish between the different types of protons in the sample. By the very nature of the pulsed NMR measurement it is difficult to make this distinction, except in the case of adsorbed water, an example of which is shown in Figure 3.2. Here the effect on the FID of drying the shale sample to remove water is illustrated. The signal that persists in the undried samples for times greater than about 50 μsec shows the effect of adsorbed water because, upon drying, the signal is significantly reduced. This indicates that organic hydrogen relaxation times are shorter than those of adsorbed water and suggests that signal contributions due to adsorbed water can be corrected for by subtracting FID amplitude measurements at 50 μsec from

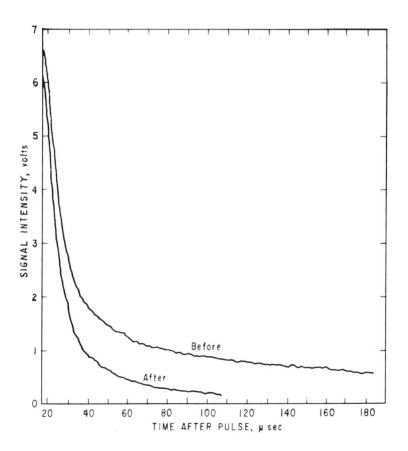

Figure 3.2 Effects of drying oil shale samples on free induction decay.

those made at 20 μsec. The corrected FID amplitude was assumed to more closely represent the organic hydrogen content of the oil shale. This procedure was followed for the Group II but not the Group I shales.

Another parameter that might aid in minimizing signal contributions due to inorganic protons is the spin-lattice relaxation time, T_1. This is the characteristic time during which equilibrium is restored along the applied field direction, after the application of a pulse. T_1 determines the frequency at which the 90° pulse sequence can be repeated and ultimately determines the rapidity of the pulsed assay method. Typically, one should wait at least 5 T_1 to allow for equilibrium to be restored before applying a second, third, or further 90° pulse.[2] For oil shales the T_1 values for the organic material are quite short (10-300 msec) whereas some inorganic protons apparently have longer T_1 values. Evidence to illustrate this is presented in the next section of this chapter.

RESULTS AND DISCUSSION

Pulse Repetition Rate

Shown in Table 3.1 are the results of a preliminary study made to determine how T_1 values of inorganic and organic protons affect the pulsed assay method. Here, two FID amplitude measurements were made on 10 oil-shale samples containing substantial amounts (up to 53%) of nahcolite ($NaHCO_3$). The first NMR measurement was made with a pulse repetition rate of 1 sec, and the second was made with a repetition rate of 30 min. The results in Table 3.1 show that the NMR measurements

Table 3.1 Correlations Between Oil Yields and Total Hydrogen
for Different Pulse Repetition Rates

Regression	Pulse Rate	Index of Determination r^2
Oil yield (gal/ton) versus free induction decay amplitude	1 sec	0.97
Total hydrogen (wt %) versus free induction decay amplitude	1 sec	0.95
Oil yield (gal/ton) versus free induction decay amplitude	30 min	0.90
Total hydrogen (wt %) versus free induction decay amplitude	30 min	0.98

of one second correlate better with the oil-yield determinations; whereas those made at 30 min correlate better with the total hydrogen. Total hydrogen includes both organic and inorganic hydrogen and was determined by the combustion method. These results suggest that a fast repetition rate tends to minimize some effects due to inorganic protons.

Fischer Assay Repeatability

Previous work[1] related NMR signals to Fischer assay oil yields using single measurements. Repeatability measurements for each of these experimental methods was not determined. Because the reliability of the NMR assay method is dependent on that of the Fischer assay, a series of tests was made to determine the reliability of the Fischer assay oil yields. Seventy-five samples (three each of 25 Group I samples) were Fischer assayed, and average oil yields and standard deviations were calculated for each of the 25 samples. These results are presented in Table 3.2.

Table 3.2   Summary of Data for Fischer Assay Repeatability Test

Sample Number SBR71-	Average F.A. gal/ton	Standard Deviation S	Dispersion Coefficient K
10164	38.7	11.2	0.289
10178	35.2	3.1	0.088
10335	15.5	1.3	0.083
10446	18.2	1.1	0.059
10648	14.2	6.7	0.472
10262	24.7	5.7	0.230
9522	21.7	6.6	0.303
9993	9.4	0.7	0.074
10296	17.9	1.0	0.056
10650	11.9	0.5	0.039
10352	30.7	0.8	0.025
10026	22.0	0.6	0.028
9947	8.8	0.5	0.061
10162	9.5	4.2	0.436
10115	14.1	0.3	0.019
10531	22.1	1.3	0.059
9587	21.4	0.8	0.038
10444	28.5	1.0	0.033
10603	6.4	2.4	0.381
10452	28.7	5.8	0.202
10254	21.5	1.6	0.073
10137	18.8	0.26	0.014
10564	21.9	6.9	0.317
10217	29.0	0.82	0.028
10224	27.0	1.2	0.045

If one defines the dispersion coefficient as the standard deviation divided by the average value, then the calculated "average" dispersion coefficient is 0.138 for the 25 samples and represents the uncertainty in Fischer assay oil yields.

Group I Oil Shale Samples

Results of linear regression analyses made with the 30 standard samples chosen from Group I were used to calculate oil yields of the remaining 111 samples. The correlation between the measured Fischer assay oil yields and calculated oil yields is shown in Figure 3.3. The value of 0.93 for the index of determination is remarkably good, considering the small sample size (0.5 g) used in the NMR measurements compared with the much larger size (100 g) typically used for Fischer assay. It appears

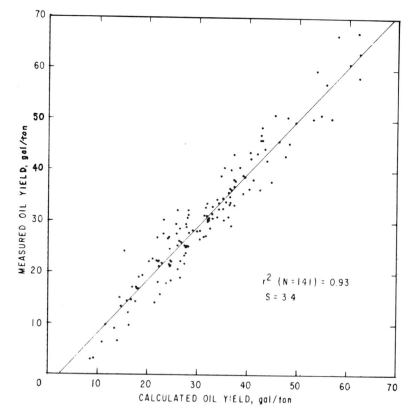

Figure 3.3   Measured oil yields vs. calculated oil yields, Group I.

that the procedure for preparing the NMR samples effectively duplicated the quality of the larger Fischer assay samples. Furthermore, these results were obtained for a single FID amplitude measurement, suggesting an insignificant adsorbed water contribution from these samples.

Group II Oil Shale Samples

The Group II shales were run in a more routine assay type operation than the Group I shales. In this case, the oil-shale samples were run by NMR before, during or after the Fischer assay of the same samples. Thus, the reported Fischer assay oil yields were not known prior to making the NMR measurements. Thirty-six samples were processed at any given time by the NMR method. When Fischer assay data became available, linear regression analyses were made on the FID measurements and reported oil yields. The results for each run are shown in Table 3.3. The poorer index of determination for run 1 was due to improper tuning of the pulsed spectrometer and, in subsequent runs, this problem was remedied as evidenced by the better correlations in runs 2-9. These data also indicate that day-to-day tuning of the pulsed spectrometer on a standard sample can be accomplished readily and with good reliability.

Table 3.3   Indexes of Determination for the Pulsed NMR Assay Method

Run	r^2 (Index of Determination)
1	0.78
2	0.91
3	0.96
4	0.94
5	0.93
6	0.97
7	0.96
8	0.98
9[a]	0.92

[a]This run totaled 12 samples; all other runs contained 36 samples each.

The 36 samples of run 3 were chosen as "standards" to determine how well the pulsed NMR measurements could predict oil yields for the remaining samples. The correlation between the measured and calculated oil yields is shown in Figure 3.4. Again a good correlation was obtained between the predicted and measured oil yields. The data for the 36

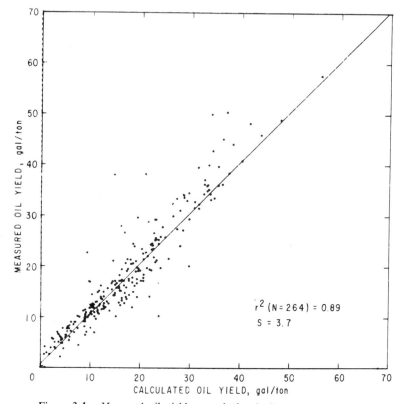

Figure 3.4   Measured oil yields vs. calculated oil yields, Group II.

samples in run one were not included in the correlation in Figure 3.4. It should be emphasized that the correlations in Figures 3.3 and 3.4 assume complete reliability in the Fischer assay. No uncertainties in the Fischer assay data were incorporated in our regression analyses, although the data in Table 3.2 show that the Fischer assay method is subject to errors. This could account for some of the scatter in Figures 3.3 and 3.4. Another reason for the scatter in these figures is probably due to sample size and sampling procedures. The indices of determination, however, indicate that our sampling procedures tended to give NMR samples representative of the total samples.

Time Savings

Thus far, data have been presented to show that pulsed NMR measurements can be used to predict potential oil yields of oil shales. We have not stressed an important advantage of the pulsed NMR assay method over the Fischer assay method—namely, the savings in time offered by the NMR method. To obtain a gallon-of-oil-per-ton-of-shale figure by the Fischer assay method for a single sample averages out to about 100 min per sample. This results from the number of measurements required by the Fischer assay method. Here one must weigh the sample retorts and collectors, retort the sample (60 min), reweigh the retorts and collectors, centrifuge (10 min) and measure the volume of oil and water produced and, finally, determine the specific gravity (30 min) of the shale oil. In all these steps there is chance for error, particularly when different people are doing the assays. The NMR measurements can be obtained directly in gallons-of-oil-per-ton-of-shale units with a suitable calibration line. To obtain an oil yield by NMR requires about two minutes per sample, including the time spent in riffling and weighing the sample. In the NMR method, a simple voltage measurement is made and, if coupled to a programmable calculator or minicomputer, an instantaneous assay can be obtained. Thus a factor of 50 in rapidity of assay is easily obtainable with NMR methods over the conventional Fischer assay.

CONCLUSIONS

The free induction decay amplitude measured on oil-shale samples by pulsed NMR linearly correlates with Fischer assay oil yields. This has been shown from analyses of 405 samples from two different oil-shale cores. In cores for which adsorbed water may be an important contributor to the NMR signal, it was necessary to make two NMR measurements of the free induction decay amplitude to correct for these interferences.

ACKNOWLEDGMENTS

The work upon which this report is based was done under a cooperative agreement between the Energy Research and Development Administration (E.R.D.A.) and the University of Wyoming.

Reference to specific equipment does not imply endorsement by the E.R.D.A.

REFERENCES

1. Decora, A. W., F. R. McDonald and G. L. Cook. "Using Broad-Line Nuclear Magnetic Resonance Spectrometry to Estimate Potential Oil Yields of Oil Shales," *U.S. Bur. Mines Rep. Invest.* **RI 7523** (1971).

2. Farrar, J. C. and E. D. Becker. *Pulse and Fourier Transform NMR* (New York: Academic Press, 1971), p. 21.

4

THE TOSCO-II OIL SHALE PROCESS

John A. Whitcombe and R. Glenn Vawter

The Oil Shale Corporation
Los Angeles, California

THE TOSCO-II PROCESS

This chapter describes the TOSCO-II retorting process and other processing facilities included in the design of a commercial oil shale plant. It also presents economic projections for production of hydrotreated shale oil and, alternatively, for crude shale oil.

Process Description

In the TOSCO-II Process, crushed oil shale is heated to approximately 900°F by direct contact with heated ceramic balls. At this temperature, the organic material in oil shale rapidly decomposes to produce hydrocarbon vapor. Cooling of the vapor produces crude shale oil and light hydrocarbon gases. Figure 4.1 is a schematic diagram of the process.

The thermal decomposition reaction takes place in a rotating kiln (referred to as the pyrolysis reactor or retort) shown in the central portion of Figure 4.1. The feed streams to the retort are 1/2 in. diameter ceramic balls heated to about 1100°F and preheated shale are crushed to a size of 1/2-in. or smaller. The rotation of the retort mixes the materials and causes a high rate of heat transfer from the ceramic balls to the shale. At the discharge end of the retort, the ceramic balls and shale are at substantially the same temperature, and the shale is fully retorted.

The hydrocarbon vapor formed by the retorting reaction flows through a cyclone separator to remove entrained solids and then into a fractionation

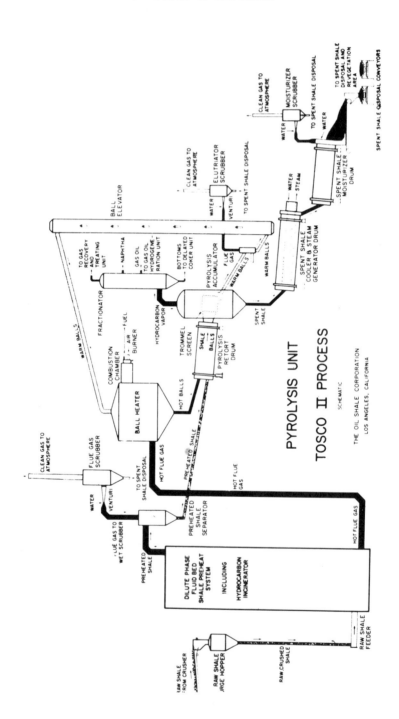

Figure 4.1   Tosco II Process.   (The Oil Shale Corporation, Los Angeles, California)

system similar to the primary fractionator of a catalytic cracking unit. In the fractionator the oil vapor is cooled to produce heavy oil, distillate oils, naphtha and light gases.

The ceramic balls and processed shale (referred to as spent shale) flow from the retort into a cylindrical trommel screen. Spent shale passes through the screen openings and into a surge hopper. The ceramic balls flow across the screen and into a bucket elevator for transport to the ball heater where they are heated by direct contact with flue gas. The ceramic balls are then recycled to the retort.

Spent shale, discharged from the retort at 900°F, is first cooled in a rotating vessel containing tubes in which water is vaporized to produce high pressure steam. It then flows to a rotating vessel in which it is further cooled by direct contact with water. The water flow is controlled to obtain about 12 wt % moisture in the spent shale discharged from the vessel. The moisture is added to control dust emissions and to make the spent shale suitable for compaction in disposal procedures described later in this chapter.

As noted earlier, the crushed oil shale is preheated prior to its entry into the retorting vessel. The preheating is achieved by direct contact of the crushed shale with the flue gas effluent from the ball heater.

The principal gaseous effluent from the process is the flue gas used to heat the ceramic balls and to preheat the shale. The process includes a wet scrubber system to control the particulate content of the gas and an incinerator to control its hydrocarbon content. Emission of oxides of sulfur and nitrogen are controlled by the selection of fuels used in the process and, in the case of nitrogen oxides, the firing temperatures of process heaters.

Process Yield

Tests in a pilot plant and semiworks plant (Figure 4.2) have shown that the TOSCO-II process recovers substantially 100% of the recoverable hydrocarbon in oil shale as determined by the Fischer assay procedure. Table 4.1 shows results from a seven-day, continuous operating period of the semiworks plant, in which the plant was operated substantially at its design capacity and operations were particularly directed to reliable measurement of product yields. The average plant yield during this period was 322.2 lb of hydrocarbons per ton of oil shale processed, some 1.7% greater than produced by Fischer assay of a composite sample of shale representative of the average plant feed during the operating period.

Figure 4.2 Seventeen-story tall semiworks structure at Parachute Creek houses the retorting system developed by TOSCO. Crushed oil shale ore is first preheated by hot flue gases, then rapidly retorted at about $900°$F by mixing with heated ceramic balls. The system permits virtually 100 wt % recovery of contained hydrocarbons. Facility is a 1000 ton/day model of each of the 11,000 ton/day retorting units to be used in commercial production. Semiworks plant was shut down in the spring of 1972, following completion of successful runs which met design, operability and environmental protection objectives.

Table 4.1   Semiworks Plant Yield Data

Hydrocarbons	Plant Yield lb/ton	Fischer Assay Yield lb/ton
C_1 - C_4	49.6	24.3
C_5 and heavier	272.5	292.4
Total Hydrocarbons	322.1	316.7
Other Gas Products		
H_2 + CO	4.5	3.7
CO_2 + H_2O	32.7	31.3

Crude Shale Oil Product

Table 4.2 shows the quality of the crude shale oil (C_5 and heavier) produced by the TOSCO-II retorting process. The whole oil has a sulfur content of 0.7 wt % and an API gravity of 21°.

Table 4.2 also shows that nitrogen compounds are present in substantial quantity in all fractions of the crude shale oil. The nitrogen content of the whole oil is about 1.9 wt %. This is an unusually high level compared to the nitrogen content of conventional crude oils. For example, heavy crude oil from the Los Angeles basin, one of the highest nitrogen content crudes processed in this country, contains about 0.6 wt % nitrogen. The principal purpose of the hydrotreating facilities is removal of nitrogen compounds, which are catalyst poisons in many refining processes, including reforming, catalytic cracking and hydrocracking.

Table 4.2   Properties of Crude Shale Oil

Component	Vol. %	°API	Wt % S	Wt % N
C_5 - 400	17	51	0.7	0.4
400-950	60	20	0.8	2.0
950+	23	6.5	0.7	2.9
Total	100	21	0.7	1.9

Crude shale oil normally has a pour point above 80°F; however, this pour point can be reduced to below 30°F by heating the heaviest portion of the oil to 700-750°F for about 30 minutes and then combining the heat treated heavy oil with the lighter fractions.[a] Analysis of this process shows that heat treating of the heavy oil generates substances that are effective pour point depressants.

Gas Product

Table 4.3 shows a typical analysis of the C_4 and lighter components produced in the TOSCO II retorting process. Because air is excluded from the TOSCO-II retort, the gas is substantially free of nitrogen and contains only the amount of carbon dioxide produced by pyrolysis.

Table 4.3   Semiworks Plant Composition of C_4 and Lighter Gas

Component	Wt %
H_2	1.50
CO	3.51
H_2S	5.16
CO_2	33.08
CH_4	11.93
C_2H_4	8.67
C_2H_6	8.43
C_3H_6	11.08
C_3H_8	5.45
$C_4's$	11.19
Total	100.00

COMMERCIAL PLANT DESIGN

The proposed Colony commercial plant (Figure 4.3) is located in Western Colorado in the southern part of the Piceance Basin which contains the world's largest known oil shale reserve. This oil shale deposit is, in turn, the world's largest known hydrocarbon reserve.

---

[a]U.S. Patent 3,284,336.

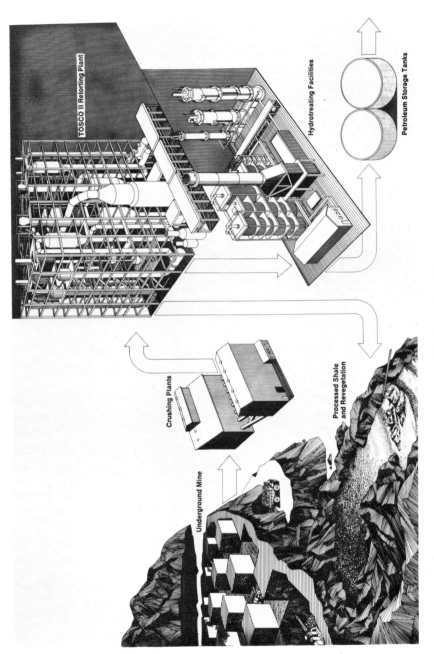

Figure 4.3   Commercial plant schematic.

The plant is to be constructed on Parachute Creek north of Grand Valley, Colorado. This property has considerable topographical relief, including narrow canyons in the southeast and south central parts of the property. The existing 1000 ton per day semiworks plant is located in the canyon valley at an elevation of 6600 ft. On the high plateau above the canyons, surface elevations generally range from 7500-8300 ft. The commercial processing facilities will be located at an elevation of 8100 ft. The decision to locate the commercial plant on the plateau was made principally because meteorological studies showed the canyon to be subject to extreme atmospheric inversion conditions.

Except where the deposit has been eroded away in the formation of the deep canyons, the property is continuously underlain by a thick, rich oil shale deposit referred to as the mahogany zone of the Green River formation. The commercial operation will mine a 60 ft interval of this zone, with an average Fischer assay grade of 34.8 gallons of oil per ton of rock. The reserves in the 60 ft interval are sufficient to support the 66,000 ton per stream day processing rate for 17-20 years.

Mining and Crushing

The top of the 60 ft interval to be mined is at an elevation of 7100 ft. Entry to the deposit will be by horizontal drifts through adits located in the cliff face above the floor of the canyon.

Mining will be by the underground, room-and-pillar method. Mining equipment of the size and type to be used commercially has already been tested in a prototype mining operation in which 1.2 million tons of rock were mined. This operation included programs designed to provide a sound basis for projection of commercial mining costs. It also included one of the most extensive rock mechanics investigations ever carried out in preparation for commercial mining. Results from the rock mechanics work provide a good basis for design of the commercial mine, including projection of room and pillar sizes and mine recovery factor.

The various elements of the mining operation are depicted in Figure 4.4. As shown, the mining is by a heading and bench operation in which the upper half of the deposit is mined before the lower half.

The upper level mining operation starts with drilling a number of holes at least 20 ft deep into a face some 50 ft wide and 30 ft high. Because the rock is soft and has a built-in lubricant, extremely high drill penetration rates, in excess of 8 ft/min, are routinely achieved. When the drilling of a face is completed, a mixture of ammonium nitrate and fuel oil is loaded into the holes and then detonated to produce more than 2000 tons of broken rock from a single face. This rock is loaded

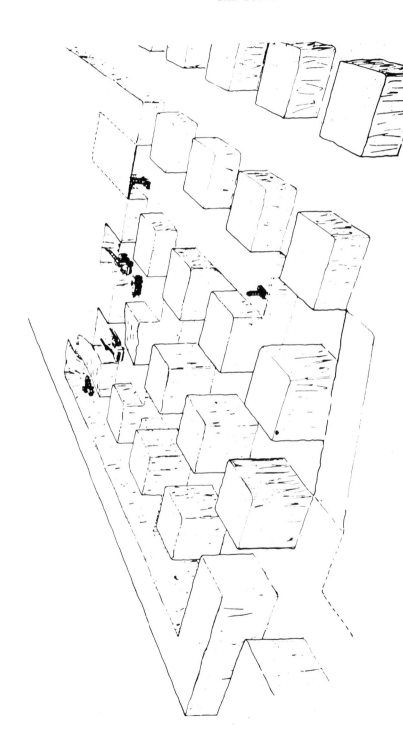

Figure 4.4 Perspective drawing of oil shale room and pillar mining cycle.

into trucks and delivered to the primary crusher. After the broken rock is removed, the newly formed faces are scaled to remove loose rock, and bolts are installed into the newly formed mine roof.

The lower level mining operation is substantially the same as used for the upper level except that the holes for blasting are drilled vertically downward.

The large underground workings in an oil shale mine make possible the use of large and productive mining equipment generally associated with surface mining. For example, in the prototype mining operation, rock was transported out of the mine in a 75-ton truck, and the truck was loaded with a front end loader with a bucket capacity of 10 tons.

The design basis for the crushing and screening facilities included in the commercial plant was derived from test programs that included testing of five different types of crushing machines installed at the semiworks plant.

In the proposed commercial plant, rock from the mine is reduced to below 10 in. in size in a primary crusher located near the mine adit and then conveyed, partially in an inclined tunnel, more than half a mile to a stockpile with a capacity of 5 million tons. Rock is reclaimed from this stockpile and conveyed to a secondary crushing plant consisting of ten crushing and screening units operating in parallel.

The minus 1/2-in. product from the secondary crushing plant is conveyed to surge facilities and then to the retorting units.

Process Units

Figure 4.5 is a block flow diagram showing the process units included in the proposed commercial plant.

After mining and crushing, the shale is fed to the retorting unit, which consists of six 11,000 ton/day TOSCO-II retorting trains operating in parallel. As noted earlier, the vapor formed by retorting flows to a fractionation system where it is cooled to produce several liquid fractions and uncondensed gas. The heaviest oil fraction, consisting of material boiling above 950°F and comprising 23 vol % of the whole oil is fed to a delayed coker.

The commercial plant includes two hydrotreating units. One of these, the distillate hydrotreater, processes the 400-950°F oil formed in the retorting reaction plus similar boiling range components formed in the coker. The second hydrotreater processes C_5 to 400°F naphtha formed in the retort, the coker and the distillate hydrotreater. The distillate hydrotreater is designed to reduce the nitrogen content of the 400°F plus product from the unit to less than 1000 ppm. The naphtha

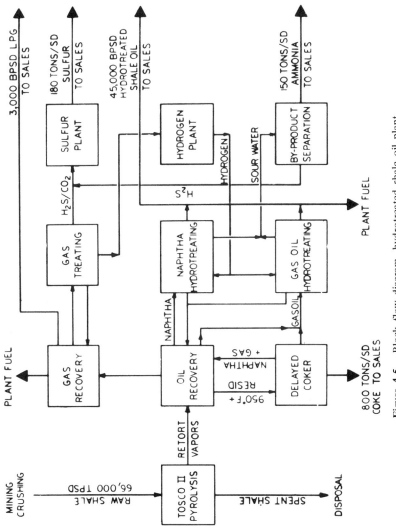

Figure 4.5 Block flow diagram—hydrotreated shale oil plant.

hydrotreater is designed for a product nitrogen content of about one ppm. Sulfur removal is substantially complete in each of the hydrotreating units.

The process designs for the hydrotreating reactors were prepared by Atlantic Richfield Company after pilot plant investigations of the hydrotreating of shale oil produced by the TOSCO-II process.

In addition to the facilities described above, the commercial plant includes units for gas processing, production of hydrogen, separation of ammonia from hydrogen sulfide and conversion of hydrogen sulfide to sulfur.

The principal products from the plant described above are 48,000 BPSD of hydrocarbon distillates consisting of 45,000 BPSD of C_5 –950°F, sulfurfree, 40° API oil and 3000 BPSD of a mixture of propane and propylene. By-products include 180 tons of sulfur, 150 tons of ammonia and 800 tons of coke per stream day.

The plant outputs noted above are net production rates after internal supply of all fuel consumed in the processing operation, including the process gas used for hydrogen generation, and after internal supply of diesel fuel for mobile equipment for mining and spent shale disposal. The projected fuel consumption for the commercial plant process units include all the C_2 and lighter components and all the C_4s produced in the retorting and oil upgrading operation plus some 5300 BPSD of hydrotreated oil. Diesel fuel is obtained by fractionation of the products from the distillate hydrotreater.

The product slate shown in Table 4.3 can be altered by changing the fuels selected for burning in the process facilities. The production of C_5-plus product can, for example, be increased by burning the C_3-products in place of hydrotreated oil.

Table 4.4 shows properties of the C_5 –950° oil noted above. This oil is a blend of sulfur free distillate products, and refining it into a slate of high value products is a relatively simple matter. Facilities for such purpose consisting of only an atmospheric distillation unit and reformer

Table 4.4   Properties of Typical Hydrotreated Shale Oil

Component	Vol %	°API	ppm Nitrogen
C_5 - 400	43	50	1
400 - 650	34	35	800
650 - EP	23	30	1200
Total	100	40	

would produce gasoline, sulfur-free light distillate fuels (No. 1 and No. 2 heating oils and diesel fuel) and a sulfur-free heavier distillate fuel oil suitable for use as industrial fuel oil or as blendstock to reduce the sulfur content of residual fuel oils.

Crude Shale Oil Production

Figure 4.6 is a block flow diagram for a plant for production of crude shale oil instead of hydrotreated oil. In this case, the fuel requirement for the plant is supplied by combustion of gas formed in the retorting process after scrubbing of the gas to remove hydrogen sulfide. The total production of oil and LPG of 55,000 BPSD is higher for this case because liquid yield is not reduced by coking or fuel consumption for oil up-grading. Sulfur is the only by-product of the crude shale oil plant.

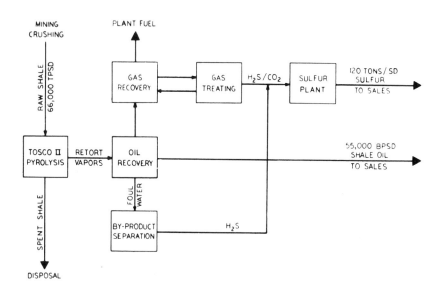

Figure 4.6   Block flow diagram—crude shale oil plant.

Spent Shale Disposal

The spent shale produced by the TOSCO-II process is a fine-grained, dark material comprising about 80 wt % of the raw shale feed. It contains about 4.5 wt % organic carbon formed in the thermal decomposition reaction because of a hydrogen shortage in the organic material contained in the raw shale. The mineral constituents of spent shale consisting of principally dolomite (calcium-magnesium carbonate), calcite (calcium carbonate), silica and silicates, are substantially unchanged by the retorting process. The retorting temperature used in the TOSCO-II process is well below the decomposition temperature of either dolomite or calcite.

Essentially all of the spent shale is finer than 8 mesh, and 60 wt % of it is finer than 200 mesh. Considerable size reduction occurs in the retorting process because the retorting destroys the organic material which holds together the finely divided sedimentary particles that form oil shale.

The spent shale disposal plan incorporated in the commercial plant design is based on safe and environmentally sound disposal procedures developed and demonstrated in an extensive program started more than ten years ago. Field investigation of spent shale disposal technology began in 1965 after completion of construction of the 1000 ton/day semiworks plant at Parachute Creek. Early work at Parachute Creek included demonstration of a satisfactory technique for adding moisture to spent shale to control dust and to permit compaction to form a stable embankment. Small revegetation test plots were constructed in 1966 to evaluate plant growth factors and plant species, and in 1967 the first field demonstration revegetation plot was constructed and seeded. This plot produced a good growth of grass and is still in good condition today. Field work was expanded beginning in 1970 with testing of various kinds of compaction equipment and construction of additional revegetation demonstration plots at various elevations and exposures. The plots are still being monitored at the present time. Extensive off-site studies relating to spent shale disposal have also been carried out. These include measure of the permeability of compacted spent shale, analysis of the quality of water runoff from spent shale embankments, and additional soil mechanics investigations to provide a basis for design of stable embankments.

In the commercial plant, spent shale will be disposed of in an embankment formed in Davis Gulch in the northwest area of the property. This gulch has more than sufficient volume to hold all the spent shale produced during the life of the mine without the embankment height exceeding the elevation of the adjacent, surrounding surface.

In the disposal operation, moistened and cooled spent shale will be conveyed to the disposal area and loaded into 150-ton trucks for transport to the active disposal site. It will then be spread in thin layers to form the embankment and compacted to increase the dry density of the material from 65 to above 90 lb/cu ft. The compaction makes the embankment stable and causes it to be, for practical purposes, impermeable to flow of water through it. The embankment will be revegetated as portions of it are completed.

The commercial disposal plan also provides for dams upstream and down-stream of the disposal area. The upstream dam protects the embankment against flash floods. The downstream dam is designed to collect precipitation run-off from the pile for use in spent shale moisturizing.

COMMERCIAL PLANT ECONOMICS

Table 4.5 presents projections of capital investment, direct operating costs and by-product credits for commercial production of hydrotreated oil and crude shale oil. All costs are in mid-1974 dollars.

Table 4.5   Commercial Plant Costs

	Hydrotreated Oil	Crude Shale Oil
Oil Plus LPG Product		
Barrels per stream day	48,000	55,000
Barrels per calendar day	43,200	49,700
Millions of barrels per year	15.7	18.1
Capital Investment, $ millions	653	510
Direct Operating Cost		
$ millions per year	68	57
$/bbl of oil products	4.30	3.20
By-Product Value[a]		
$ millions per year	9.5	1.2
$/bbl of oil products	0.60	0.07

[a]The ammonia, sulfur and coke by-products are valued at $125, $30, and $6 per short ton, respectively.

Capital Investment

The capital investment estimates include all on-site facilities and equipment required for the mining and processing operations. Also included are the costs for the plant access road; flood control and run-off dams; off-site by-product terminal and staging area; pipeline and pumping facilities to transport water from the Colorado River to the plant site; mine predevelopment work; catalysts, chemicals, spare parts and supplies for the plant; community development assistance; operator recruitment and training; environmental monitoring; plant owner's supervision of the design and construction; and working capital. The capital investment estimates do not include either the cost of the oil shale reserve or the cost of the pipeline for the oil product.

Approximately 90% of the total investment shown in Table 4.5 for production of hydrotreated oil was estimated by C. F. Braun & Co. and its subcontractors. This portion of the estimate includes an allowance of approximately 15% for contingency and to provide for possible incentives that may be required to attract construction labor to the job site. The remainder was estimated by TOSCO or the Operator for the Colony joint venture.

Due solely to business conditions at the time of its preparation, the design and cost estimate is less reliable than it would have been if prepared in more normal times. In the period in which the design and estimate were prepared (June 1973 to August 1974), and particularly toward the end of this period, the demand for construction materials, process equipment and shop space was so intense that it was in many cases impossible to obtain reasonable bids on materials and equipment. The reliability of the estimate was also adversely affected by the high rate of escalation, without precedent in recent years, then occurring in the quoted prices for materials and equipment.

The capital investment for the crude shale oil plant presented in Table 4.5 is approximate and was prepared by TOSCO as a modification of the C. F. Braun & Co. estimate.

Operating Costs

The operating cost estimates presented in Table 4.5 provide for all direct operating costs of the project and exclude depreciation, other capital related costs and reserve costs. Specific comments on items included and not included in the operating cost estimate are noted below:

1. The cost of transporting the products and by-products to their marketing area is not included in the estimate of direct operating costs.

2. The operating cost estimate provides for maintenance of the mobile equipment used for mining and spent shale disposal but does not include an allowance for deferred capital expenditure for periodic replacement of the equipment. Such deferred capital expenditures are estimated to average about $4 million per year over the life of the project.

3. The operating cost estimates provide for purchase of all the electric power required in the operations.

4. All fuel consumed in the process units is produced by the plant and none is purchased, except for diesel fuel for the case in which crude shale oil is the plant product. In the case of the hydrotreated oil plant, the diesel fuel is supplied from plant production.

The operating cost projections shown in Table 4.5 were prepared by TOSCO with the assistance of data and information provided by the operator of the Colony joint venture and from the results of the commercial plant design work. Because of the recent economic conditions, these projections are also not as reliable as would normally be the case for a project in an advanced design stage. The principal uncertainties are in the costs of process plant maintenance, power, insurance and taxes. Because of enormous escalation in the cost of construction, traditional methods of projecting costs in these areas must be re-evaluated; such re-evaluation is now in progress for this project.

Projected Selling Price

The selling price required for the oil has been computed as a function of discounted case flow rates of return on investment, consistent with the capital and operating cost projections presented in Table 4.5. The computations were made on an all equity basis, in accordance with present regulations with respect to federal and state tax rates and depletion and investment credit allowances, and with maximum depreciation rates permitted under present regulations. The computations also presume that the plant participants can utilize tax credits generated by the project in the year the credit occurs. The calculations further presume that deferred capital expenditures (principally for mine mobile equipment) will be derived from project cash flow.

For a 12% post-tax discounted cash flow rate of return on investment and with the premises noted above, the required average selling prices for the oil products from crude shale oil and hydrotreated oil plants, are $9.50 and $13.20 per barrel respectively. Reduction of the required rate of return to 10% reduces projected selling prices to $8.20 per barrel for crude shale oil case and $11.50 per barrel for the hydrotreated oil case. These projections are in 1974 dollars and do not provide for inflation or deflation or other changes in economic conditions compared to those in effect when the C. F. Braun & Co. estimate was prepared. The projections also do not provide for interest on debt or recovery of the cost of the oil shale reserve.

The current price of landed foreign crude oil is between approximately $12 and $13 per barrel with the prospects for ever rising prices. The long range viability of shale oil production is thus indicated, especially considering the severe oil shortage in this country. However, on the short term, owing to the economic and political uncertainties discussed above, and owing to the fact that this is a first-of-a-kind project, it is doubtful that conventional private financing will be available for the first plant. Government support in some form is considered necessary to stimulate the construction of pioneer plants. Once an oil shale industry is established, however, participants in plant construction will likely find that a substantial portion of the plant can be financed by a long-term loan secured only by the plant assets. Such financing can be expected to have a material and favorable effect on the required selling prices of the oil product while maintaining a satisfactory rate of return in equity capital.

NOTE

The Oil Shale Corporation (TOSCO) has been a leader in the development of technology for recovery of oil from oil shale for more than 15 years. In this period, TOSCO and joint venture associates have spent more than $55 million on such development in a program that has included demonstration of the TOSCO-II retorting process in a 25 ton/day pilot plant and a 1000 ton/day semiworks plant. The development program is complete, and technology covering all aspects of oil shale processing is now ready for commercial use.

The readiness for commercial use includes completion of a detailed design and cost estimate and an environmental analysis for commercial facilities processing 66,000 tons per stream day of oil shale and producing 48,000 barrels per stream day of hydrotreated, sulfur-free distillate products.

The detailed design and cost estimate were completed in August 1974 at a cost of more than $12 million by C. F. Braun & Co. as managing contractor and Fluor Utah, Inc. as the principal subcontractor for a four-party joint venture referred to as Colony Development Operation (Colony). The participants in the venture are TOSCO, Atlantic Richfield Company (Operator), Ashland Oil, Inc., and Shell Oil Company. Field construction of the commercial plant had been scheduled to begin in May 1975; however, pending resolution of economic uncertainties then affecting this and other projects the participants agreed in October 1974 to suspend the start of field construction. The absence of government policy relating to oil pricing and to the nation's need for supplemental oil supplies was also a factor in the decision to suspend the start of field construction.

The environmental analysis, which covers the oil shale plant and related off-site facilities, including a pipeline for the oil product, was submitted to the Department of the Interior about April 1974. The Department is preparing a draft Environmental Impact Statement for the proposed plant and off-site facilities.

5

MILD OXIDATION OF BIOLEACHED OIL SHALE

D. K. Young, S. Shih and T. F. Yen

University of Southern California
Los Angeles, California 90007

The study of organic matter present in the Green River shale formation is of considerable geochemical interest as evidenced by past reports dealing with isolation and identification of the hydrocarbon fraction contained in both the solvent soluble organic portion (bitumen) and the generally insoluble organic portion (kerogen) of the shale. Depending on the location of the shale sample collected for analysis, the amount of organic matter averages 15%. However, due to the extensiveness of the oil shale formation, the potential use of the entrapped organic matter as a possible source of liquid fuel ($\sim$ 1.5 trillion barrels of known reserves)[1] has provided an incentive to industry to develop the most efficient process for extracting this reserve.

Major industrial investigative efforts are presently centered around destructive pyrolysis (or retorting). The basic retorting techniques themselves are not new; they were known at least 50 years ago.[2] The most ideal adaptation of these basic techniques to the present problem of shale oil recovery would be the *in situ* retorting process. This technique obviates the high costs of mining, crushing, transporting and, ultimately, of disposing the spent shale. To date various *in situ* schemes, such as injection of hot gas or steam, electrical discharge, and underground nuclear explosion have been considered to provide the necessary source of heat to start the retorting process and overcome the low permeability of the formation. Estimate of the recovery efficiency is about 50% of the organic matter with 25% burnt for the retorting process and another 25% as unrecoverable carbon-rich residue (coke).

As an alternative way of releasing the organic material, primarily the kerogenic portion since the bitumens are easily extracted with solvent from the mineral matrix, we have investigated the feasibility of mild oxidative degradation. Oxidation has been used as a tool for structural oxidants, and the starting material is usually a kerogen concentrate with a major portion of the mineral matrix removed by concentrated hydrofluoric acid treatment. In the present study, the shale sample has been pretreated with dilute acid ($\sim$ 0.1 N) for the removal of soluble mineral (dolomite and calcite) only. This can also be accomplished by leaching the shale sample with the acid medium produced by sulfur-oxidizing bacteria (*Thiobacillus* spp.) as has been demonstrated in this laboratory.[3] The shale sample, which has undergone this bioleaching process, is about 70-75% mineral constituent, composed largely of quartz and clay. Starting with this "bioleached" shale, the release of the entrapped kerogen will be carried out in mild oxidative steps using alkaline potassium permanganate solution and ozone separately. Mild stepwise oxidation is intended to prevent further fragmentation of released organic matter, since it is more reactive than the still entrapped kerogenic material. Permanganate solution and ozone[4] are known to oxidize saturated hydrocarbons; however, the mode of oxidation is not likely to be the same. The basic skeletal structure of kerogen has been postulated to compose of largely cross-linked aliphatic chains;[5] it would be of interest to compare the effect of these two oxidants on the kerogen entrapped in a resistant mineral matrix. Results of the permanganate oxidation are presented in the rest of this report.

EXPERIMENTAL

The shale sample was collected from the Mahogany Ledge of the Green River formation and crushed to pass a 150-mesh screen. From elemental analysis, the shale was estimated to contain about 13% organic matter by weight. The solvent extractable material, bitumens, was found to be about 2%. Direct bioleaching of the raw shale with the acid medium of the sulfur oxidizing bacteria was not done; instead it was pretreated by dilute hydrochloric acid, resulting in a similar weight loss of 40% as compared with directly bioleached shale. The dilute acid-treated shale was Soxhlet extracted with a (4:1) benzene:methanol mixture for 84 hr to remove the soluble material. The hydrocarbon fraction from the soluble material was analyzed by gas chromatography (Hewlett-Packard Model 5750) on a 9 ft x 1/8 in. stainless-steel column, packed with 3% SE-30 on Chromosorb Q. The branched and cycloalkane components are essentially identical with an earlier report.[6]

Stepwise permanganate oxidation of 10 g of the shale treated above was carried out in a manner similar to that of Djuricic et al.[5] For each step, 25 ml of a solution with 0.08 M $KMnO_4$ were warmed with the shale to a temperature of 75°C. Upon completion of oxidation, the solid residue (oxidized shale and MnO_2) was separated from the aqueous layer by centrifugation, and a fresh portion of $KMnO_4$ solution was added to continue the oxidation. Oxidation was terminated after the 28th step. At this point the shale still contains entrapped organic matter, since carbon analysis showed a carbon content of 0.83% in the solid residue.

The aqueous layer from each step of the oxidation was combined, and acidification with hydrochloric acid yielded a precipitate (fraction I) which turned into a lustrous dark brown material when dried. An amount of 1.24 g of the precipitate was isolated, corresponding to about 7.45% of the untreated raw shale. This fraction was analyzed further. The organic material that remained in the aqueous layer was isolated by first evaporating the solution to dryness with a rotary evaporator under reduced pressure, and then the residue was extracted thoroughly with diethyl ether. Evaporation of the diethyl ether left behind 0.39 g of extract (fraction II). Together the two fractions constituted 9.78% of the raw shale.

A portion of the oxidation product (fraction I) was dissolved in pyridine-d_5 and subjected to NMR analysis (Varian Model TC-60) to characterize its overall structure (Figure 5.1). BF_3 esterification in methanol and subsequent heptane extraction yielded 293 mg (per gram of material) of heptane-soluble esters. Gas chromatography of the heptane soluble esters, under conditions mentioned above, is shown in Figure 5.2. Identification of the unbranched aliphatic esters (both mono- and di-basic) was done by co-injection of methyl ester standards. The presence of branched and cyclic carboxylic esters was inferred from urea clathration method that removed the unbranched esters to a considerable degree.

RESULTS AND DISCUSSION

The products of the oxidation reaction are potassium salts of carboxylic acids. The compounds were identified using various techniques; a comparison of the gas chromatograms with a collection of standard samples confirmed the presence of saturated unbranched aliphatic mono-carboxylic acids (C_{11}-C_{31}), saturated straight-chained aliphatic di-carboxylic acids (C_{12}-C_{18}), and branched aliphatic (or naphthenic) carboxylic acid ($\sim C_{12}$-C_{20}). NMR spectra of the oxidation products in pyridine-d_5 solvent revealed the absence of a significant amount of aromatic protons. Since it has been shown that alkyl-substituted aromatic compounds are converted

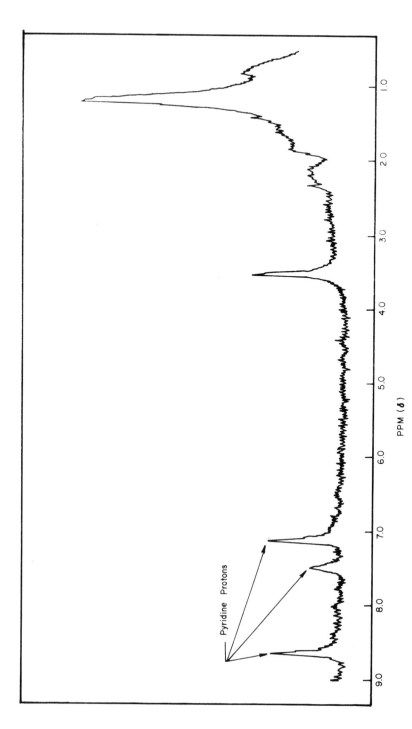

Figure 5.1   NMR spectrum of fraction I dissolved in (99.9%) pyridine-d_5.

N — unbranched aliphatic carboxylic methyl esters
D — unbranched aliphatic dicarboxylic methyl esters
B — branched or cyclic acid methyl esters.

The numbers refer to the number of carbon atoms (not including the methoxyl carbon).

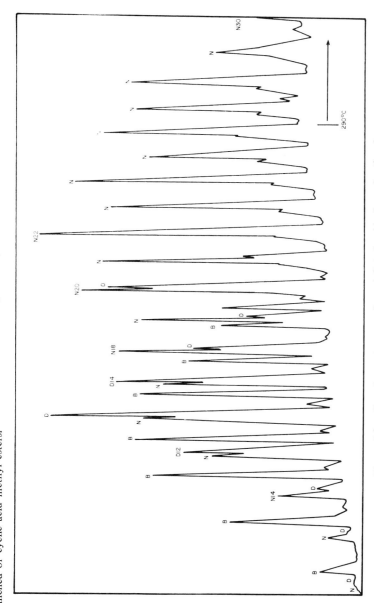

Figure 5.2   Gas chromatogram of precipitated acids from fraction I.

to aromatic carboxylic acids, one can conclude that Green River kerogen contains few aromatic sites, which agrees with the results of Djuricic *et al.*[5] There is, however, no apparent dominance of the unbranched aliphatic dibasic acids as observed by Djuricic and co-workers. A likely cause for this may be incomplete oxidation of the kerogen "nucleus," since the presence of mineral (*e.g.*, quartz and clay) that is resistant to mild chemical conditions would tend to hinder oxidation of the kerogen bound to it. This is consistent with the drastic increase of polyfunctional aliphatic acids (especially dicarboxylics) as oxidation of kerogen concentrate progresses.[7]

The results of the present investigation indicate that oxidative release of the entrapped organic material in an aqueous medium is possible without disaggregating or dissolving the resistant mineral. Under the mild oxidative conditions used, a significant amount of the organic matter is released as soluble acids ($\sim$ 9.78% of the total raw shale). If an efficient method can be devised to quickly remove the released acids so that further oxidative degradation is prevented, a stronger oxidizing medium could be used.

Pyrolysis of Green River shale at high temperature ($\sim 500°C$) tends to yield some aromatic hydrocarbons,[8] possibly due to rearrangement of aliphatic hydrocarbons. Oxidation in an aqueous medium can proceed at much lower temperature ($75°C$) while the product is mainly aliphatic in nature. Apparently all available organic material present can be released by oxidation, and there is no coke formation as in pyrolysis.

Permanganate is not a suitable oxidant for large scale oxidation even though it is a very effective oxidant for analytical purposes. Once the permanganate is reduced to MnO_2, there is no simple and economical method of oxidizing it back to MnO_4-. Besides one must be wary of the possible environmental effects of excessive usage of a metal such as manganese. Ozone has been considered as an alternative oxidant as it can be readily generated from oxygen, and excess ozone can be easily destroyed (by a catalyst) before releasing to the atmosphere as oxygen. Robinson *et al.* have partially oxidized the Green River shale with ozone; Bitz and Nagy have used ozone on coal and kerogenic materials.[10]

ACKNOWLEDGMENT

This work is supported by NSF Grant No. GI-35683.

REFERENCES

1.   Prien, C. A. *Ind. Chem. Eng.* **56**, 32 (1964).

2.   McKee, R. H. *Shale Oil.* (New York: Chemical Catalog Co., 1925).

3.   Findley, J. E., M. D. Appleman, and T. F. Yen. *J. Appl. Microbiol.* **28**, 3 (1974).

4.   Hamilton, G. A., B. S. Ribner and M. T. Hellman. "Oxidation of Organic Compounds III," In *Advances of Chemistry Series* (R. F. Gould, Ed. (1967), p. 15.

5.   Djuricic, M., M. D. Vitorovic and K. Biemann. *Geochim. Cosmochim. Acta* **35**, 1201 (1971).

6.   Andres, D. E. and W. E. Robinson. *Geochim. Cosmochim. Acta* **35**, 661 (1971).

7.   Burlingame, A. L. and B. R. Simonet. *Nature* **222**, 741 (1969).

8.   Dinneen, G. U. *Chemical Engineering Progress Symposium Series* **61**(54), 42 (1965).

9.   Robinson, W. E., D. L. Lawlor, J. J. Cummins and J. Fester. *U.S. Bur. Mines, Rep. Invest.* **6166** (1963).

10. Bitz, M. C. and B. Nagy. *Proc. Nat. Acad. Sci.* **56**, 1383 (1966).

6

OPERATIONS AND ENVIRONMENTAL CONSIDERATIONS, OCCIDENTAL PETROLEUM CORPORATION *IN SITU* OPERATIONS

Randall T. Chew, III

Director, Geology/Environment
Occidental Oil Shale, Inc.

Operations commenced at OXY's "Logan Wash Property" ten miles northeast of DeBeque, Colorado in June, 1972 (Figure 6.1). Ground was broken for the first buildings and mining commenced in September, 1972. The property consists of approximately 4000 acres of which about 2000 are underlain by oil shale. Although there had been no previous operations on the Logan Wash property itself, a small amount of mining and an unsuccessful pilot plant using a surface retort was operated in the 1920s on Logan Mountain about three miles west of the current operations.

The Logan Wash property is in the southwestern part of the Piceance Creek Basin in Colorado, about 30 miles south of the center. High-grade oil shale is considerably thinner on the Logan Wash property than in the center of the basin where sections as much as 2000 ft thick average 15 gal/ton. The 15 gpt section at the Logan Wash site ranges from 300-350 ft thick. It includes the Mahogany Ledge and the rocks about 200 ft above the Mahogany Ledge. The depositional center of the basin moved southwest late in the history of its formation and the thickest ore grade oil shale lies above the Mahogany Ledge there whereas it lies as much as 1500 ft below the Ledge (or Zone) in the center of the basin.

In the OXY process low-grade material below and within the sections selected for mining is broken and mined out so that the void created amounts to 15-20% of the material to be processed. The ore is then

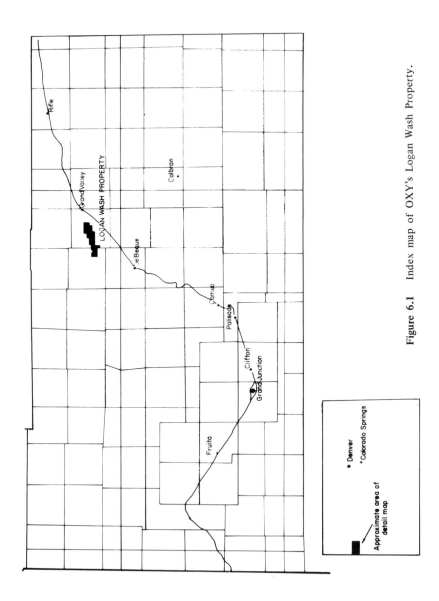

Figure 6.1   Index map of OXY's Logan Wash Property.

drilled and blasted and the void literally transferred to the ore grade material. The space where the ore previously existed, plus the space mined out is filled with rubble. The low-grade seam selected for mining may lie below the ore or may be one of two common low-grade seams, the A-groove and B-groove that occur within the ore grade material.

Air, plus recycle gas, is introduced at the top of the broken rubble pile and removed at the bottom. The pile is fired at the top and the flame front moves downward. In the retorting process the kerogen molecule is cracked into smaller molecules of crude oil. The products are oil, light hydrocarbons, water and carbon. The carbon provides the fuel for the process. Retorting occurs at the forward end (bottom) of the retorting front at a temperature of about 900°F. The flame front at a temperature of 1300-1500°F follows behind. Shale oil formed at the retorting front moves downward by gravity ahead of the front and never "sees" the flame. Figure 6.2 shows an elevation of a typical retort arrangement and Figure 6.3 shows a plan of a typical production panel.

Through the early part of 1975, all retorting operations took place at the "Experimental Mine," begun in 1972. Three retorts 35 ft square varying in height from 85 to 105 ft have been fired. These have produced from 15-40 barrels per day of shale oil. The rubble piles in these three retorts have been accessed through drill holes from the surface about 500 ft above the top of the retort. The surface plant has contained most of the pumping facilities and all of the control and monitoring equipment.

Figure 6.4 shows conventional mining operations in the Experimental Mine. Figure 6.5 shows the Topside Plant above the Experimental Mine. The building contains the control center, instrumentation, and pumps. Figure 6.6 shows the bulkhead in the drift to Room 3, outlet pipes, and instrumentation.

Commencing with the second retort (Room 2), certain of the pumps and monitoring and control equipment were moved underground, setting the pattern for future commercial operations where essentially all equipment will be underground.

In conjunction with the construction and firing of the third retort (Room 3), a large retort approximately the size of a commercial retort has been commenced in a new "Commercial" mine about one-half mile west of the Experimental Mine. The retort (Room 4) will be 120 ft square by 250 ft high and is expected to be fired in September, 1975.

Access is via two sets of drifts 24 ft square with the upper about 280 ft above the lower. All operations at the Commercial Mine will be underground setting the pattern for future genuinely commercial operations which would utilize the same mine openings. When the mine is in

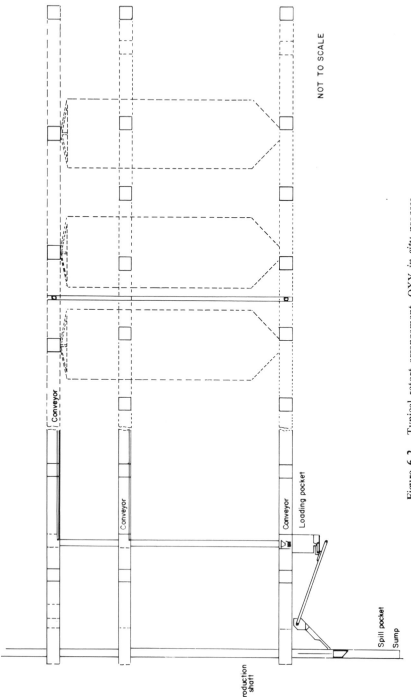

Figure 6.2 Typical retort arrangement, OXY *in situ* process.

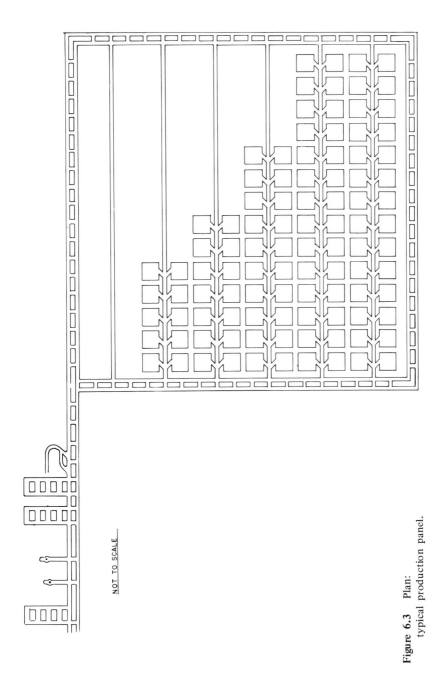

NOT TO SCALE

Figure 6.3 Plan: typical production panel.

Figure 6.4   Conventional mining operations.

Figure 6.5   Topside plant above the experimental mine.

Figure 6.6   Bulkhead and drifts to Room 3.

normal operation all offices, pumps and instrumentation will be underground. The only surface installation will be connected with shipping the
oil. Room 4 is expected to produce several hundred barrels per day.
Figure 6.7 shows the Commercial Mine drifts and the access road.

Products of the OXY modified *in situ* oil shale process are crude shale
oil and power. The off-gas is expected to be burned by gas turbines to
produce power. A 30,000 bbl/day commercial operation is envisioned
for the Logan Wash property and would be expected to produce about
200 Mw of surplus power.

The OXY modified *in situ* process is environmentally desirable compared with other shale oil processes for several reasons. Perhaps the most
important of these is that no spent shale is produced to be disposed of
at the surface. The mined material is raw oil shale that can be dumped
in the adjacent canyons and is identical with naturally eroded oil shale
now forming talus slopes in the same canyons. It is expected that the
dumps will be revegetated in a manner similar to the existing talus slopes.

Another consideration is that the OXY modified *in situ* process has
essentially no water consumption since none is used for cooling or for
stabilizing spent shale dumps. Drilling water necessary for mining operations can come from the mine itself.

Figure 6.7   Commercial drifts and access road.

The OXY modified *in situ* process will use fewer employees than other processes. About 600 employees will be needed for the 30,000 bbl/day plant. It has been announced that 800-1000 employees would be needed for a 50,000 bbl/day plant using a surface retort. Just as important, no construction force as large as or larger than the normal work force will be needed during the construction phase. The initial construction phase in the OXY modified *in situ* process consists of mine development with only a minimum of surface construction work to be done. The mine development will be accomplished by crews that will stay on with the company to do the mining connected with commercial operations. The work force will steadily increase over the first two years past time zero rather than having a large construction that will move out to be replaced by a smaller operating force.

The OXY modified *in situ* process will recover more barrels of oil per acre because it is capable of economically handling lower-grade ores than the other processes. The grade cut-off for the OXY process is between 15 and 20 gal/ton. For the other processes it is rarely below 30 gal/ton.

Environmental work on the Logan Wash project has two parallel thrusts. The first is acquiring and preparing data for permit applications required for the operation. Some 50 permits are currently in force on the project. The second thrust is that of acquiring the baseline data needed to prepare a complete Environmental Impact Statement that will be required when the decision is made to go commercial on the Logan Wash site. Since OXY is also vitally interested in actions related to the Federal Prototype Oil Shale Leasing Programs, the Environmental group monitors these activities closely.

Operations at the Logan Wash project have expanded rapidly since its inception in June, 1972. In June 1972 the number of people employed on the project doubled from 1 to 2 and tripled when a third person was hired later in the month. In June 1975 about 240 persons were employed on the project, plus about 60 others working for contractors. The Environmental group was formed in September 1973, in the midst of this rapid expansion. The project was and is still in the experimental stage so it was decided to contract essentially all the technical environmental work and use in-house personnel only for data collecting, which would also function as a training program.

The system has worked well and the Geology/Environment group consists of eight persons. All professional activities involved in baseline data acquisition and in dealing with various state and county agencies at the technical level is handled by an engineering consulting firm. Preparation of Environmental Analysis Reports and permit applications is handled in-house. Emphasis has been on short "tight" reports containing precisely the information required by regulations.

Environmental baseline data projects have been completed or committed in the following areas: archeology, paleontology, hydrology, engineering geology, fauna, flora, meteorology, sound and seismic. An elementary socioeconomics study, probably confined to a statement of the number of employees anticipated, the education and training required for them, and the pay scale distribution, remains to be prepared. A Water Quality study related to the quality and improvement, if needed, of the small amount of water to be released from a commercial operation is also expected to be prepared. Target date for completion of the Environmental Impact Statement is February 1976.

It is anticipated that a decision to go commercial at the Logan Wash site could come as early as the first quarter of 1976. The Environmental group expects to have baseline data acquired for the period of one year, collated, and interpreted at the time the commercial decision is made so that there need be little or no delay in submitting the Environmental Impact Statement known to be required. In addition, the group is attempting to anticipate environmental problems that may arise associated with such factors as pipeline and powerline routes that cannot be determined until the commercialization decision is made.

7

ELECTROLYTIC OXIDATION
AND REDUCTION OF OIL SHALE

C. S. Wen and T. F. Yen

Department of Chemical Engineering
University of Southern California
Los Angeles, California 90007

INTRODUCTION

Reserves of oil shales and related minerals in the world represent an important potential source of fuel. Most methods of yielding a crude shale oil have been based on heating oil shale to a high temperature ($\sim 500°C$).

The high temperature retorting of oil shale tends to yield many aromatic hydrocarbons.[1] It has been found that at high temperatures, aliphatic C–C and ether C–O bonds are easily broken and rearranged in shale oil[2] where radical species containing carbon atoms can combine in rapid fashion at a high temperature ($\sim 500°C$) to form carcinogenic agents (such as PAH—polycyclic aromatic hydrocarbons). This very significant health problem combines the disposal of vast amounts of spent shale with groundwater contamination, causing serious environmental impact. Therefore, it appears that present retorting techniques at high temperatures are not the most favorable recovery shale oil methods.

It is shown in Chapter 2 that bioleaching effectively removes carbonate minerals from the shale, and thus develops its porosity and permeability. Increasing the extent of the internal surface will increase the ability to break down the mineral organic matrix in oil shale. To avoid high temperature heat treatment, the applicability of electrolytic oxidative degradation and the low-pressure and low-temperature electrolytic hydrogenation of oil shale have been studied as the method to produce commercially valuable organic compounds and to drive out the clean oil from bioleached oil shale.

According to the literature, the use of oxidative degradation for the exploration of oil shale has been done effectively by using oxidizing agents, including potassium permanganate,[3] hydrogen peroxide,[4] and chromic acid.[5]   For bioleached oil shale in an alkaline medium, organic material (kerogen) bound to inorganic residues can be removed almost entirely by permanganate oxidation (See Chapter 5). The chemical oxidation of oil shale yields valuable hydrocarbons that could be converted readily to diesel fuel; however, for large scale application, the excessive usage of permanganate and the vast amounts of spent reduced form MnO_2 will cause a very significant environmental problem and limit the feasibility of this technique.

In principle, any successful chemical oxidation should have its electrochemical counterpart. Electrochemical oxidation of coal has been tried by Lynch et al.[6] and Belcher,[7] who reported that the use of anodic oxidation led to the formation of ulmic acids and some water-soluble compounds. By contrast to chemical methods, none of the spent reacting agents appear as environmental pollutants or as impurities in the products produced by the electrolytic oxidation. This could be a stepwise process controlled by anodic potential, electrode materials, overvoltage, and concentration of products. Also, valuable metallurgy from the oil shale could be extracted as by-products by using the electrolytic technique at the same time and with the same reactor.

The insoluble organic substance in oil shale, kerogen, contains considerable quantities of nitrogen-, sulfur-, and oxygen- compounds that cause the major factors in the high decomposition temperature for kerogen and produce the significant pollutants during the retorting process. Hydrogenation is recommended to remove these undesirable elements and to upgrade shale oil to conventional petroleum characteristics. Since mild chemical reducing agents do not greatly affect the kerogen, extremely strong reducing conditions are needed. Chemical reduction of kerogen requires high pressure (4200 psig) and temperature (355°C).[8]   However, the possibility of molecular rearrangements under such drastic conditions limits this technique.

In the bioleached oil shale, at the beginning of electrolytic reduction, the interconnected pore characteristics will help release the bridge portion of kerogen (i.e., amide, cycloalkadiene, ester, and heterocyclic compounds).[9] These released bridge components of kerogen serve as the proton-donor for further electrolytic refining of enriched bioleaching oil shale. Further electrochemical addition of hydrogen decreases the organic sulfur and

nitrogen content in oil shale.   This chapter presents preliminary work relating to the electrolytic oxidation and reduction of bioleached oil shale.

EXPERIMENTAL

Electrolytic Oxidation of Oil Shale

Electrolytic oxidations were carried out using an H-type cell of 150-ml
total capacity; apparatus used for these works is shown diagrammatically
in Figure 7.1.   The anode and cathode compartments were separated by
a porous frit.   The anode electrodes were made of 45 mesh copper and
platinum gauzes (2.5 x 5 cm) rolled into cylinders, and a lead sheet (12
cm^2) served as the cathode.   A current density was maintained constantly
throughout the oxidation.

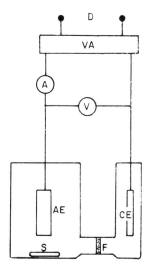

D: D.C. source

VA: Voltage adjuster

A: Ammeter

V: Voltmeter

AE: Anode electrode (platinum gauze)

CE: Cathode electrode (lead sheet)

S: Stirrer

F: Frit

Figure 7.1   Apparatus of electrolytic oxidation.

Shale samples, which were collected from the Mahogany Ledge of the Green River formation and the high grade shale (Anvil Point, Colorado), were ground to pass a 150-mesh screen and leached with 20% hydrochloric acid for 24 hours instead of the acid medium of the sulfur oxidizer bioleaching, which resulted in a weight loss of 33%, similar to that of bioleached shale. After leaching, samples were placed in the anode chamber, together with the total 100 ml of 3 N sodium hydroxide solution to fill the level in two chambers. The mixture in the anode chamber was kept well stirred with a magnetic stirring bar to avoid foaming. The kerogen concentrate was Soxhlet-extracted with a mixture of benzene:methanol (4:1) for 48 hours to remove the soluble organics (bitumen) (See Chapter 5). The residue kerogen concentrate contained 9.75% ash after analysis.

Upon completion of the oxidation, the contents of the anode chamber were filtered and washed well with hot water. The aqueous layer was acidified with hydrochloric acid to yield a precipitate which was analyzed by gas chromatography with BF_3 esterification in methanol, and subsequent heptane extraction. The filtrate from the acidification was extracted with carbon tetrachloride. An example of separation and analysis of kerogen concentrate is shown in Figure 7.2.

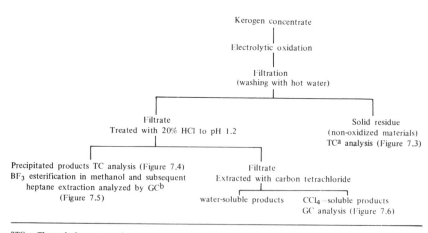

Kerogen concentrate

Electrolytic oxidation

Filtration
(washing with hot water)

Filtrate
Treated with 20% HCl to pH 1.2

Solid residue
(non-oxidized materials)
TC^a analysis (Figure 7.3)

Precipitated products TC analysis (Figure 7.4)
BF_3 esterification in methanol and subsequent
heptane extraction analyzed by GC^b
(Figure 7.5)

Filtrate
Extracted with carbon tetrachloride

water-soluble products CCl_4–soluble products
GC analysis (Figure 7.6)

[a]TC = Thermal chromatography
[b]GC = Gas chromatography

Figure 7.2 Separation and analyses of the products obtained by the electrolytic oxidation of kerogen concentrate.

The hydrocarbon fraction of the oxidization product was analyzed by gas chromatography (Hewlett-Packard Model 5750) on 10' x 1/8" glass columns packed with 3% SE-30 (silicone gum rubber) on Chromosorb Q and 5% Carbowax 20 M on Chromosorb W. The analysis of solid residue and the precipitated product of kerogen oxidation was carried out by MP-3 thermal chromatography with heating at 40°C/min to 620°C with a TC (thermal conductivity) detector, and the effluent gases were trapped and back-flushed to the gas chromatographic analysis. Table 7.1 summarizes the various fractions of oil shale that have been tested by the electrolytic oxidation.

Table 7.1   Electrolytic Oxidation of Oil Shale

	Leached Shale	Leached Shale	Kerogen Concentration
Sample source	Anvil Point, Colo..	Green River	Green River
Pretreatment	7.4% HCl leaching to 33% wt loss	7.4% HCl leaching to 30% wt loss	Extracted with benzene/methanol (4:1) 84 hr after acid leaching (Ash 9.75% W)
Sample weight	2.0 g	1.0 g	0.5 g
Anode	pt	pt	Cu
Current density (amp/cm^2)	0.01	0.01	0.005
Temperature	25°C	25°C	25°C
Time of oxidation	25 hr	40 hr	40 hr
Weight of ppt (acidify to pH 1.2)	0.30 g	0.05 g	0.02 g
Weight of residue	1.50 g (elemental analysis in Table 7.2)	0.72 g	0.30 g

Electrolytic Reduction of Oil Shale

The electrolytic reduction of kerogen concentrate was carried out by a 250-ml flask with three necks that were fitted with reducing tube adapters. The center adapter was fitted with a thermometer that could be immersed in the solution. An aluminum sheet was sealed through the right adapter neck into the flask with total 12 cm^2 immersed surface in the electrolyte serving as the cathode. A carbon rod, 3.5 cm long and 0.5 cm in diameter, was used as the anode passing through the left neck. During electrolysis, the mixture was kept well stirred by a magnetic stirrer and the cell was cooled by an ice bath to maintain a constant temperature ($\sim$ 35°C). A current was kept constant, 0.05 amp/cm^2, by a little regulation of applied voltage ($\sim$ ±5 volts).

In a typical run, a sample of 1 g of 100-150 mesh kerogen concentrate (the Green River formation) in 100 ml of ethylenediamine containing 1.4 gm of LiCl was electrolyzed for 30 hr. The reagents used were the same as that described for the electrochemical reduction of coal with LiCl in ethylenediamine.[10] To isolate the products, the reduced mixture was poured into 100 ml ice water and centrifuged to separate the reduced kerogen. Repeated washings and centrifugations were continued until the washings had a pH of 8 (test paper). The residue was transferred to a round flask and dried by a stream of nitrogen, then kept in an oven at 75°C. A portion of the solid residue was analyzed by infrared spectroscopy (Beckman Model AccuLab 6) and was sent to ELEK Microanalytical Laboratories, Torrance, California, for elemental analysis. The remaining portion of the solid residue was Soxhlet-extracted with heptane for 10 hr, then dried and extracted again with a mixture of benzene/methane (4:1) for 48 hr. The heptane and benzene/methanol extracts were analyzed by gas chromatography. A 10 ft x 1/8 in. glass column packed with 5% Carbowax 20 M on Chromosorb W was used. The centrifuged liquid layer from the electrolyzed mixture was evaporated to remain at 50 ml, neutralized with carbon dioxide gas to a pH of 8, then extracted with heptane and chloroform.

RESULTS AND DISCUSSION

Electrolytic Oxidation of Kerogen Concentrate

The thermogram of kerogen of the Green River Formation[11] shows a sharp peak at 480°C, which represents the decomposition of kerogen at this temperature. For the solid residue after electrolytic oxidation of kerogen, the initial decomposition temperature occurs at 280°C followed by the second breakdown peak at 375°C and the smallest third peak at 420°C (Figure 7.3). All these are lower than that of the decomposition temperature of kerogen concentrate (480°C). The trailing peaks at 100°C and 580°C belong to the water and CO_2, respectively. The corresponding gas chromatogram of effluent-trapped gas from the above decomposition shows that almost all hydrocarbons have been oxidized and have disappeared, leaving only some low carbon number materials.

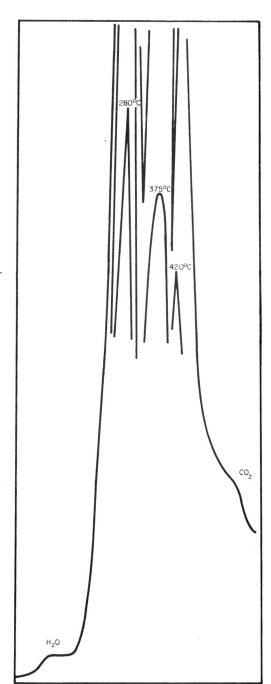

Figure 7.3 Thermal chromatogram of nonoxidized residue of kerogen concentrate.

Another thermogram (Figure 7.4) shows the thermal decomposition of the precipitated product. The first peak of thermogram at 110°C could be the water removal and some easily decomposed products. The other two peaks present at 170° and 250°C are expected, owing to the water-insoluble carboxylic acid. The minor trailing peak at 430°C could belong to the long chain of water-insoluble aliphatic fatty acids. The gas chromatogram of BF_3 esterification of precipitated product shows a predominance of mono- C_{14} to C_{22} carboxylic acid and C_{12} dibasic acid (Figure 7.5).

The extract from carbon tetrachloride was analyzed by gas chromatography. Two fractions of CCl_4-soluble product are present on the gas chromatogram (Figure 7.6). The low-boiling point fraction could be due to the oxidation of short-chain components that are cross-linked on the outside of kerogen.

Electrolytic Oxidation of Leached Oil Shale

After 25 hours electrolytic oxidation of 2.0 g acid leached high grade shale (Anvil Point, Colorado), the oxidized residue shale was separated from the aqueous layer by filtration. The filtrate was acidified to yield a precipitate (0.30 g) that corresponds to about 10% of the original raw shale. As shown in Figure 7.7 by the gas chromatogram, the heptane-soluble compounds from the BF_3 esterification of the oxidized precipitated products were composed of saturated monocarboxylic acids (C_{10}-C_{22}), normal dicarboxylic acids (C_6-C_{11}), and branched aliphatic carboxylic acids.

The ultimate elemental analysis of the original leached shale and solid residue (Table 7.2) shows that about 76.3% of organic hydrocarbons have been oxidized and dissolved in a liquid layer. The carbon tetrachloride extract of the water-soluble filtrate showed a group of peaks from the gas chromatographic analysis. Some of them were identified as saturated fatty alcohols from C_{14} (1-tetradecanol) to C_{20} (1-eicosanol). Identification of peaks was done by co-injecting known standards (obtained from the Applied Science Laboratories Inc.), and by comparing the chromatographic retention time of each compound with those of standard kits.

The result of the present investigation of electrolytic oxidation shows an efficient stepwise process to the oxidative degradation of leached oil shale. By controlling the anodic potential, further degradation of kerogen could be prevented entirely and could produce the valuable chemicals from oil shale at room temperature. Impurities from an oxidizing agent are not present in the product mixture. This will be helpful for developing

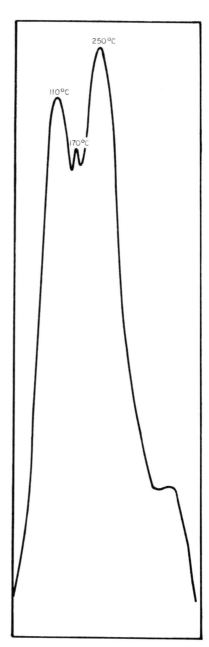

Figure 7.4 Thermal chromatogram of oxidized precipitated product from electrolytic oxidation of kerogen concentrate.

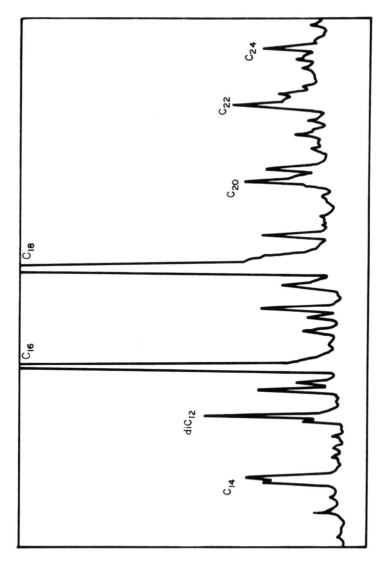

Figure 7.5   Gas chromatogram of BF$_3$ esterification of precipitated product from electrolytic oxidation of kerogen concentration.

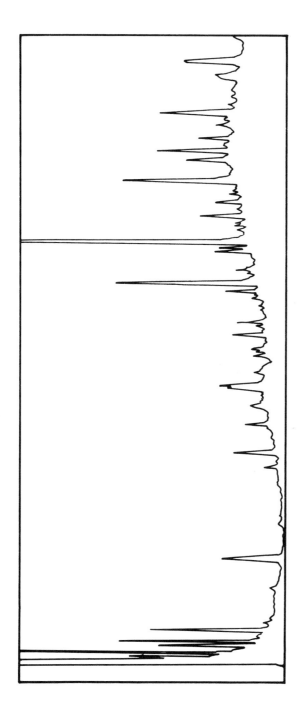

Figure 7.6   Gas chromatogram of carbon tetrachloride extraction of electrolytic oxidation of kerogen concentrate.

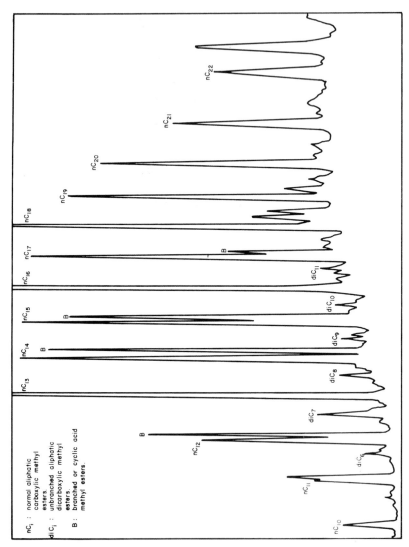

Figure 7.7 Gas chromatogram of BF$_3$ esterification of precipitated product from electrolytic oxidation of leached oil shale.

Table 7.2   Ultimate Analyses of Solid Residue from
Electrolytic Oxidation of Leached Oil Shale

	Carbon (wt %)	Hydrogen (wt %)	Ash (wt %)
Original leached shale[a]	41.7	4.65	54.3
Residue from 25 hr oxidation	9.46	1.59	85.41

[a]Based on 33% weight loss

electrolytic bioleached oil shale oxidation into procedures suitable for large-scale preparative work.

As mentioned in Chapter 5, the bioleached oil shale can be oxidized easily with potassium permanganate in the alkaline solution.   Therefore, further search is made for the use of oxidant agents present in the electrolyzed solution or adsorbed on the electrode surface serving as oxidative catalysts.   In such cases, the bioleached oil shale to be oxidized reacts chemically with the catalyst oxidant which is electrolytically re-generated.   The other oxidants, with the exception of permanganate, include rhenium, osmium, hydrogen peroxide and pyrite.   Among them, pyrite (Fe^{3+}-Fe^{2+}) will be demonstrated, since pyrite does exist in oil shale and can be removed by two aerobic bacteria (*i.e., Thiobacillus thiooxidans* and *Ferrobacillus ferrooxidans*).[1][2]   The scheme for the re-moval of pyrite with bacteria and the reaction of kerogen from bioleached oil shale is described by Figure 7.8.

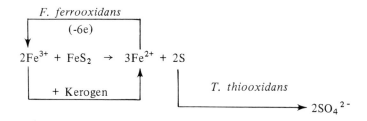

Figure 7.8   The scheme for the removal of pyrite with bacteria
and the reaction of kerogen.

Thiobacillus thiooxidans has been found to be an efficient bioleaching medium of oil shale (see Chapter 2) and has a definite oxidation potential which can be enhanced by exerting an electrolytic oxidation potential.[13,14] Kerogen in the scheme is the compound irreversibly oxidized by Fe(III) which is generated electrolytically. Owing to this chemical reaction, the electroactive form Fe^{3+} is regenerated by *Ferrobacillus ferrooxidans* and enhanced by exerting an electrolytic oxidation potential. From this observation, it is possible to develop an electrolytic oxidation system to the sulfur- and iron-oxidizing bacterial culture.

Electrolytic Reduction of Kerogen Concentrate

Gas chromatogram of normal alkanes found in heptane extract from reduced kerogen is shown in Figure 7.9. Peaks were identified as described before. The predominant normal alkanes obtained are nC_{22} to nC_{28}.

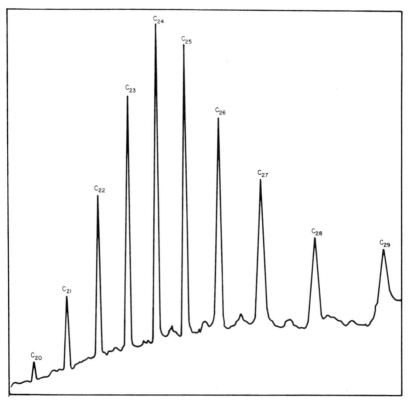

Figure 7.9 Gas chromatogram of normal alkanes founded from electrolytic reduction or kerogen concentrate.

Distribution of n-alkane is presented in Table 7.3. The total yield of this heptane-soluble product is about 3.7% on the original kerogen concentrate. The extract of benzene/methanol (4:1)-soluble fraction of reduced kerogen consisted of an orangish-brown semisolid, which was about 6.4% of the original kerogen concentrate.

Table 7.3   Normal Alkanes Obtained from Electrolytic Reduction
of Kerogen Concentrate

n-Alkane	Relative Quantity[a]
C_{19}	0.01
C_{20}	0.03
C_{21}	0.15
C_{22}	0.39
C_{23}	0.72
C_{24}	1.00
C_{25}	0.90
C_{26}	0.70
C_{27}	0.60
C_{28}	0.38
C_{29}	0.23
C_{30}	0.18
C_{31}	0.15
C_{32}	0.08

[a]Relative to the area of $n\text{-}C_{24}$.

The infrared spectra (potassium bromide pellets) of original and reduced kerogen concentrate are given in Figure 7.10. Using the baseline intensity technique, bands above 1600 cm^{-1} of the spectra were almost the same, except the broad absorption centered at 3470 cm^{-1} could be due to the O-H hydroxyl groups and the N-H stretching vibration. The latter may come from the reaction agent (ethylenediamine). It was found that reduction produced increased intensity for the symmetrical bending mode of CH_3 groups at 1370 cm^{-1}, but the other aliphatic CH bands at 1452, 2922 and 2959 cm^{-1} were kept constant. Bands below 1250 cm^{-1} of reduced kerogen are quite different from the original sample. The strong absorption of this region is probably caused by a concentration of the inorganic minerals that were present originally in the fixed kerogen mineral matrix.

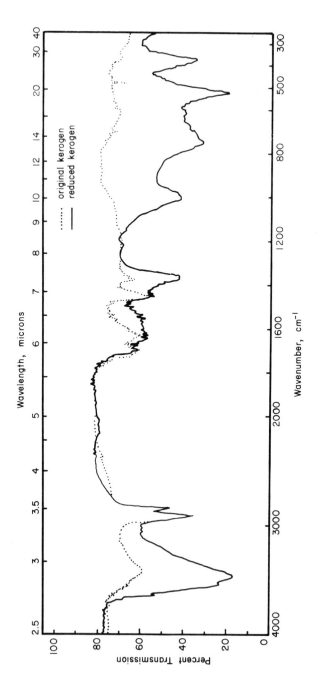

Figure 7.10 Infrared spectra of original and reduced kerogen concentration (KBr pellets).

The elemental analysis of the original and reduced kerogen concentrate (Table 7.4) indicated little significance, because a certain amount of reduced components have been dissolved in a liquid layer. The increase in ash content could be due partly to incomplete removal of lithium chloride and contamination of aluminum electrode, and partly to a concentration of the original ash by dissolving the "soluble" fractions of the reduced kerogen. The contamination of aluminum may have been due to erosion or may have removed some of the eroded surface layer mechanically by stirring the electrolytic solution during electrolysis. The calculation of atomic ratio of hydrogen to carbon is put on an ash-free basis. Increase in oxygen content is probably due to oxidation during the electrolysis and recovery of the sample. An interesting result of electrolytic reduction of kerogen concentrate is the great decrease in sulfur content, as seen in Table 7.4. Some of the sulfur loss undoubtedly is caused by elimination of sulfur from heterocyclic organic structures.

Table 7.4   Electrolytic Reduction of Kerogen Concentration[a]

	Original Kerogen Concentrate	Reduction[b] Sample 1	Reduction[c] Sample 2
Carbon, %w	68.60	40.71	40.55
Hydrogen, %w	8.42	6.41	6.47
Nitrogen, %w	3.48	3.25	3.34
Sulfur, %w	2.41	0.14	0.22
Oxygen, %w	8.75	15.24[d]	18.38
Ash, %w	9.76	34.25	30.75
H/C atomic ratio[e]	1.47	1.82	1.84

[a]Samples were dried in vacuo overnight at $50°C$ prior to analysis.

[b]Reduced sample obtained from washings and centrifugations (pH 8).

[c]Reduced sample obtained after heptane and benzene/methanol extraction.

[d]By difference.

[e]Based on the assumptions that the added oxygen was present as oxygen and not as water;[15,16] the ratio of nitrogen retained in residue to nitrogen dissolved in liquid is the same as those of carbon and hydrogen, and nitrogen added as ethylenediamine ($C_2H_8N_2$).

The heptane and chloroform extracts from the liquid layer were analyzed by gas chromatography. The gas chromatogram showed normal C_{20}, C_{21} and C_{22} alkanes present among a group of peaks.

Electrolytic reduction of kerogen concentrate appeared to be a powerful technique to break down the cross-linked matrix of kerogen. The decrease of sulfur content of shale oil will be an important advantage in the electrolytic hydrogenation process. Normal alkane extract from reduced kerogen also offers feasible large-scale electrolytic solvent refining in the future.

ACKNOWLEDGMENT

This work is supported by NSF No. GI-35683 and PRF 6272-AC2.

REFERENCES

1. Dinneen, G. U. "Effect of Retorting Temperature of the Composition of Shale Oil," *Chem. Eng. Prog. Symp. Series* **61**(54), 42 (1965).
2. Shulman, A. I. and V. A. Proskuryakov. "Mechanism of the Decomposition of Kerogen from Baltic Sea Kukersity in the Bitumenization State," *Khim. Tverd. Topl.* **6**, 73 (1971).
3. Djuricic, M. V., D. Vitorovic, V. D. Andresen, H. S. Hertz, R. C. Murphy, G. Preti and K. Viemann. "Acids Obtained by Kerogens of Ancient Sediments of Different Geographic Origin," (Oxford, Braunschweig: Pergamon Press, 1972), p. 305.
4. Down, A. L. and G. W. Himus. "A Preliminary Study of the Constitution of Kerogen," *J. Inst. Petrol.* **27**, 426 (1941).
5. Burlingame, A. L. and B. R. Simoneit. "High Resolution Mass Spectrometry of Green River Formation Kerogen Oxidations," *Nature* **222**, 741 (1969).
6. Lynch, C. S. and A. R. Collett. "Electrolytic Oxidation of Coal," *Fuel* **11**, 408 (1932).
7. Belcher, R. "The Anodic Oxidation of Coal. I. Introduction and Preliminary Experiments," *J. Soc. Chem. Ind.* (London), **67**, 212 (1948).
8. Hubbard, A. B. and J. I. Fester. "A Hydrogenolysis Study of the Kerogen in Colorado Oil Shale," *U. S. Bur. Mines, Rep. Invest.* **5458** (1958).
9. Yen, T. F. "A New Structural Model of Oil Shale Kerogen," *ACS, Div. Fuel Chem. Preprint* **19**(2), 109 (1974).
10. Sternberg, H. W., C. L. Delle Donne, R. E. Markby and I. Wender. "Electrochemical Reduction in Ethylenediamine," in *Coal Science*, R. F. Gould, Ed. (Washington, D.C.: ACS Publications, 1966), Chapt. 33.
11. Scrima, D. A., T. F. Yen and P. L. Warren. "Thermal Chromatography of Green River Oil Shale. I. Bitumen and Kerogen," *Energy Sources* **1**(3) (October 1974).
12. Silverman, M. P. "Mechanism of Bacterial Pyrite Oxidation," *J. Bacteriol.* **94**(4), 1046 (1967).

13. Fischer, D. J., A. E. Herner, A. Landes, A. Batlin and J. W. Barger. "Electrochemical Observations in Microbiological Processes. Growth of *Thiobacillus thiooxidans*, I," *Biotech. Bioeng.* **VII**, 471 (1965).

14. Fischer, D. J., A. Lander, M. T. Sandford, II,, A. E. Herner and C. J. W. Wiegand. "Electrochemical Observation in Microbiological Processes. Growth of *Thiobacillus thiooxidans*. II," *Biotech. Bioeng.* **VII**, 491 (1965).

15. Reggel, L., R. Raymond, W. A. Steiner, R. A. Friedel and I. Wender. "Reduction of Coal by Lithium-Ethylenediamine. Studies on a Series of Vitrains," *Fuel* **40**, 339 (1961).

16. Reggel, L., I. Wender and R. Raymond. "Reduction of Coal by Lithium-Ethylenediamine. A Re-evaluation of Previous Data," *Fuel* **43**, 75 (1964).

8

RETORTING INDEXES FOR OIL SHALE PYROLYSES FROM ETHYLENE/ETHANE RATIOS OF PRODUCT GASES

I. A. Jacobson, Jr., A. W. Decora and G. L. Cook

Laramie Energy Research Center
Energy Research and
    Development Administration
Laramie, Wyoming 82070

INTRODUCTION

Production of shale oil from oil shale is currently practical only by thermally decomposing (retorting) the organic materials in the shale and collecting the liquid products. Investigations to develop processes for retorting oil shale have resulted in many proposed designs for the equipment. However, to maintain control of any of the processes, measurements of appropriate input and output parameters are required to indicate conditions during the decomposition and the subsequent collection of products. The direct measurement of retorting temperatures is not always possible. Flow rates through the retorts give only an indirect measure of residence times for material in the heated zones. Both residence times and temperature are important control parameters—related to economy of operation and quality of product.

The pyrolysis of oil shale kerogen is a very complex reaction or group of reactions that results in the production of a myriad of hydrocarbons and hydrocarbon derivatives. These products range from compounds containing one carbon atom per molecule (methane) to compounds containing greater than 30 carbon atoms per molecule. It is not currently feasible to set forth the mathematical relationships of the pyrolysis reactions with great certainty. This inability to set down the exact mathematical relationships of the overall pyrolysis reaction should not preclude the gleaning of certain useful empirical data that can be used to assist in the interpretation or control of the retorting processes.

Shale oil production by thermal decomposition of the organic material in the shale has been described as a pseudo first-order process.[1,2] In a practical process the shale is heated to the maximum temperature over a finite period of time. The products of retorting remain in a heated zone for varying periods of time. The nature of the products depends on both the temperature range over which thermal decomposition takes place and on the residence time of the products in a hot zone. Temperature measurements in a retort are not readily related to the product even if coupled with flow rates through the retort. This chapter develops a parameter that combines the elements of temperature and residence time into a single number that can be used to indicate instantaneous retorting conditions or to compare various thermal processing techniques for oil shale.

The parameter developed for comparison or control of the retorting process has the dimension of temperature. It could be defined as an "effective temperature" or a "Retorting Index." In the laboratory, this index was developed by relating the ethylene/ethane ratio in the product gases from retorting of shale to a measured temperature in the retorting zone. Residence times of the products in the hot zone were nearly constant. In a commercial-size retort, residence times could vary over wide ranges. Residence time variation causes a change in the observed ratio. The calculated parameter also changes and so reflects the changing retorting conditions. Application of the parameter to Fischer assay retorts, gas combustion retorts, and to entrained solids retorts is illustrated with examples. The easily calculable Retorting Index is applicable to *in situ* retorting as well as those retorts used as examples.

EXPERIMENTAL PROCEDURE

Equipment

The equipment consists of an electrically heated quartz tube 2.1 cm i.d. by 83.8 cm long with 24/40 standard taper joints at the ends. A section of the tube, 15 cm minimum length, 43 cm from the inlet was heated to the desired retorting temperature. Heating was accomplished by a three-unit tube furnace, and the temperature was maintained by potentiometer controllers. Oil shale samples were contained in a 1.25 cm by 7.62 cm boat made from stainless-steel screen. The sample boat was moved in and out of the retorting zone by means of a 1-mm stainless steel rod that extended from the boat out through the quartz tube inlet.

A tube receiver, a U-tube trap, and an evacuated gas receiver made up the product collection system. The receiver and U-tube were cooled with liquid nitrogen when nitrogen was used for the sweep gas and with dry ice when oxygen was used in the sweep gas for oxidative retorting runs. Sweep gases into the retort tube were metered through a metering valve. Pressure in the retorting section, as monitored by an open-end manometer, was maintained at atmospheric pressure by venting gases from the U-tube through a stopcock into the gas collection system.

Oil Shale Samples

Oil shale samples from Colorado, Wyoming and Utah were used in this study. The sizes of the oil shale used were (A) 20 to 30 mesh, (B) 10 to 14 mesh, (C) 1/8 in. to 30 mesh, and (D) 1/4 in. to 1/2 in. Most of the retorting work was performed on size C shale. Three different Colorado oil shale samples were obtained from the Bureau of Mines mine at Rifle, Colorado and assayed 53.8, 52.5 and 22 gpt. The 53.8-gpt oil shale had been ground to sizes A and C, the 52.5-gpt shale ground to size D, and the 22-gpt shale ground to sizes B and C. Wyoming oil shale samples were a 12.4-gpt sample from a Washakie Basin, Sweetwater County corehold and 13.4-, 19.9-, 30.5-, and 34.4-gpt shales from the Bureau of Mines Rock Springs site 6, well No. 6-2 core. The Utah shales were from the Gulf Evacuation No. 1 core drilled by Gulf Minerals, and the shale samples assayed 14.5, 20.3, 29.0, and 42.7 gpt. All of the Wyoming and Utah oil shales had been ground to size C. A summary description of the oil shale samples used is presented in Table 8.1.

Pyrolysis Procedure

Temperature profiles of the reaction tube were determined by measuring the temperature inside the tube at 2.54-cm intervals with a thermocouple and potentiometer with sweep gas flowing. Determination of temperature profiles was performed only when work at a new temperature was begun. The temperature at which the furnace was set remained constant, and the temperature variation at any point within the quartz tube would fluctuate ± 2°C (3.6°F) maximum.

In making a retorting run, about 7 g of oil shale were weighed into the sample boat, and the boat was placed at the inlet of the cold reaction tube. The entire retorting system was flushed by evacuation and filling several times with the intended sweep gas. Both the receiver and U-tube trap were cooled, the sweep gas flow adjusted to the desired rate, and the vent opened to the atmosphere.

Table 8.1   Description of Oil Shale Samples Used in the Procedure

Sample No.	Geographical Source	Assay gpt[a]	Sample Mesh Size
1	Colorado	53.8	20 to 30 mesh
2	Colorado	53.8	1/8 in. to 30 mesh
3	Colorado	52.5	1/4 in. to 1/2 in. mesh
4	Colorado	22.0	10 to 14 mesh
5	Colorado	22.0	1/8 in. to 30 mesh
6	Wyoming	34.4	1/8 in. to 30 mesh
7	Wyoming	30.5	1/8 in. to 30 mesh
8	Wyoming	19.9	1/8 in. to 30 mesh
9	Wyoming	13.4	1/8 in. to 30 mesh
10	Wyoming	12.4	1/8 in. to 30 mesh
11	Utah	42.7	1/8 in. to 30 mesh
12	Utah	29.0	1/8 in. to 30 mesh
13	Utah	20.3	1/8 in. to 30 mesh
14	Utah	14.5	1/8 in. to 30 mesh

[a]Potential oil yields were determined by the modified Fischer assay method.[3]

The furnace was then turned on and allowed to heat to temperature. After retorting temperature was reached, the sample boat was moved into the retorting zone and kept there for 20-25 minutes to insure complete retorting. The boat was then moved back to the inlet, and the furnace turned off. To insure complete collection of the gaseous products, gas collection was started 10 minutes before the furnace reached temperature and continued 10 minutes after the furnace was turned off. The coolant baths were removed from the receiver and U-tube trap, the traps were warmed to room temperature, and any liberated gases were swept into the gas collection system. When the retorting run was finished, the pressure in the gas collection system was measured and the shale oil and spent shale were weighed.

For the cracking runs the sample boat was not placed as far down the reaction tube. For these runs the boat position was generally 15.24 cm upstream from the "normal" position, and the retorting temperature was about 100-150°F lower.

The majority of the retorting runs were made with a nitrogen sweep through the retort tube. Gas flow was maintained at 2.5 standard cm^3/min (superficial space velocity of 0.023 ft^3/min/ft^2). Several runs were made with the nitrogen flow increased to 20 standard cm^3/min (superficial space velocity of 0.19 ft^3/min/ft^2). In addition to these basic retorting runs, others were made using air and nitrogen as sweep gas with the oxygen content varying from 3-21% and a total gas flow of 2.5 to 20 standard cm^3/min, steam and nitrogen as the sweep gas with the nitrogen flow at 2.5 standard cm^3/min and a steam rate of 1 g/min.

Gas Analyses

Gas analyses were performed by gas liquid chromatography (GLC) using a 1/8 in. o.d. by 10 ft stainless-steel column packed with 150 to 200 mesh Porapak Q.* GLC operating conditions were a helium flow of 18 cm^3/min and oven temperature programed from 50° to 180°C at 4°C/min. Detection was by thermal conductivity. For quantitative analyses the GLC peak areas were corrected for molar response by the method of Messner.[4]

RESULTS AND DISCUSSION

Table 8.2 is a tabulation of the recoveries and ethylene/ethane ratios for retorting runs performed at 1,064.4° and 1,297.5°F. These data show the type of recovery experienced during the work. It is felt that most of the loss was due to nonrecovery of liquid that condensed in inaccessible parts of the system. As can be seen, the ethylene/ethane ratio changes when the retorting temperature changes.

The change in ethylene/ethane ratio is not linear with change in temperature. A linear relationship can be obtained by using logarithm of the ethylene/ethane ratio and reciprocal of the temperature. Other combinations of saturates and unsaturates, while showing similar changes with temperature, cannot be transformed to linear relationship as readily.

When a linear least squares regression of the log (ethylene/ethane) with reciprocal temperature is performed, the resulting regression equation has a coefficient of determination (100 r^2) of 95. This means that all but 5% of the variation of log (ethylene/ethane) can be explained as reciprocal temperature dependence. Data from retorting runs on oil shales from different locations, of different particle size, and of different assay richness were included in the regression.

The regression equation so derived is

$$\frac{1000}{T} = 0.8868 - 0.4007 \log (\text{ethylene/ethane}) \tag{8.1}$$

where T = temperature, °F.

---

*Reference to a specific brand or trade name is made to facilitate understanding and does not imply endorsement by the Bureau of Mines.

Table 8.2 Recovery and Ethylene/Ethane Ratio for Selected Temperatures of Laboratory Retorting Using Nitrogen Sweep Gas

Oil Shale			Total Flow cm³/min	Retort Temp. °F	Charge g	Recovery, wt %				Wt % Ratio Ethylene/Ethane
Source[a]	Assay gpt	Size[b]				Spent Shale	Oil + Water	Gas	Loss	
C	53.8	C	2.5	1,064.4	7.6052	71.69	22.27	5.05	0.73	0.7012
C	53.8	C	20.0		7.3051	71.82	20.86	6.30	1.02	0.7124
C	53.8	A	2.5		5.9429	72.14	20.84	5.22	1.80	0.7638
C	53.8	C	2.5		7.5043	71.82	22.29	5.15	0.74	0.7207
C	52.5	D	2.5		7.4783	73.73	19.73	5.29	1.25	0.7867
C	53.8	A	2.5		6.1041	72.02	21.36	5.27	1.35	0.7565
C	52.5	D	2.5		8.2537	73.98	19.46	5.02	1.54	0.7979
C	53.8	C	20.0		7.4921	71.99	20.91	6.42	0.67	0.7213
W	12.4	C	2.5		7.5210	88.25	8.49	2.46	0.80	0.6968
C	c	B+C	2.5	1,297.5	8.4510	80.83	14.70	3.44	1.03	0.7950
C	53.8	C	2.5		7.7834	66.29	13.57	15.88	4.26	1.6135
C	53.8	C	2.5		7.8141	66.13	14.97	15.85	3.05	1.7003
C	53.8	C	2.5		7.8151	66.95	13.53	16.92	2.60	1.6762
C	53.8	C	2.5		7.8141	66.38	13.59	17.32	2.71	1.6975

[a]C = Colorado, W = Wyoming.

[b]Particle size, A = 20-30 mesh, B = 10-14 mesh, C = 1/8 in.-30 mesh, D = 1/2 in.-1/4 in.

[c]A mixture of 53.8- and 22-gpt oil shales to give an approximate 36-gpt oil shale.

When Equation (8.1) is recast for the prediction of the Retorting Index, it is

$$RI = T = 1,000/(0.8868 - 0.4007 \log (\text{ethylene}/\text{ethane})) \qquad (8.2)$$

When ethylene and ethane are determined with a two percent accuracy, it is possible to calculate the Retorting Index to $\pm 25°F$ (95% confidence).

Oxygen was added to the sweep gas to determine its effects, if any, on the ethylene/ethane ratio. Total amounts of oxygen had to be kept low so the exothermic oxidation reactions would not upset the thermal balance in the retorting zone by increasing the shale temperature above the furnace temperature. In Table 8.3 are listed the results from the retorting runs made with added oxygen. These runs were made at $1,187°F$ using the 53.8-gpt, size C, Colorado oil shale. When the Retorting Index is calculated for the oxidation retorting runs, it is not significantly different from the furnace temperature. This shows that the presence of oxygen in the sweep gas has no effect on the Retorting Index. A similar conclusion can be drawn from the one retorting run in which steam was included in the sweep gas.

Table 8.3 also lists data obtained from the cracking runs. These data produce a Retorting Index which generally is higher than the retorting temperature. The retorting temperatures for these runs were $100\text{-}150°F$ lower than the furnace temperature. This apparent anomaly can be readily explained. Both ethylene and ethane production in retorting and cracking are controlled by the laws of kinetics. The ethylene/ethane ratio is increased in a thermal cracker by increasing the temperature. The ratio can also be increased by holding the temperature constant and increasing the residence time. The same temperature-residence time control of the ethylene/ethane ratio is found in oil shale retorting. Therefore, increasing the temperature with a small decrease in residence time or holding the temperature constant with an increase in residence time will increase the ethylene/ethane ratio, and the products of retorting will be essentially the same in either case. In most retorts the retorting products are in the high-temperature zone for only a small fraction of a second before they are swept to a cooler temperature. When the retort products were cracked in the bench retort, they spent a longer time in the high-temperature zone so more cracking could take place. Consequently, the products are the same as if they were produced at a higher temperature. Because we cannot determine the residence time for the retorting process, the composition of the retort products is compared to temperature and a higher Retorting Index is correct.

For further information on the validity of the Retorting Index the calculations will be applied to data from four different retorting methods. Table 8.4 lists the reported retorting temperature, ethylene/ethane ratio,

Table 8.3 Recovery and Ethylene/Ethane Ratio for Cracking, Oxidative, and Steam Laboratory Retorting

Oil Shale[a]		Oxygen %	Total Flow cm³/min	Retort Temp. °F	Charge g	Recovery, wt %				Wt % Ratio Ethylene/Ethane
Source[b]	Assay gpt					Spent Shale	Oil + Water	Gas	Loss	
Cracking										
U	29.0	0	2.5	1,187.0	7.5527	83.72	7.52	6.38	2.38	1.6077
C	53.8	0	2.5	1,257.4	7.1671	68.05	13.27	15.48	3.20	1.5911
C	53.8	0	2.5	1,469.1	7.2269	62.32	11.91	24.24	1.53	3.6810
C	53.8	0	2.5		7.6531	61.07	11.69	25.84	1.40	3.6319
C	53.8	0	2.5	1,064.4	7.3948	76.19	13.40	6.56	3.85	0.9411
C	53.8	0	2.5		7.8100	72.75	18.40	7.18	1.67	0.9066
Oxidative										
C	53.8	2	4.1	1,187.0	6.8099	69.02	15.59	9.21	6.18	1.2307
C	53.8	3	3.0		6.5100	69.67	15.58	9.29	5.46	1.2325
C	53.8	5	3.3		6.0910	70.24	15.49	9.12	5.15	1.2671
C	53.8	6	3.2		6.7263	70.09	15.62	8.92	5.36	1.2280
C	53.8	7	3.8		6.8567	69.51	15.94	9.72	4.83	1.2167
C	53.8	8	4.2		6.7088	70.03	16.24	9.46	4.27	1.2312
C	53.8	9	4.2		6.5680	70.27	16.07	9.22	4.44	1.2476
C	53.8	10	4.1		6.6326	69.71	16.20	9.47	4.62	1.2374
C	53.8	11	4.0		7.1970	70.49	15.52	9.38	4.61	1.2559
C	53.8	12	4.0		6.4717	70.46	15.72	9.26	4.56	1.2499
C	53.8	21	2.5		6.9395	66.90	16.06	8.60	8.44	1.2412
C	53.8	21	5.0		6.7760	69.88	15.71	10.45	3.96	1.2646
C	53.8	21	20.0		6.1027	69.69	15.05	11.66	3.60	1.3012
Steam										
C	53.8	0	—	1,187.0	6.7067	c	c	c	c	1.2056

aParticle size, 1/8 in. to 30 mesh. bC = Colorado, U = Utah. cData not available.

Table 8.4   Reported Retorting Temperatures and Retorting Indexes

Retort	Wt % Ratio Ethylene/Ethane	Reported Retorting Temp. °F	Retorting Index °F
Fischer assay	0.3107	932	918
	0.2585	932	892
	0.3472	932	934
	0.2933	932	909
	0.4338[5]	932	969
Entrained solids, steam[7]	1.8884	1,000	1,287
	2.3494	1,100	1,353
	3.8667	1,200	1,532
	5.5556	1,300	1,695
	6.6316	1,400	1,787
	9.6216	1,500	2,020
	12.9153	1,650	2,252
Entrained solids steam + air[7]	5.3243	1,085	1,674
	8.4408	1,205	1,932
	5.2889	1,230	1,670
	12.9937	1,295	2,258
	13.5381	1,315	2,294
Gas combustion[6]			
6 ton/day, Run 311-C	1.8000	1,400[a]	1,273
150 ton/day, Run 25-1	1.4000	1,310[b]	1,206
150 ton/day, Run 25-3	0.5333	1,625[b]	1,004

[a]Maximum bed temperature.
[b]Maximum distributor temperature.

and Retorting Index for Fischer assay, gas combustion, and entrained solids retorting.

Fischer Assay

Ethylene/ethane ratios are listed for five Fischer assay runs. Four were reported in intra-Bureau reports, and the fifth was reported by Goodfellow.[5] The Retorting Index for these data cluster around the 932°F point, which is the maximum temperature used in the assay. In Fischer assay the oil shale is heated at a relatively slow rate to the maximum temperature of 932°F. Variation in heating rate could easily affect the Retorting Index.

Gas Combustion

Results from three gas-combustion retort runs are reported.[6] These data are for one run of the 6-ton-per-day retort and two runs of the 150-ton-per-day retort, and the reported temperatures are for maximum bed temperature and maximum distributor temperature, respectively. Maximum distributor temperature is the highest combustion temperature in the retort and does not give an indication of the temperature of retorting any more than the maximum bed temperature does. Here, the use of the calculated Retorting Index gives a meaningful value for a temperature of retorting. Reported yield data follow more closely with the Retorting Index than the maximum distributor or maximum bed temperature.

Entrained Solids

Retorting Indexes calculated from the data from the Bureau of Mines entrained solids retort[7] deviates greatly from reported retorting temperatures. In fact, it is possible to calculate two new regression equations that have essentially the same slope as Equation (8.1), but different intercepts. One equation would be for the steam only entrainment, and the other for steam plus air entrainment. The fact that the entrained-solids retort data give regression equations with essentially the same slope as was obtained from the laboratory data indicates that the same kinetic mechanism producing ethylene and ethane is applicable. The steam entrainment data show a higher ethylene-ethane ratio and therefore a higher Retorting Index because of the effect of residence time in the retort. The retort products in this retort have to pass through about 35 ft of heated retort that would give the products a residence time of several seconds. This is considerably longer than the contact time found in most other types of retorting. At $1000°F$, for example, the residence time in the entrained solids retort is about 2.5-3 sec as compared with less than 0.5 sec estimated for the bench retort. Severe cracking of the retorted products takes place in the entrained solids retort producing final products that appear to have been made at a higher temperature, hence a higher Retorting Index. This argument is also borne out by the increased aromaticity of the oil produced in the entrained solids retort. The steam plus air retorting data show even higher Retorting Index than the steam-entrained data because of the added heat from the exothermic, oxidation reactions.

Ten-Ton Aboveground Retort

Two retorting runs of the 10-ton aboveground retort[8-10] provided the necessary data (unpublished) to allow the calculation of Retorting Indexes. Temperatures of the shale bed were measured every five hours with thermocouples placed at about 18-in. intervals in bed depth. Gas analyses were performed at the same time. Retorting run 28 had an average maximum bed temperature of 1,020.9°F and an average Retorting Index of 1,070.9°F. This run suffered from extreme channeling resulting in a retorting rate of 2.28 ft/day. In this retorting run the calculated Retorting Index follows quite closely the maximum bed temperature. Retorting run 29 had no channeling, and its retorting rate was 1.59 ft/day so that the shale bed could soak and obtain a higher temperature. For this run, the Retorting Index is lower than the maximum bed temperature. The average Retorting Index was 964.7°F, and the average maximum bed temperature was 1,180.3°F.

SUMMARY

A method of calculating a Retorting Index for oil shale retorting has been presented. The method utilizes the relative amounts of ethylene and ethane in the retort gas and allows determination of the Retorting Index or effective retorting temperature to ±25°F. Calculation of the Retorting Index is possible for aboveground and *in situ* retorting. Factors such as particle size, rate of heating, and oil shale assay have no apparent effect on the Retorting Index. Because of the kinetics involved, such things as retort product residence time and cracking are reflected in the Retorting Index. Thus, the Retorting Index will be more nearly associated with retort-product composition than such things as maximum temperature of the oil shale bed.

ACKNOWLEDGMENTS

The work upon which this report is based was done under a cooperative agreement between the Bureau of Mines, U.S. Department of the Interior, and the University of Wyoming.

REFERENCES

1.   Allred, V. D. *Chem. Eng. Prog.* **62**, 55 (1966).
2.   Hubbard, A. B. and W. E. Robinson. *U. S. Bur. Mines Rep. Invest.* **4744** (1950).

3. Stanfield, K. E. and I. C. Frost. *U. S. Bur. Mines Rep. Invest.* **4477** (1949).

4. Messner, A. E., D. M. Rosie, and P. A. Argabright. *Anal. Chem.* **31**, 230 (1959).

5. Goodfellow, L., C. E. Haberman, and M. T. Atwood. *ACS Div. Petrol. Chem., Preprints* **13**(2), F86 (1968).

6. Matzick, A., R. O. Dannenberg, J. R. Ruark, J. E. Phillips, J. D. Lankford, and B. Guthrie. *U. S. Bur. Mines Bull.* **635** (1966).

7. Sohns, H. W., E. E. Jukkola, and W. I. R. Murphy. *U. S. Bur. Mines. Rep. Invest.* **5522** (1959).

8. Carpenter, H. C. and H. W. Sohns. *Colo. School Mines Quart.* **63**, 71 (1968).

9. Carpenter, H. C., S. S. Tihen, and H. W. Sohns. *ACS, Div. of Petrol. Chem. Preprints* **13**(2), F50 (1968).

10. Dockter, L., A. Long, Jr. and A. E. Harak. *ACS, Div. Fuel Chem. Preprints* **15**(1), 2 (1971).

POLYCONDENSED AROMATIC COMPOUNDS (PCA) AND CARCINOGENS IN THE SHALE ASH OF CARBONACEOUS SPENT SHALE FROM RETORTING OF OIL SHALE

J. J. Schmidt-Collérus, F. Bonomo,
Kishor Gala and LaRose Leffler

Denver Research Institute
Denver, Colorado 80210

INTRODUCTION

General

The presentation described below discusses research carried out during the first year of the Disposal and Environmental Impact of Carbonaceous Solid Waste from Commercial Oil Shale Operations Project, supported by the National Science Foundation's program of Research Applied to National Needs (NSF-RANN) under Grant No. GI 34282X1.

It is obvious that some aspects of the objectives of these investigations might appear insufficiently detailed or too limited in scope—or, on the contrary, as too broad in scope or too concerned with problems considered solved; or some aspects might appear to them at this time rather inconsequential or exaggerated in their concern, depending on the perspective and the observer's vantage point.

The objective of this investigation was to determine experimentally possible specific physical environmental effects from solid carbonaceous material from an oil shale industry, the full impact of which might only be felt many years after full-scale operations have begun. Consequently, these investigations rely on material and data obtained from rather small pilot plant operations. With the foreseeable development of actual larger-scale demonstration plants (about 50,000 barrels of oil per day), these investigations appear timely and, hopefully, might contribute some new experimental data useful for a better evaluation of potential environmental problems.

A major concern of potential injection in the environment of organic compounds, albeit of small percentage quantities, is the sum total of large quantities of such carbonaceous material that might have to be disposed of on the surface and underground (Tables 9.1, 9.1A); and in most cases the as yet unknown mode of transportation, fate and effect on the ecology of these trace organic compounds and/or their derivatives.

Table 9.1   Estimated Schedule of Oil Shale Development and Spent Shale Ash (Solid Waste) Produced for Disposal[a]

End of Year	Production Level (bbl/day)	Raw Shale Processed (tons/day)	Spent Shale Produced (Solid Waste) (tons/day)
1977	8,000	11,500	9,800
1979	48,000	69,000	59,000
1984	407,000	586,000	496,000
1987	600,000	864,000	732,000

[a]Assumption: surface retorting (No commercial *in situ* processing)

Table 9.1A   Estimated Schedule of Oil Shale Development and Spent Shale Ash (Solid Waste) Produced[a]

End of Year	Production Level (bbl/day)	Raw Shale Processed (tons/day)	Spent Shale Produced (Solid Waste) (tons/day)
1977	8,000	11,500	9,800
1979	48,000	69,000	59,000
1984	432,000	622,000	527,000
1987	700,000	1,010,000	854,000

[a]Assumptions: major production by surface retorting. (Modified *in situ* production: 25,000 bbl/day (1984);   100,000 bbl/day (1987).

The imminent development of commercial oil shale operations in the Piceance Creek Basin in Colorado (and possibly also in the Uintah and Green River Basins) will generate solid waste of staggering proportion in the form of spent oil shale ash.

Assuming the construction of the first commercial plant to begin in 1976, the evaluation of a number of industrial and government reports allows a fairly good prediction of industry development and rates of spent shale production (Table 9.1).

On the basis of these estimates the amount of spent shale generated in 1979 approximates 59,000 tons/day or approximately 21.5 million tons/yr and in 1987 approximately 312 million tons/yr (if one includes *in situ* production)—an impressive figure.

The basic philosophy of this research program is to investigate these problems experimentally (in cooperation with the industry and government agencies interested in shale oil production), and make the results available to all interested private and government organizations.

The composition and properties of the solid waste will depend on the type of retorting process used and the conditions of retorting. In some retorting processes, the resulting spent shale still contains up to five percent carbon residue from the original organic matter present. This carbonaceous matter is present, in part, as organic compounds that are soluble in organic solvents. Due to the pyrolytic process used during retorting, part of this organic matter consists of polycondensed organic matter (POM) that might include polynuclear or polycondensed aromatic hydrocarbons (PAH) and azarines (AA) in addition to other types of high-molecular-weight organic compounds.

While formation of POM compounds in small quantites is ubiquitous wherever pyrolysis of organic matter occurs and could, therefore, be disregarded, systematic and long-range investigations carried out in the last few decades have shown that chronic exposure to certain polluting inorganic trace elements as well as trace amounts of polycondensed aromatic pollutants can have detrimental biological effects.

An impact on the ecosystem is possible because of potential leaching and accretion of this material in the aquifer, potential concentration during recycling operations of impounded water, and the possible translocation into the vegetation and/or partial transfer into the surrounding atmosphere. All these factors must be considered. However, some of this rationale applies not only to above-ground operations, but might also apply to potential *in situ* operations.

From these introductory remarks, one finds it easy to define the major specific objectives of the research program:

1. Determination of the amount and kind of organic compounds in carbonaceous spent shale and in the process water from retorting operations.

2. Isolation and identification of the structure and composition of those compounds that are of known or suspected biological activity.

3. Investigation of the changes compounds may undergo in large dumpsites and investigation of their impact on the receiving environment, including (a) solubilization and leaching by ground and runoff water resulting in their pollution, (b) volatilization of compounds from the waste and transfer into air, (c) identification of POM absorbed on or present in airborne carbonaceous particulate matter from oil shale processing operations, and (d) effect of possible auto-oxidation phenomena on the volatilization of organic compounds from the waste and their transfer into air.

4. Examination of potential beneficial uses for carbonaceous solid shale waste.

The major activities and preliminary results of these investigations can be summarized as follows:

1. Samples of soil, water, vegetation, and air from various pristine areas of potential future oil shale operations were collected and partially analyzed for their content of polycyclic organic matter, in particular polycondensed aromatic hydrocarbons. This was done to establish a base line for future comparative studies.

2. Samples of carbonaceous spent shale from various pilot plant retorting processes were collected and analyzed for their content of volatile organic as well as for polycondensed aromatic compounds.

A major portion of these studies has been completed; however, more detailed comparisons await additional experimental data from potential retorting processes such as the Union Oil-B-Process, which may be the first one ready for commercial operation.

Summary of Specific Results

1. Carbonaceous spent shale with up to 5% organic carbon content contains material soluble in organic solvents. The benzene-soluble fraction ranges from 0.02-0.2%, depending on the retorting conditions and the age of the spent shale.

2. The benzene-soluble portion contains a fairly large amount of polycondensed organic matter (POM) such as polycyclic aromatic hydrocarbons (PAH) and also azarines. The PAH compounds identified to date are summarized in Table 9.2.

3. In addition to these PAH compounds, the presence of a larger number of azarines and some carbazoles is indicated. While these have not

Table 9.2   Polycondensed Aromatic Hydrocarbons Identified in Benzene Extracts of Carbonaceous Spent Shale

Compound	TLC, R_B, Color	Detection Method Fluorescence Spectrum	HPLC Retention Time	Remarks
Phenanthrene	X	–	–	
Benz(a)anthracene	X	X	X	
Dibenz(a,h)anthracene	X	X	–	
7,12-Dimethylbenz(a)anthracene	X	X?		Fluorescence spectrum indicates a possible mixture with another compound separation of these by HPLC progress
Fluoranthene	X	X	–	
3-Methylcholanthrene	X	X	–	Further confirmation by HPLC in progress
Pyrene	X	–	–	
Benzo(a)pyrene	X	X	X	
Dibenz(c,d,j,k)pyrene	X	X	X	Separated by HPLC from BaP
Perylene	X	X	X	
Benzo(g,h,i)perylene	X	–	–	Fluorometric identification in progress

as yet all been identified, the presence of acridine, dibenz[a,j] acridine and other higher-molecular-weight bases has been established. Furthermore, a relatively large diffused fluorescent area is evident on the TLC plates (corroborated by a very broad peak in the chromatogram of the HPLC) that might indicate possible homologous series of alkyl–substituted PAH compounds. Their separation might be possible only by capillary gas chromatography. Nonfluorescent hydrocarbons (and possibly heterocompounds) are also present in the benzene extract, and their separation by HPLC using differential refractometry is in progress.

4. The amount of benzene soluble material in carbonaceous spent shale is about one or two orders of magnitude *higher* that that found in soils from pristine areas, but about one order of magnitude *lower* than that found in airborne particulate matter, such as that collected in industrial areas.

5. In a traverse of a gulch projected as a future disposal area, the extractable material in soil is one or two orders of magnitudes lower than in the spent shale, but varies with the density of vegetation growing at the particular sampling site; this is because endogenic PAH compounds generated by the vegetation can eventually end up in the soil.

6. Preliminary data indicate that a larger number of polycyclic aromatic compounds (including those with known adverse biological activity) can be leached from the carbonaceous shale and migrate with the saline water. The extracted water-soluble salts from carbonaceous spent shale contain from 20-40% of the total benzene-extractable organic matter of the original carbonaceous spent shale, depending on the type of retorting process and the age of the spent shale.

7. The benzene-soluble and leachable organic matter (and probably all organic carbonaceous matter) from carbonaceous spent shale appears to be subject to slow oxidation processes and part of the lower-molecular-weight organic compounds can be subject to volatilization.

Discussion

The investigation of trace organic compounds injected into the environment is significant because some cause adverse biological effects, and others, the fate of which is as yet unknown, might also exhibit such deleterious effects, either by themselves or in their altered form. On the other hand, changes in structure during weathering and/or migration may cause inactivation. Certain classes of polycondensed aromatic compounds present in airborne particulate matter as well as in water and food have received increased attention since conclusive evidence proved their biological and pathological effect among habitual cigarette smokers, as well as increasing evidence of rising death rate in the U.S. due to cancer.

Polycyclic aromatic hydrocarbons in man's global environment might be of endogenic and/or of exogenic origin. Some investigators in this field contend that endogenic polycyclic aromatic hydrocarbons (many of which are strong carcinogens) are synthesized in plants, and investigations, particularly by Borneff and Fischer,[4] Blumer, Mallet and Heros, Graff and Diehl,[1] point to the regular presence of a number of polycyclic aromatic hydrocarbons (in many cases up to eight compounds of which at least five have blastomogenic properties) in most growing plants, including those far removed from man's technological activity. Other investigators (*e.g.,* Grimmer, Jacob and Hildebrandt) carried out experiments that indicate that polycyclic aromatic compounds such as benzo[a]pyrene are exclusively of exogenic origin.

Polycyclic aromatics may be synthesized during germination and plant growth, which takes place independent of photosynthesis, *i.e.,* even in the absence of light.[1] Polycyclic aromatic hydrocarbons (PAH) occur in petroleum and are also synthesized by living organisms such as higher plants, algae and microorganisms.[2,3] Thus, there appears to exist in nature what one could call a normal peg of polyaromatic material. At present this natural normal peg corresponds to about 1-2 μg of 3,4-benzopyrene/100 g dry vegetable substance that might always have existed in our environment. Significant deviations from this normal peg would then indicate the presence of exogenic material. Most of the latter are man-made.

The most significant factors that might have to be considered in the *disposal* of vast quantities of carbonaceous solid waste are: (a) the presence of polycondensed organic matter (POM), its possible solubilization in saline ground and runoff water, and its possible translocation and effect on the ecosystem; (b) the presence of other organic materials in the carbonaceous spent shale and their potential impact on the ecosystem and on the water resources; and (c) re-emission of hydrocarbons (adsorbed during the retorting process) due to surface evaporation and possible self-heating of the solid carbonaceous waste.

Let us now examine a few of the characteristic aspects of potential environmental effects from carbonaceous-spent shale.

Translocation in Plants

Plant roots could solubilize the organic matter in the spent shale, absorb the PAH and/or AA material and eventually translocate them (with possible simultaneous concentration) in such other parts of the plants as the leaves, stems and seeds, thus bringing these compounds into the ecological food chain. There is experimental evidence that exocellular enzyme systems of plant roots can solubilize large organic molecules in the soil environment and translocate them into the plants; subsequent translocation into the fauna is a further possibility. Since polycyclic aromatics by themselves, or in the presence of organic (or inorganic) solubilizers, can migrate with the groundwater, subsoil water, or can be picked up by runoff water, this effect may not be localized to the dumpsite itself but could have similar effects at more remote locations. If the water movement is localized by impounding, this type of migration can perhaps be minimized. However, the PAH compounds may in this case concentrate by accretion.

Effect of POMs on Groundwater,
Runoff-Water and Soil

Borneff[4] has established that groundwater can solubilize POM compounds
in colloidal form. The stronger the blastomogenicity of the compounds,
the higher the solubilization in water. Even subsoil water of irreproach-
able origin contains traces of polycyclic aromatics deemed harmful.
Groundwater passing through carbonaceous deposits could be considerably
enriched in POM materials.

Kelus[5] could show that organic substances such as polycyclic aromatic
hydrocarbons, aromatic amines and carbamates emitted by the chimneys
of industrial plants or leached from asphalt roads and soil around petroleum refinery plants, form emulsions with water and, in this form, can
migrate long distances and end up in rivers and lakes. They accumulate
and concentrate on the bottom of reservoirs, in deposits on sewage filters
and in organisms living in water.

It is therefore plausible that the potential presence of materials in the
spent shale dumps, especially where a slurried or wetted spent shale is disposed of on the surface (or underground) could pollute groundwater and
surface waters of local creeks and ponds. This could become acute if
the retention capability of the dams used for the impounded water is
insufficient or the route of seepage changes. Such contaminated water
could noticeably affect the ecological habitat downstream, at the outcrop
of the water tables or in wells.

Potential Impact of Other Solubilizable POM-Type
Organic Pollutants on the Ecological System

In addition to PAH compounds potentially present in the carbonaceous
spent shale, the latter also contains a larger number of other polyaromatic
and lower-molecular-weight organic compounds. While these might not
possess demonstrated blastomogenic effects, they may be mutagenic or
in other ways affect the environment.

These compounds can also be solubilized by the root systems of the
local vegetation (or revegetation) and could subsequently influence adversely their metabolism. Prolonged exposure to such external influences
could lead to mutagenic changes. Both effects could weaken plants'
resistance to external climatic factors or diseases.

It appears, therefore, that other organic components in carbonaceous
spent shale might be important. The solubilization and fate of these
compounds by leaching and percolating water and their influence on the
ecology of the environment and pollution of surface waters is presently
being investigated.

It was found that the presence of normal and branched hydrocarbons and of aliphatic acids and/or their salts increases considerably the solubility of polycondensed aromatic hydrocarbons thus contributing to an increase in their mobility within the spent shale dump or out of it. Furthermore these compounds exert a synergistic effect in the translocation of POM compounds into plants and, in the case of airborne particulate matter into animal tissue (*e.g.*, alveolar epidermis).

The Possible Impact of Solid Waste Disposal
of Carbonaceous Spent Shale on Air Pollution

A significant aspect is potential air pollution due to volatile hydrocarbons released by surface evaporation and by possible self-heating processes that might occur inside extensive and deep dumpsites. Initial GC and MS analysis of the volatiles released from reheated carbonaceous spent shale (from retorting of Green River oil shale) showed saturated and unsaturated hydrocarbons up to C_{25}, in addition to the release of aromatic compounds such as benzene and toluene. The presence of these hydrocarbons in the carbonaceous spent shale might be due to readsorption of pyrolysis vapors onto the inorganic matrix and/or carbonaceous surface prior to removal of the spent shale from the retort. Readsorption of this type has been demonstrated experimentally.

If the mechanisms of chemisorption and subsequent oxidation reactions are similar to those found in other finely divided carbonaceous matter such as coal dust or charcoal, one could expect similar reactions in spent shale. The first stages in oxidation processes in coal were studied extensively by Jones and Townend,[7] who found that adsorption of oxygen at low temperatures leads to a very activated form of the chemisorbed oxygen. The presence of traces of water is essential for the formation of this complex. Particle size and temperature were also important; above $80°C$ the adsorption complex starts to decompose, producing mainly CO. Thus, chemisorption at low temperature is important in the initiation of oxidation of carbonaceous materials.

Heat evolution during such processes could be considered. Garner and co-workers[8] have shown that the heat effect in the initial states of chemisorption reactions might wholly or partly cause the self-heating of coal and other finely divided carbonaceous matter.

Another possible mechanism for the self-heating of coal is the oxidation of pyrite. In the presence of moisture and entrapped air, the exothermic oxidation of finely divided pyrite under proper conditions can increase the temperature of a carbonaceous dump to the point of self-heating and then to spontaneous ignition.

Spent shale from the oil shale of the Green River Formation has a carbon content of perhaps a maximum of 5%, and the temperature required for self-ignition (or spontaneous ignition) is probably too high (approximately 470°C) to be of great concern. The problem of self-heating, or accidental ignition of carbonaceous spent shale is, however, real enough to require a more detailed investigation of the physical and chemical parameters involved and study of possible reaction mechanisms in this solid waste. Composition and extent of air pollution resulting from such reactions and potential impact of this type of pollution on the ecology should be considered seriously.

The Influence of Carbonaceous Material on
the Erosion and Leaching of Oil Shale Dumps

Investigations carried out by the Denver Research Institute on the disposal and uses of spent oil shale[9] led to the conclusion that suitably processed spent shale (*i.e.,* finely divided burned spent shale that does *not* contain residual carbonaceous matter), when wetted, will develop sufficient cohesion so that stabilized dumps with high angle of slope can be constructed.

From the data it appears that relatively low retorting temperatures (~ 900°F) and the presence of carbonaceous material (3-5%) may adversely affect the compaction strength of the spent shale, limiting the allowable safe-slope angles and heights that can be built.

EXPERIMENTAL ANALYTICAL APPROACH

Sampling and Sample Preparation

Carbonaceous Spent Shale

Four types of carbonaceous spent shale samples were collected for investigation:

1. Carbonaceous spent shale from the TOSCO Process. By the courtesy of Colony Operation (ARCO) and the Oil Shale Corporation, two varieties of spent shales were available: spent shale obtained about five years earlier and fresh spent shale produced about six months earlier.

2. The second type of carbonaceous spent shale was sampled at the dump site of the former Bureau of Mines gas retort operations at Anvil Points near Rifle, Colorado. Two types of spent shale were collected: spent shale from the Bureau of Mines earlier operations (about 10 years

old), and spent shale from the gas retort pilot experiments operated by the Colorado School of Mines.

3. The third type of carbonaceous spent shale (presently under investigation) was obtained from the Paraho Corporation. This spent shale originates from an oxidative process (as opposed to a reductive process such as the TOSCO Process) in which part of the organic material present in the raw shale is actually combusted by injection of air. However, even under these conditions the resulting spent shale still contains about 3% organic carbon, and part of this is present as organic compounds soluble in conventional solvents (*e.g.*, benzene).

4. The fourth type of spent shale being investigated was obtained by courtesy of the Union Oil Company from their Modified B-Type Retort. In comparison to the clinker-type spent shale from the original Union Oil Shale Retort, the spent shale from the modified type B retort is carbonaceous and also contains soluble organic material.

There is also some morphological difference between these three spent shale types. While TOSCO spent shale has a small particle size (average particle size -35 mesh) the Paraho spent shale varies from very fine (-200 mesh) particles to larger chunks (+4 mesh). Union Oil spent shale ranges between these two types.

The samples were stored in 50-gallon sealed drums in a storage area protected from weather. Sampling for the preparation of analytical samples was carried out by quartering and riffeling to obtain homogeneous samples. A sieve analysis was carried out, and the samples were air dried in the laboratory at humidity levels of from 10-15% and stored in the closed polyethylene containers. Before actual extraction the moisture content was determined by the Dean-Stark method.

Soil Sampling

Soil sampling was conducted during three field trips. The soil samples were collected by auger, following standard procedures, and stored in metal containers. They were ground to -65 mesh, air dried, and the moisture determined before extraction.

Soil samples were collected from pristine sites and also from a traverse of one gulch. Additional soil samples were collected from Parachute Creek close to the Colony and Union Oil pilot plant operation sites.

Soil samples in the Piceance Basin were collected from dry river flood plains.

Sampling of Vegetation

Typical vegetation from the pristine area of the Piceance Basin was collected near the sites of soil sampling. The vegetation collected at the beginning was not segregated by the various species except for leaves and young branches of sage brush. The various grasses and other vegetation were taken collectively. The collected plant material was dried at 80°C in a forced-air oven until constant weight was achieved. The dried material was then stored for future sampling in polyethylene bags.

The plant material was originally fragmented in a large capacity blender for extraction. However, because of formation of fine particles (which slowed subsequent extraction), this method was changed in favor of chopping the plant material to 1/2-in. size, followed by extraction.

Water Sampling

Water samples were obtained from wells, springs, creeks and rivers. Artesian well water from the deeper part of the Piceance Creek Basin is highly saline and may have an average content of 25,000 mg/l. At the edges of the Basin there are wells with much lower salinity values (2000 mg/l). Samples from these wells were collected in 5-gallon glass water jugs. These were previously cleaned with detergent and much water rinsing, followed by an acetone rinse and a rinse with pure benzene. River water was collected from the White and Colorado Rivers.

Air Sampling

Air sampling was done on two field trips. The first was in the Parachute Creek Valley about 1000 ft upstream from the spent shale dump of the Union Mine.

The second air sampling was made several months later. In both cases a Hi-Vol sampler was used for long period sampling (3½ and 23 hr, respectively). A second air sampler was used to monitor air near the generator. This was 1000 ft removed from the Hi-Vol sampler. Finally air samples were collected in MSA organic vapor sampling tubes.

After sampling, the filters were folded and hermetically sealed in polyethylene bags for subsequent weighing and extraction in the laboratory.

Extraction and Concentration Procedures

Extraction of Carbonaceous Spent Shale

The homogeneous- and air-dried samples of spent shale were extracted in large Soxhlets with an average thimble charge of about 400 g. Usually five were run simultaneously to extract 2000 g of spent shale in a single charge.

After a number of pre-trials it was decided to use double distilled benzene as solvent. Absence of polycyclic material in the solvent was tested by concentrating 500 ml of benzene to 0.1 ml and spotting the solution on a TLC plate. This benzene showed only slight fluorescence, if any. Each Soxhlet was charged with 500 ml of solvent, and the extraction continued for 2000 extraction cycles. The entire extraction apparatus was protected with black shields to prevent changes induced by fluorescent light.

After extraction the benzene solution was first stripped of the solvent by a rota-vacuum procedure. However, this procedure was later changed to fractional distillation to prevent loss of volatiles in the material and in particular PAH compounds. The benzene solution was concentrated to about 50 ml, then transferred to a pre-weighed vial, and the residual benzene removed at room temperature in a gentle stream of nitrogen.

All extraction, concentration and drying procedures were carried out with exclusion of fluorescent light and only incandescent light was used when needed. The concentrated extract in the vial was capped, wrapped in aluminum foil and stored in the refrigerator for subsequent analytical separation work.

The extracted material is a dark-brown waxy solid with the typical odor of shale oil. It is completely soluble in benzene and a number of other organic solvents.

The raw carbonaceous spent shale (TOSCO) received had an average moisture content from 13.5-20%. Upon drying one-inch layers in large flat trays with periodic tilling, the moisture content dropped to about 1%. It is interesting to note that extraction of wet carbonaceous spent shale (15-20% moisture) will yield more benzene solubles than dried material. The color of the benzene extract is red-brown and the dry carbonaceous spent shale extract is more yellow-brown. It is thought that the moisture might extract some water-soluble inorganic or complexed material, which is much less soluble in dry benzene.

Used benzene is recovered and purified by fractional distillation as is the freshly received benzene. High purity solvents, *i.e.*, solvents "distilled in glass" supplied by Burdick and Jackson Laboratories, Inc. are used for extraction and/or analytical separations.

An attempt to extract spent carbonaceous shale with benzene in a vapor-proof sealed ball mill yielded a sticky material impossible to separate from the solvent. This approach was abandoned.

Extraction of Soils

The extraction of soils is accomplished by the same method used for spent shale.

Extraction of Vegetable Materials

Leaves of sage brush and/or grass and other local vegetation were dried at 80°C to constant weight. Extraction with pure benzene was continued until no more extracted material was detected by GC in the solvent. The extract is quite intractable and difficult to remove from residual amounts of solvents and/or chlorophyll, carotenes and lipids.

Extraction of Water

Water samples were extracted in a 1:1 benzene-to-water ratio in the high power blender. Three extractions per sample were necessary. The method worked well, although occasionally emulsions formed that had to be separated by centrifugation.

Extraction of Particulate Airborne Samples

Extraction of the particulate matter collected from the glass filter of the Hi-Vol sampler and the Gelman sampler was carried out by folding the filter and placing it into the thimble of a small Soxhlet extractor.

Extraction of Volatile Organic Compounds
from the Atmosphere

Collection of volatile organic vapors from the atmosphere was carried out by passing a measured amount of air through a charcoal-filled tube, which is now standard practice in air pollution sampling. Volatile hydrocarbons were displaced by carbon disulfide and analyzed directly by GC or GC-MS techniques.

Extraction of Carbonaceous Spent Shale with Water

A water extraction of carbonaceous spent shale was carried out to determine the amount of water-soluble inorganic salts, and to investigate whether the presence of salts solubilizes organic material to the extent that it might be carried into the aqueous solution.

This was done with distilled water in the large Soxhlets as was the extraction with benzene. Concentration of the saline aqueous solution was done by fractional distillation and/or evaporation with nitrogen.

Results of this experiment were interesting in connection with potential leaching of PAH compounds from spent shale piles, and will be discussed later.

Leaching of Carbonaceous Spent Shale

Leaching of carbonaceous spent shale by natural weather conditions was accomplished by constructing a lysimeter consisting of a bed of 32.6 ft x 4.3 ft x 1 ft of carbonaceous shale layered on top of a 5-in. bed of gravel, in which are imbedded three parallel perforated PVC sampling lines (2 in. I.D.) that collect the seepage water from rain and snowmelt in a glass sump from where it is automatically pumped into a rotovac and evaporated. Periodically the concentrated salt solution in the rotovac flash is replaced with an empty flask, the concentrated solution further evaporated to dryness, and the salt removed and stored under inert atmosphere in the dark in a refrigerator. The lysimeter was installed in the open on the south side of one of the Denver Research Institute laboratories and the leacheate collected for over a period of about 3½ months, from December 1973 to March 1974. The dried salt collected by this method was subsequently extracted with benzene by Soxhlet extraction using the same method as applied for the extraction of the non-leached carbonaceous-spent shale. It is noteworthy that during this collection time the lysimeter plot was surrounded by abundant weeds and grass growing on regular topsoil, but no vegetation germinated on the spent shale of the lysimeter.

Development of Separation and Analysis Methods

General Considerations

A major portion of the initial research effort was expanded to find suitable optimal separation and identification methods for the type of material extracted. An extensive literature survey showed that frequently what appears to work well for simple synthetic mixtures of pure standard compounds was difficult to translate to complex extracts. Materials from various pollution sources required the adoption of various approaches and the development of a methodology best suited to the particular case. The reason for the rather extensive methodology work was that the extracts from carbonaceous spent shale were more complex in nature than anticipated, and in this respect resembled the complexity of the soluble bitumen from raw shale itself, *i.e.,* the molecular weight range is broad, and the type of organic compounds ranges from alkanes to azarines, and probably includes also a number of metallo-organic complexes and elementary sulfur. For the same reason, known methods, although satisfactory in many ways, are being further refined with respect to separation capability, sensitivity, expediency, and reduction of losses in quantitative evaluation.

The major methods used in the PAH analysis were Thin-Layer Chromatography (TLC), High-Pressure Liquid Chromatography (HPLC), Gas Chromatography (GC), Ultraviolet and Infrared Spectroscopy (UV-IR), Fluorescence Emission Spectroscopy (FL), Mass Spectrometry (MS), and Nuclear Magnetic Resonance (NMR).

Development of TLC Methodology

Originally it was felt that fluorescence in combination with TLC would be most adaptable to the separation and detection of trace amounts of PAH compounds. This approach was further consolidated after consultation with Professor Joachim Borneff[6] who, with his staff, has conducted continuing analysis of carcinogens in water and soil.

In particular, the method developed by H. Kunte[10] in Borneff's laboratory, using two-dimensional mixed layer TLC, combined both the advantages of adsorption and reversed phase TLC. This method gave good separation and shortened the time normally required to run the sample sequentially on separate plates. Furthermore, losses were reduced, since the separation was accomplished on the same plate. We conducted a series of experiments using the same adsorbents and developers originally used by Kunte, which proved not very satisfactory when applied to the separation of POM mixtures obtained from spent shale extracts. Modifications were then tried, resulting in plates that did not contain silica gel. While this improved the migration of the individual components, diffusion of the spots increased. A series of other combinations were subsequently evaluated.

It appears that a mixed TLC plate, solvent mixture, and technique has been developed that is satisfactory not only with mixtures of standards, but also with PAHs from extracts of spent shale, soils, and plant material. The glass plates, 20 x 20 cm, are coated with a mixture of aluminum oxide, silica gel, and 40% acetylated cellulose in a ratio of 1:1:1, w/w, mixed to a slurry with 95% ethanol, and spread to a 0.33-mm thick coating. After air drying, the plates were deactivated, spotted and run. As much as 8 mg of a POM mixture can be loaded on the starting spot. Figure 9.1 shows an example of this separation. Development in the first direction uses isooctane for 80 minutes. Then the plates are dried at ambient temperature and subsequently developed in the same direction with a second solvent mixture, n-hexane:benzene, 95:5, for 60 minutes. After drying at ambient temperature, the plates are developed again in

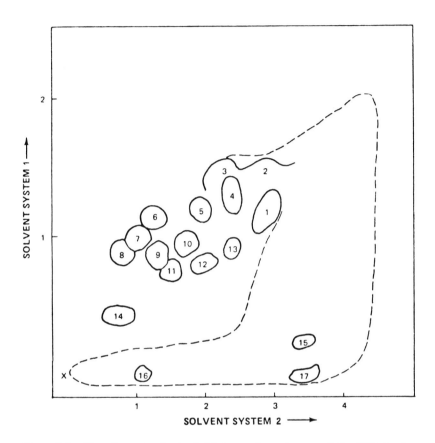

Figure 9.1   Two-dimensional mixed thin-layer chromatogram of the PAH fraction of benzene solubles from carbonaceous spent shale [CSA II (1)]. Layer: 40% acetylated cellulose, aluminum oxide G, silica gel G (1:1:1). Solvents: System I, isooctane, drying followed by n-hexane, benzene (95:5). System II, methanol, ether, water (4:4:1). Compounds: 2, phenanthrene; 3, pyrene; 4, fluoranthene; 7, benzo[a]pyrene and anthanthrene; 13, benzo[ghi]perylene; – – diffused fluorescent area.

the same direction using the same solvent system for another 60 minutes. The plates are humidified overnight, then run in the second direction for 3 hr with methanol:ether:water (4:4:1) and dried. The fluorescent PAH spots are detected under UV light (254 nm), and documented by photography on Polaroid film. After marking the spots, they can be scraped off, eluted with methanol, and subjected either to fluorometry, mass spectrometry, GC-MS and/or HPLC for further identification.

TLC Pre-Separation Studies

Since the samples to be analyzed were rather complex mixtures, the POMs were pre-separated by column chromatography on activated alumina early in the program. This, however, led to large losses. This method was replaced by pre-separation on a silica-gel plate. A 20-x-20-cm glass plate was spread with a silica gel-G slurry in water:acetone (95:5) of 0.5 mm thickness. A benzene solution of the sample was streaked and developed in one direction with benzene:cyclohexane (3:2) for 45 minutes. Mixtures of standards were spotted on the side to indicate the position of these compounds on the plate. As much as 15 mg of spent shale extract, and up to 400 mg of plant extract, could be streaked on one plate. Experiments with test solutions have indicated that the total loss from streaking to the spectrophotometric identification in the case of benzo[a] pyrene was approximately 6%.

A typical example of such a separation is shown in Figure 9.2. This method allows the separation of alkanes from the PAH compounds and from the AA compounds. Within the AA compounds, it is possible to separate the azarines from the carbazoles all on one plate.

Test mixtures of PAH standards could thus be separated into strongly fluorescent PAH and AA bands of acridines and carbozoles. The PAH band is well defined and separated from the azarines and other hydrocarbons that migrate with the solvent front and accumulate at the edge of the plate.

An interesting phenomenon was observed in pre-separating the benzene extract from carbonaceous spent shale. Nearly in the center of the PAH band appeared a quenching band. The band was removed by scraping, eluted with methanol, and the solvent evaporated. A solid precipitated out. Direct probe mass spectrometry indicated that the material was elementary sulfur, S_8. Extraction of this sulfur from the PAH band is possible with mercury and gives about 11%, which corresponds actually with the elementary analysis value obtained from the benzene extract. This means that practically all the sulfur of the benzene extract concentrates in the PAH region. Pre-separation of the sulfur-free benzene extract by shaking repeatedly with fresh mercury removes the sulfur and on the TLC plate the PAH band is free of the quenching S-band. By the same method one can remove the sulfur present, for instance in soil extracts or plant extracts, and obtain a clear PAH band.

Analytical TLC Separations

Once the PAH band has been separated, it can be scraped off and desorbed from the silica gel by methanol. The resulting extract is

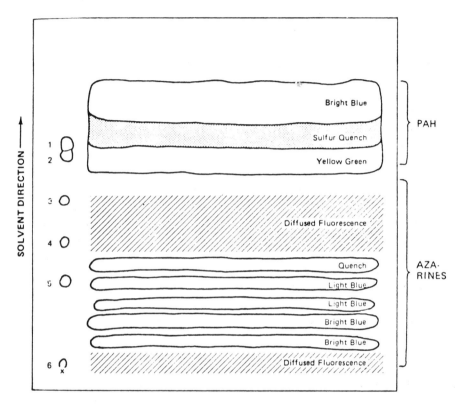

Figure 9.2   One-dimensional pre-separatory thin-layer chromatogram of benzene
solubles from carbonaceous spent shale [CSA II (1)] with sulfur. Layer: silica gel G.
Solvents: benzene, cyclohexane (1.5:1). Compounds: 1 and 2, PAH composite
mixture; 3, acridine; 4, carbazole; 5, 1,2,7,8-dibenzacridine; 6, phenanthridine.

concentrated by evaporation in the dark and at ambient temperature in a
nitrogen stream. The concentrated solution is then spotted onto an analytical TLC plate coated with a mixed layer and the plate is developed as
described previously.

It can be seen from Figure 9.1 that the system works well for the
separation of up to 20 standards, although some do overlap to an extent,
but can be differentiated frequently by their difference in fluorescent
colors. However, in runs with extracts from actual samples, such as
carbonaceous spent shale and soil, one always finds some diffuse fluorescent areas. This was particularly bothersome in the spent-shale samples
and for the two-component systems; this diffuse area extends into the

portion of the plate that contained the PAH spots. With the three-component system developed and described above, this area is confined to the right edge of the plate. It is suggested that these diffuse fluorescent areas represent homologous compounds of alkyl-substituted PAH, which retain their fluorescent properties. Therefore, no specific spots are formed, but a fairly continuous fluorescent area develops. This was corroborated later by HPLC runs.

Sulfur does not interfere with either system because it forms a nearly rectangular quenching area in the upper left-hand corner of the analytical TLC plate, which is well separated from the PAH spots. Therefore, in subsequent runs the samples were not desulfurized before TLC separation.

The pre-separation run shown in Figure 9.3 is of great interest. It was obtained from a benzene extract of the water-leached salts of carbonaceous spent shale. The water extracted about 5% of inorganic salts. After drying, these salts were re-extracted with benzene. The TLC pre-separation runs on silica gel show distinctly a PAH band, a very strong and broad aza-rine band and a sulfur band. This supports the fact that water-leached inorganic salts are solubilizing PAH compounds and carrying them along wherever the saline solution migrates. Recycling the saline solution through the spent shale could enrich it in inorganic salts as well as in PAH compounds. Analytical TLC runs of this PAH band and spectro-photometric determinations show that, in addition to PAH compounds such as fluoranthene, the salts also contain a number of other, as yet not identified, PAH and AA compounds that have not yet been investigated. The dotted area in Figure 9.1 is the diffuse band mentioned further above. This represents perhaps one of the more significant findings during this phase of investigation. The phenomenon is actually the reversal of the well-established geochemical reaction in which rather complex organic materials such as humates or fulvates or nucleosides, proteins or serum present in aqueous solutions of subsurface or groundwater are capable of solubilizing inorganic compounds and/or minerals that otherwise are quite insoluble in water.[11] The opposite appears true, as well. Inorganic salts can solubilize PAH compounds in soil and in spent carbonaceous shale. However, a detailed proof of this influence is still outstanding, and investigations of this question are underway at the present time.

The solubilization of PAH and AA compounds might be rather significant with respect to the transport and possible accretion of POM compounds and PAH or AA compounds from carbonaceous spent shale waste. However, more intensive and in-depth studies will be required to establish quantitatively the extent of this phenomenon in carbonaceous spent shale.

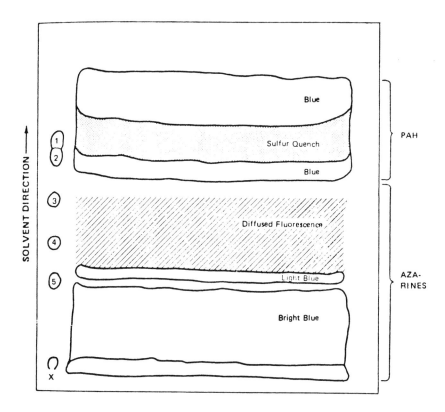

SOLVENT DIRECTION →

Figure 9.3 One-dimensional pre-separatory thin-layer chromatogram of the benzene solubles from the water extract of carbonaceous spent shale [CSS II (2)]. Layer: silica gel G. Solvents: benzene, cyclohexane (1.5:1). Compounds: 1 and 2, PAH composite mixture; 3, acridine; 4, carbazole; 5, 1,2,7,8-dibenzacridine; 6, phenanthridine.

Infrared Spectroscopy

Infrared spectra of the benzene extract from carbonaceous spent shale were investigated. Spectra were obtained from extracts of an old and a recent carbonaceous spent shale, respectively. These are rather similar to each other as they show low aromaticity but a surprisingly high degree of alkane character. The band around 1700 cm^{-1} likely indicates organic acids. Another IR spectrum was obtained from the PAH band from a silica-gel TLC pre-separation. This spectrum shows more aromaticity (which would be expected) and a smaller 1700 cm^{-1} band, but still a strong aliphatic band at 2900 cm^{-1}. All this indicates that the PAH fraction of the extract must still contain some moieties of highly aliphatic character. The IR spectra were prepared as capillary films, using a Beckman IR-8 instrument.

Nuclear Magnetic Resonance

A NMR spectrum of the benzene extract from carbonaceous spent shale was obtained with a Varian Model 3005. The spectrum corroborates conclusions from the elementary analysis and IR spectra, indicating low aromaticity of about 12% of the total organic matter in the benzene extract. The region around $\delta = 1\text{-}2$ indicates a high percentage of saturated alkane-type compounds or alkane moieties associated with the aromatic part.

UV and Fluorescence Spectroscopy

Because of the small amounts of materials present in the TLC spots or in the HPLC fractions, one method of identification and quantitative determination is by UV and/or emission fluorescence spectroscopy. The latter is the more sensitive and is also used to detect the PAH spots on the TLC plates. Calibration curves were made for standards to be used in connection with TLC techniques. An example of these FL curves is shown in Figure 9.4. An example of the fluorescence spectra for quantitative determination of benzo[a]pyrene from a standard and the TLC spot of a spent shale extract is shown in Figure 9.5.

High Pressure Liquid Chromatography

A high-pressure liquid chromatograph was obtained. Its adaptability for the separation of complex PAH mixtures was studied. Several papers indicate that HPLC shows strong promise for separation of PAH compounds.[1 2] The instrument is equipped with UV and fluorescence detectors, allowing the detection of compounds with weak UV absorption but strong fluorescence and vice versa. The method appears particularly adaptable to combination with TLC and/or mass spectrometry.

After a series of trial runs with standards and standard mixtures and various gradient elution profiles, it is now possible to separate reasonably well the 26 components of one of our standard mixtures. Table 9.3 is a listing of the compounds in the mixture in order of increasing retention time.

When this method is applied to the benzene extract of spent carbonaceous shale, one obtains the chromatogram shown in Figure 9.6. The

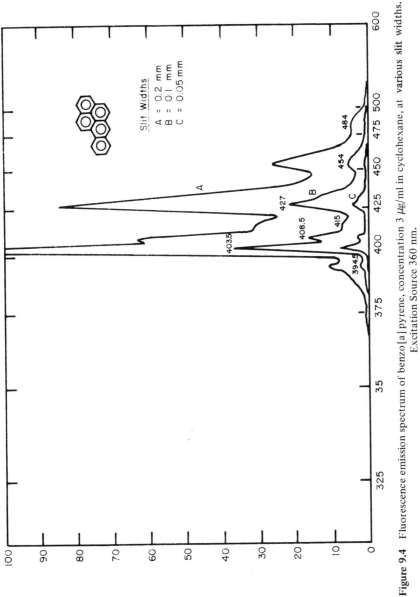

Figure 9.4 Fluorescence emission spectrum of benzo[a]pyrene, concentration 3 μg/ml in cyclohexane, at various slit widths. Excitation Source 360 nm.

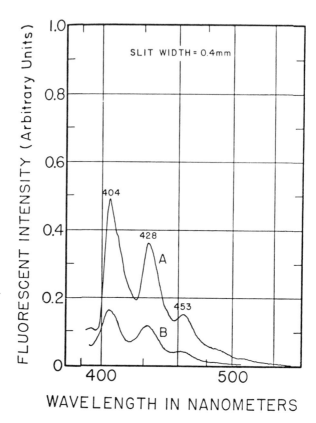

Figure 9.5 Fluorescence emission spectrum of TLC benzo[a]pyrene spot from
[CAS II (2)] benzene extract of carbonaceous spent shale (A). Stand. BaP
spectrum. Concn. in cyclohex. 0.03 mcg/ml (B).

components were detected from a 10 μl injection of a diluted benzene
solution. Figure 9.6 shows an extract of a PAH band from a TLC plate
still containing the sulfur (S_8). It is noteworthy that the fluorescent
trace indicates rather distinct peaks (many of which correspond to PAH
peaks on the UV absorption trace). However, at the longer retention
end of the chromatogram there is a broad and very intensive peak
(showing smaller shoulders) indicating a diffuse fluorescence mixture
leaving the column. This corroborates the findings by IR, NMR, and
TLC indicating the possible presence of homologous alkyl substituted
PAH compounds or azarines with strong fluorescence. The possible
resolution of this band, or at least its breakdown into smaller increments

Table 9.3   Retention Times of POM Standards by HPLC[a]

	Compound	Retention Time, Min
1	Naphthacene	3.9
2	Phenanthridine	4.9
3	7,12-dimethylanthracene	5.1
4	Acridine	5.3
5	Carbazole	5.7
6	Fluorene	5.9
7	Phenanthrene	7.1
8	1,2,7,8-dibenzacridine	10.9
9	Fluoranthene	11.5
10	Pyrene	13.1
11	1-methylphenanthrene	13.5
12	Benzo(c)phenanthrene	17.1
13	1,2-benzanthracene	23.1
14	1,2,7,8-dibenzcarbazole	23.1
15	7H-dibenzcarbazole	26.4
16	Perylene	32.0
17	1,2,3,4-dibenzpyrene	34.0
18	1,2,3,4-dibenzanthracene	38.1
19	Benzo(a)pyrene	39.2
20	Benzo(ghi)perylene	45.5
21	1,2,5,6-dibenzanthracene	48.3
22	3-methylcholanthrene	49.8
23	Benzo(rst)pentaphene	54.0
24	9,10-diphenylanthracene	54.7
25	Anthanthrene	55.8
26	Coronene	64.0

[a]Operating conditions: Column: 1 meter Sil X II (Octadecyl);   Function: Gradient Elution in 80 min;   Starting Solvent Condition: 60% Methanol, 40% Water;   Curvature: Convex 0.5;   Flow Rate: 0.75 ml/min.

by gel permeation chromatography as an example, is being investigated. In general, this detector is so sensitive that HPLC lends itself very well to use with TLC. Using a silica gel preparatory column, one could replace the pre-separation TLC plate. The retention times T of compounds in a mixture are very reproducible. The HPLC method might also be used as a pre-separator by Gel Permeation Chromatography (GPC) that pre-separates the compounds on the basis of their molecular size.

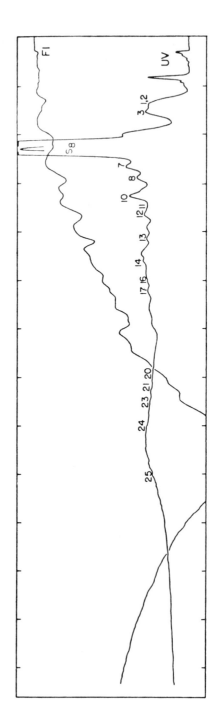

Figure 9.6   High-pressure liquid chromatogram of POMs obtained from separation of [CSA II (1)] benzene extract on a TLC plate, using two detectors, ultraviolet absorption (UV) and fluorescence (FL).

Gas Chromatography and Mass Spectrometry

The two methods have been used separately and in conjunction with each other. In one heating experiment it was indicated that possibly there are volatile hydrocarbons present in the carbonaceous spent shale that will volatilize at relatively low temperatures. Between 100-300°C (on Corasil SCOT columns of 50 ft length) a large number of compounds can be separated, none of which have been studied yet by GC-MS. However, there appear to be hydrocarbons in a benzene extract present from C_{10}-C_{25} and even higher molecular weight. MS will be utilized to identify some of these GC peaks.

The use of TLC or GC in conjunction with mass spectrometric methods is of advantage if new unknown compounds are present in a mixture. Mass spectroscopy by itself, while quite sensitive, cannot differentiate between two isomeric compounds of the same molecular weight, since the strongest peaks are the parent ion peaks, and the fragment ion peaks are very weak. However, intensity ratios of the $(M-1)^+$ $(M-2)^+$ could be utilized for closer differentiation. The presence of $(M-15)^+$ peaks are of use in identifying methyl-substituted PAH compounds and also breakdown products of POM compounds in general. The spectra of PAHs have very characteristic and strong parent ion peaks. Low-voltage scans can be used advantageously if mixtures of PAH compounds are present. In alkyl substituted POMs with larger alkyl chains, the intensity of the alkyl peaks may obscure the parent ions of lower-molecular-weight homologues. However, in conjunction with GC and/or HPLC, the method is very useful providing sufficient material is available to obtain a good mass spectrum.

DISCUSSION OF RESULTS

Summary of Analytical Results

Mineral Composition and Elementary Analysis

The composition of the mineral matter in carbonaceous spent shales is not much different from that in the raw shale itself, since the temperature of retorting is not sufficiently high to decompose the carbonate of the dolomite and/or calcite mineral. The mineral composition of carbonaceous-spent shale contains soluble sodium and potassium salts (mostly as sulfates) in addition to some soluble calcium, magnesium and aluminum. However, compared with oil shale retorted at high temperature (1800°C), the carbonaceous spent shale contains up to 5% residual carbonaceous material, which is partially soluble in organic solvents. Elementary analysis of spent shale and of the benzene extract of various origin shows that the older spent shale (CSA I) that was stored for about 12 years, is much lower in organic carbon and hydrogen, whereas the mineral carbon (carbonates) remained about the same. This could be due to a slow oxidation process of the organic matter.

The elementary composition of the benzene-soluble material is remarkably similar to that of the soluble bitumen extractable with benzene from raw shale, except for sulfur, which is considerably higher in the extract of the spent shale. This might indicate elementary sulfur that originates probably from pyrite decomposition under the reducing atmosphere in the retort.

Benzene Extraction of Carbonaceous Spent Shales

Extraction of carbonaceous spent shale samples was carried out to determine the presence and amount of benzene soluble material remaining in carbonaceous spent shale from various retorting processes, and to compare these amounts with each other and with the total benzene-soluble material from soil samples obtained from a "pristine" environment and soils from other areas such as the environment of oil-shale pilot plants, refineries, and benzene extracts from water samples, plant material and airborne particulate matter.

These benzene extracts were needed as starting samples for analysis and (at a later stage) for translocation studies. Since there have been only two or three major pilot operations over the last decade, the number and type of samples are limited, and vary also in their age. This could be of interest because it allows some comparison of weathering effects. Unfortunately, some of the spent shale samples could not be taken at the same time from various depths of the dump site, particularly of the older shale dumps. This will be attempted during this research program.

The data on benzene-extractable organic materials from carbonaceous shale would lead to the following remarks, some of which might be considered as preliminary conclusions:

The older spent shale (CSA I) has a much lower value of organic solubles (0.01%) than the more recent spent shale (CSA II) (0.24%), *i.e.,* the 7-year-old carbonaceous spent shale has (in average) only about 1/20 of the extractables as the more recent sample. This could be due to gradual loss of organic carbonaceous matter by oxidation and/or volatilization. The elementary analysis on total and organic carbon content appears to corroborate this. On the other hand, this could be due in part to different operating conditions when this shale was retorted

7 years earlier. There is no record on the exact operating conditions under which this spent shale was obtained except that the temperature range and retorting times were very similar to those used in operations yielding the more recent carbonaceous spent shale (CSA II), *i.e.,* the retorting temperature was about 900-1000°F. Nonetheless, the general appearance of the CSA I spent shale and the presence inside of the un-disturbed drums of whitish-gray zones and pockets would indicate loss of carbonaceous matter in these areas over a long period of time. It is not known at present how this slow oxidation is initiated and why it starts in certain areas within the body of the spent shale. This is the objective of the oxidation studies conducted under another phase of the present research program.

Six-year-old spent shale from another retorting process [Sample CSA III (1)] yields also a relatively high percentage of organic extractable material (about 0.26% on a dry basis). This result (which will have to be corroborated by samples from other areas of the same dump sites) is rather interesting, since the sample was taken only about 1-1½ ft below the surface of the dump slope. The explanation for this relatively high value of organic extractable from a dumpsite exposed over six years to weathering could be due either to preferential leaching of the inorganic salts by runoff water, thus increasing the relative concentration of the less soluble organic components, or to the fact that the retorting method itself yielded a coke with a higher percentage of organic soluble com-ponents, or (most probably) to a combination of both factors.

This extract, although highest in amount, shows the smallest PAH con-tent. This could be due to solubilization and transportation by saline water resulting from leached salts of the surface water.

Water Extraction of Carbonaceous Spent Shale

Carbonaceous spent shale from the various retorting processes was ex-tracted with water by the Soxhlet method to determine the amount of soluble salts extracted by water leaching, to obtain comparable data with soils and lysimeter leaching experiments, to obtain soluble salts for re-extraction with benzene, and to determine how much of the soluble organic matter in the extracted spent shale was extractable after water leaching.

Determination of water leachability from carbonaceous spent shale was not the primary concern; rather, it was to obtain information about whether the saline water solutions may also leach some of the organic material (in particular, POM compounds) and thus transport these with them.

The spent shale samples of various origins were extracted by the same method used for the benzene extraction, *i.e.*, Soxhlet extraction over 6- and 12-day periods. The data indicates average values (about 5%, 2.5% and 1.9% respectively) of soluble salts on a dry weight basis. These values are much lower than those reported by Ward *et al.*,[13] whose work was conducted under different conditions and over 42 days, showing a yield of about 13% of leachable salts. Our data indicate that the older spent shale has a higher salt concentration probably due to the loss of some of the carbonaceous matter by oxidation (the soluble salts could not be leached from the closed drums) whereas some of the salts from the newer spent shale (CSA II) were wetted down and also exposed to weathering conditions in the open pile. Similarly, it is not known how much of this leaching occurs at various depths and at the edges of the deposit. This must be more closely investigated. Similar studies by Striffler *et al.*[14] have already contributed valuable data in this area.

Re-Extraction of Carbonaceous Spent Shale after Leaching with Water

It was of interest to determine how much organic extractable remains after leaching with water. To this end 400 g of the water-leached material was re-extracted with benzene under the same conditions as the original spent shale (CSA II). It became evident that, after leaching, benzene extraction yielded 0.13% of organic soluble material. There is an incongruency in the material balance of the organic extractables. Before leaching, CSA II yields about 0.24% of solubles from 2000 g dry spent shale whereas after leaching, it yields only 0.13% soluble material, and the extracted salt about 0.005%. The difference of about 41.5% of the original total organic soluble material exists as salts of organic acids (normal and branched-chain) and higher-molecular-weight bases. Both types of compounds are present in the salt leachate and, therefore, can be mobilized by seepage or surface (runoff) water.

Re-Extraction of Water-Leached Salts

To evaluate the amount of organic matter contained in the inorganic matter present in the inorganic salts leached by water from the carbonaceous spent shale, the inorganic salts were extracted with benzene, and the extract subjected to TLC analysis. Results of the re-extraction are shown in Table 9.4.

The data would indicate that the salts extracted by the Soxhlet method do contain re-extractable organic matter which corresponds to about 20% of the total benzene extractable from the original carbonaceous shale

Table 9.4   Re-Extraction of Water-Leached Carbonaceous Spent Shale with Benzene[a]

Extract Number	Compound	Sample Designation	Weight (g)	Time (days)	Moisture %	Extracted Solubles (g)	Weight %
53	Carbonaceous Shale (6 months old)	CSS-II(2)R	400	6	1.6	0.5152[b]	0.13

[a]The benzene extract is 0.131% on a dry weight basis.
[b]After shaking with Hg to remove sulfur, it yielded 0.4585 g benzene soluble material which is 0.117% based on the original weight of dry spent shale ash.

before water extraction. This is very notable since it indicates that organic hydrocarbons can be solubilized by the saline solutions percolating through the disposed carbonaceous spent shale. These organic materials contain azarines and PAH compounds, such as benzo[a]pyrene, 7,12-dimethylbenzanthracene, and others, some of which show strong biological effects. Therefore, this aspect of solubilization is being pursued quite intensively during the research program. It will also include studies of the soluble salts from a DRI lysimeter test plot which, up to now, has yielded a considerable amount of salt due to leaching by rain and snow melt, a total of 408 liters, and an expected amount of 6800 g of leached salts.

Although these findings of solubilization are based on limited data, they are considered as rather significant in connection with potential migration of organic trace compounds through the spent shale, whenever the saline leachate water would migrate.

Extraction of Pristine Soil Samples

Soil samples from various areas of the Piceance Creek Basin and other areas were collected. While the analysis of these samples is still in progress, some samples in which the benzene-soluble material has been measured show an average benzene extract of about 0.02%. This data is of interest since some of these soils were collected from gulches considered future locations for spent shale deposition and thus will eventually be filled with carbonaceous spent shale (such as Davis Gulch). In one field study, sampling of soil was made in a traverse of the West Fork of Stuart Gulch (planned as a possible dump site for spent shale). The extraction data for these six sampling sites on the valley profile is shown in Figure 9.7.

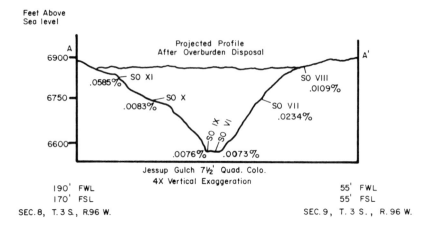

Figure 9.7 Cross section of canyon showing soil sample sites.

Extraction of Plant Material

A large quantity of plant material was collected—both grass and shrub types. However, because of difficulties during extraction procedures, there has only been time to extract the sagebrush leaves, which give (as would be expected) a fairly high percentage of benzene solubles as shown in Table 9.5.

Table 9.5 Benzene Extract of Sage (*Artemesia cana*) Leaves

Extract Number	Compound	Sample Designation	Sample Weight (g)	Extraction Time (days)	Extracted Solubles (g)	Wt % of Solubles
1 S G	Sage	PM XIV (1)	200[a]	30[b]	10.2	5.1
2 S G	leaves &					
3 S G	young stems					

[a]Dry plant material.

[b]Initial extraction in large Soxhlet. Slow extraction because too many fine particles.

Extraction of Process Water Samples

Process water from retorting of oil shale in a vertical kiln retort was analyzed for benzene-extractable material. The water was actually so rich in residual shale oil that, upon standing, it collected as a thin layer on the surface. Extraction was carried out after thorough mixing of the original solution. Results are presented in Table 9.6.

Table 9.6   Benzene Extract from Process Water[a]

Extract Number	Compound	Sample Designation	Sample Weight (g)	Extraction Time (days)	Extracted Solubles (g)	Wt % of Solubles
70	Process Water from Vertical Kiln Retort (20 Ton Retort)	PW I (1)	40	6	0.2948	0.737

[a]If process water is used for wetting the spent shale down to 13% moisture, then for 2000 g of spent shale there are added 1.92 g of organic matter to the 4.62 already present, making it a total of 6.54 = 0.32% based on dry weight.

The use of this process water for wetting down the spent shale would, of course, introduce additional soluble organic material, the total of which could amount to more than 0.327% or close to 200,000 tons of benzene-soluble organic matter per year for a 50,000 bbl/day operation.

Extraction of Air Particulate Matter

Air particulate matter was collected in pristine areas and in the Parachute Creek Canyon, about one mile below the Conoly Corporation plant. A Gelman sampler was used to determine particulates from the generator used.   The Hi-Vol sampler was placed about 1000 ft away from the generator. These values are presented together with values obtained from Hi-Vol sampler by   courtesy of the Colorado State Health Department (Table 9.7).

Content of POMs in the Carbonaceous Spent Shale

From the TLC, HPLC, fluorescence, and MS methods, the POM compounds identified to date are presented in Table 9.8.

Table 9.7   Benzene Extracts in Air Particulate Matter from Pristine Areas and
Other Locations in Colorado

Extract Number	Compound	Sample Designation	Sample Weight (g)	Extrac- tion Time (days)	(g)	Wt % Solubles	Average mcg/m^3 Air	m^3 Air Collected
1	Air Particulates from Parachute Valley	AP 1 (1)	0.02810	6	0.0023	8.22	82	344
2	Air Particulates from Parachute Creek[a]	AP II (1)	0.0697	6	0.00094	1.349	590	118
3	Air Particulates from Davis Gulch	AP III (1)	0.0750	6	0.00832	11.1	36	2067
4	Denver (1972 Average)[b]	AP IV (1)	0.5031	2	0.04085	8.12	213	2362
5	Denver Gates Sewer Plant[b]	AP V (1)	0.408	2	0.2444	5.99	170	2400
6	Rifle[b]	AP VI(1)	0.348	2	0.01249	3.59	145	2400
7	Aspen[b]	AP VII(1)	0.403	2	0.01375	3.41	168	2400
8	Rio Blanco	AP IX (1)	0.0528	2	ND	ND	22	2400

[a]Gelman sampler (10 feet away from generator)
[b]Colorado State Health Department data

Thirteen additional compounds are now being studied. The problem of separating and identifying the continuous fluorescent bands that appear on the plates and are considered to represent alkyl-substituted polycyclic condensed aromatic compounds has not been attacked.

To evaluate potential harmful properties suspect compounds among the PAH compounds in the soluble organic benzene extract it is, of course, most logical to survey for compounds that experimentally have been proved to have such harmful properties. Furthermore, it is important to establish whether these compounds can, under certain circumstances, migrate out of the large dump sites and enter into the environment. Since among the PAH compounds isolated by the TLC method benzo[a] pyrene was easily detected in the *benzene-extractable organic matter of spent shale* and can be well separated on the Kunte-type TLC plate, it was chosen as the first PAH compound for quantitative evaluation. To

Table 9.8   POM Compounds Identified in Benzene Extract of
Carbonaceous Shale Coke from Green River Oil Shale

Name of Compound	Potential Carcinogenicity[a]
Phenanthrene	— —
Fluoranthene	— —
Pyrene	— —
Anthanthrene (dibenzo[cdjk]pyrene	— —
Benz[a]anthracene (1,2-Benzanthracene)	+
Benzo[a]pyrene	+++
7,12-Dimethylbenz[a]anthracene	++++
Perylene	— —
Acridine	— —
Dibenz[a,j]acridine (1,2,-7,8-dibenzacridine)	++
Phenanthridine	?
Carbazole	— —
3-Methylcholanthrene	++++

[a]Particulate Polycyclic Organic Matter.[15]

this end, the benzo[a]pyrene (BaP) spot was removed from the TLC plate, eluted with methanol and concentrated. This was done both with CSA II extract which was desulfurized [CSA II (2)] and with material which was not desulfurized [CSA II (1)]. Upon concentration, the methanol extract of the BaP spot was transferred to a quartz cuvette and analyzed by emission fluorometry.

Quantitative BaP Determination

The characteristic emission bands at 403 and 426 nm were used for quantitative evaluation. BaP at these wavelengths gives linear fluorescent emission output within the concentration limits present in the TLC spot.

A quantitative BaP evaluation from a desulfurized benzene extract from the organic salts extracted from 2000 g of CSS II (2) is given as an example:

1. Salt recovered from water extraction of 2000 g spent shale about 50 g.
2. Benzene extract of 50 g salt yields 0.0929 g benzene extract. This corresponds to about 0.005% on the basis of the original spent shale.
3. Re-extraction of 2000 g water-leached spent shale yields 2.2925 g of benzene-soluble material. Based on the original salt-containing shale, this is 0.1122%; adding to this the 0.005% leached out with the salt gives 0.1172% soluble extract.

4. 0.4585 g of the benzene extractable were dissolved in 100 ml benzene to yield a 0.4585% solution.

5. 3.2 ml of this solution containing 14.672 mg of benzene solubles was streaked on a silica gel plate for pre-separation of PAH compounds. The loss in this operation in BaP is about 6%.

6. The PAH band was scraped off the plate, and the material eluted with 20 ml methanol. The methanol was evaporated under N_2.

7. The total recovered PAH material from the TLC plate was 4.3 mg = 4,300 μg. Total PAH in the benzene extractable is, therefore, 134.38 mg or 29.3%. Considering the 6% losses due to handling yields are: (a) Total PAH on the TLC plate 4.30 mg, (b) Total PAH in benzene soluble = 134.38 mg (29.31%), and (c) Total amount of PAH in the CSA II (2) spent shale equals, therefore, 0.034%, or 340 ppm.

8. BaP determination.
4.3 mg = 4,300 μg of PAH was taken up in 0.2 ml of methanol. Only 1,600 μg PAH went into solution. The Kunte-type TLC plate was developed in the usual manner; the BaP spot was removed, desorbed in 6 ml methanol, concentrated to 3.5 ml, and transferred into the quartz cuvette.

9. The solution for spotting contained 1,600 μg.

10. Fluorometric determination of the sample gave the following values:

λ (nm)	Peak Height (arbitrary units)	Slit Width (nm)
403	3.3	0.2
426	2.2	0.2

Fluorometry of a standard containing 0.3 μg/ml BaP gave the following values:

λ (nm)	Peak Height (arbitrary units)	Slit Width (nm)
403	18	0.2
426	10.4	0.2

11. From these values (at 0.2 mm slit width) the BaP of the spot was calculated to an average value of 0.207 μg BaP/spot. Using a similar evaluation at 4 mm slit width gives an overall average value of 0.232 μg BaP/spot.

12. Referring this value to the PAH yield for the applied 1600 μg PAH, a value of 0.0145% BaP in PAH is obtained (145 ppm).

13. Since in the analytical plate handling there is another error of 6%, there is, therefore, 0.016 μg BaP in the 1,600 μg of PAH.

14. Consequently, the benzene extract from CSS II (2) contains about 0.002% benzo[a]pyrene or 20 ppm. If one considers all the 4,300 μg of PAH obtained from the benzene extractable, the following

value is obtained:
Benzene-soluble extract from carbonaceous spent shale
Sample CSS II (2) contains 0.0045% or approximately 0.005%
benzo[a]pyrene or 50 ppm.

Since it was established (animal experiments) that a solution of 0.002% (20 ppm) benzo[a]pyrene in the presence of a promoting solvent when painted three times weekly on C3H mice produces tumors within a mean time of appearance of 48 weeks and earliest tumors even before 40 weeks, benzene extract from carbonaceous spent shale (containing perhaps as much as 50 ppm BaP) is suspect of potential harmful biological effects and, on this basis, the benzene extract could itself be considered potentially mildly blastomogenic.

However, this consideration is based upon inference from laboratory tests by using pure BaP in a promoting vehicle to a benzene extract that contains a host of other components that could either neutralize, diminish, or potentially enhance the activity of BaP. Furthermore, there is experimental evidence (Table 9.2) that the extract contains other PAH compounds with known biological effects such as dibenz[a,j]acridine; 7,12-dimethylanthracene; benz[a]anthracene; or 3-methyl-cholanthrene as possibly other alkyl-substituted PAH or AA compounds with as yet unknown biological activities. Since these compounds have as yet not been determined quantitatively, it is not possible to evaluate their potential contribution to the biological activity of the extracts. However, one could state that *mutatis mutandis*, their actual *in vivo* biological effect, are subject to the same consideration as BaP.

Furthermore, since the benzene extract represents only about 0.2% of the carbonaceous spent shale, the latter might contain only up to 60 ppb of BaP which, in comparison with other organic materials such as crude oil, coal and even some vegetation, might appear negligible and nonhazardous. However, our present knowledge as to the triggering mechanism of biological reactions to certain polycondensed aromatics is still very limited and as the presence of other PAH or POM compounds may suppress, or enhance the activity, this may be also dependent on the availability of these compounds for solubilization and/or desorption by biological fluids. Because of the experimentally demonstrated solubilization of POM compounds and their potential accretion in the dumpsites, the knowledge of their transportation and fate is now being studied. Tests for their biological activities at various stages along their migration and transformation in time will ultimately result from development of a sensitive and responsive bioassay test for trace amounts of organic materials present as potentially harmful pollutants. Because of the experimentally demonstrated solubilization of organic material from carbonaceous spent shale, such bioassay tests appear most desirable. Such a test is not only desirable for the trace organic compounds in carbonaceous spent shale, but for all energy-producing processes and on-stream compounds using fossil fuel.

Qualitative and quantitative determination of other POM compounds is underway. The combination of using TLC and/or HPLC for pre-separation and fluorescence spectrometry for final identification and quantitation have proved very useful as demonstrated on the first PAH compound discussed above.

Simultaneously, and in accord with the study of the transportation and fate of the organic compounds, translocation studies of polynuclear aromatic and other organic compounds extracted from carbonaceous spent shale into the physical and biological environment have indicated that polycondensed aromatic compounds such as ^{14}C-labeled benzo[a]pyrene will translocate in hydroponic cultures of wheat and barley and move into the above-ground stem and leaves. This is also the case in experiments using soils spiked with radioactive BaP. Studies carried out with algae and bacteria also indicate translocation of BaP from the culture medium (*i.e.,* water). The translocation in these experiments is enhanced in the presence of hydrocarbons or other organic compounds (*e.g.,* purines and pyrimidine bases or nucleic acids) which increase the solubility of BaP in the water. Experiments with spiked spent shale are being conducted at the present time, and preliminary tests yield similar results to those conducted with soils. The amount of translocated benzo[a]pyrene (BaP) depends on the concentration in the substrate and the vegetation period. The concentration in the plant is proportional to the concentration in the substrate and is highest during the growing period of the plants.

Furthermore, preliminary investigations of potential oxidation processes in large carbonaceous spent shale disposal areas and potential air pollution due to desorption of volatile compounds have also been initiated.

It could be demonstrated by gas chromatography-mass spectrometry (GC-MS) that between 100-200°C the carbonaceous spent shale will release a large number of volatile components. So far some of the major components determined are aromatic compounds such as benzene and toluene, in addition to alkanes of higher molecular weight. The relative amounts of these compounds released depend on the type of retorting process used. Retorting carried out at higher temperatures will of course yield a spent shale containing fewer volatiles.

CONCLUSIONS

Based on these investigations, the following tentative summaries and conclusions can be made:

1. Carbonaceous spent shale (coke) from retorting of Green River oil shale with up to 5% organic carbon content contains lower- and higher-molecular-weight organic material soluble in organic solvents. The benzene-soluble fraction ranges from about 0.01-0.2% depending on the retorting conditions and the age of the spent shale.

2. The benzene-soluble fraction contains organic compounds with predominantly aliphatic character and some polynuclear organic matter (POM) such as polycyclic condensed aromatic hydrocarbons (PAH) and azarines (AA).   A sizable fraction of these POM compounds appears to be alkyl-substituted.

3. The polycondensed aromatic hydrocarbon and azarine fractions contain compounds such as benzo[a]pyrene, 1,2-benzanthracene and dibenzacridine. Based on their amount present, the benzene soluble fraction from some of the carbonaceous spent shale (about 0.005%) bioassay tests might be indicated to determine the extent of their biological activity. Other PAH compounds with known biological activity are also present. However, their quantitative evaluation is as yet unknown and therefore the final quantitative evaluation will have to await results of these on-going investigations.

4. The soluble organic matter (and perhaps all organic carbon) from carbonaceous-spent shale appears subject to slow oxidation processes, and part of it is subject to water leaching or slow volatilization in the air.

5. The percent amount of benzene soluble material in carbonaceous spent shale can be one to two orders of magnitude larger than that from soils collected from pristine areas.

6. From traverse of a gulch projected as a potential disposal area the extractable organic material is, in general, also one or two orders of magnitude lower than that from spent shale; however, it varies with the density of the vegetation growing at the particular sampling site. This can be attributed to the endogenic PAH compounds synthesized by the plants and ending up in the soil.

7. The content of certain PAH compounds in the benzene extracts is about three orders of magnitude higher than that found in the soil, plant and water samples collected from the pristine areas.

8. Preliminary data indicate that a large number of polycyclic aromatic compounds (including BaP) can be leached easily from the carbonaceous

shale and migrate with the saline water. This water has a PAH content that could be at least three to four orders of magnitude higher than groundwater or surface water from pristine areas.

9. Based on these preliminary findings one can state that, in addition to the migration of inorganic trace elements, there could be uptake of solubilized trace amounts of organic compounds by saline water that might be present in the carbonaceous shale dump. These are subject to migration, possible concentration by accretion and translocation.

10. The presence of PAH compounds in the organic extracts and the water-leached extracts is established and there is evidence that the concentration of some of these PAH compounds having blastomogenic or mutagenic properties is at a level that should not be considered inconsequential, and warrants further intensive study and monitoring (both physical and biological) in view of the large quantities of spent shale that must be disposed of in commercial operations.

11. Studies on the translocation of PAH compounds to plants and aquatic life and on slow oxidation processes and potential desorption of volatile organic compounds are underway.

PROJECTED FUTURE RESEARCH

The projected immediate objectives of this project included:

1. Continued separation and identification of organic compounds present in trace quantities in the spent shale and process water, particularly polycondensed aromatics and other organic compounds in the carbonaceous spent shale.
2. Continued base line studies in pristine areas.
3. Solubilization and transportation studies of these compounds by the saline percolating water and of their fate in the spent shale deposits.
4. Translocation studies of organic compounds (in particular PAH compounds) into land plants and aquatic life.
5. Oxidation studies and its influence on potential air pollution.
6. Desorption studies of volatile components from the spent shale.

Analytical and lysimeter studies indicate that three new problem areas have arisen.

1. The potential solubilization of PAH compounds by the salts present in the carbonaceous spent shale and, therefore, their possible migration with the water-soluble salts in the runoff, subsurface, and groundwater or accretion inside or outside the dump or in impounded water. This aspect should be studied in greater detail.

2. The dynamics of inorganic salt level shifts in spent shale piles due to to periodic natural or artificial watering and evaporation processes. This could bring highly concentrated salt layers close to (or into) horizon of roots in natural or artificially vegetated areas, where active absorption by root hairs is taking place.

3. The dynamics and fate of water used to wet down the spent shale for disposal and compaction. It is presently not known whether and how long it will take for the average 13% moisture in the large shale piles to migrate deeper and sideways into the natural original soil; nor is it clear how the heavy overburden of the spent shale will affect the shift in the location of natural springs in spite of the intended culverting of these springs.

SOME FINAL CONSIDERATIONS

From these investigations it appears that the disposal of carbonaceous shale from commercial oil shale operations will inject into the environment organic compounds of various nature, the transportation, fate and ecological impact of which are not yet fully understood. Furthermore, the disposal of up to 4.5% of carbonaceous material (nearly 20-25% of the total energy extractable from the organic content of the oil shale rock) could be considered as wasting a sizable amount of potentially recoverable energy.

Therefore, why not utilize this energy source by combusting the carbon. This approach could eliminate some environmental problems in the disposal of carbonaceous spent shale and, at the same time, extract most of the available energy rather than throw it away.

Proponents of various processes have some basic disagreement as to the technological, economic and other aspects that speak for or against the combustion of the residual carbonaceous material. Proponents of some processes claim it might not be economical to do so, that compaction and/or revegetation is facilitated when using carbonaceous spent shale; others claim that the process design can be made to advantageously utilize the residual carbon in the actual pyrolysis process and yield a nearly carbon-free spent shale and thus operate more efficiently and avoid the potential environmental complications. Some processes supposedly are either in development or drawing board stage to do just that.

It is beyond the scope of the present and projected research project to evaluate the merits of the various approaches. However, any new process which in itself (or an after-treatment process) would produce noncarbonaceous spent shale would be desirable because it would eliminate a number of additional potential environmental problems and possibly involve additional capital investments at a later date for their abatements.

However, as long as it appears that large quantities of carbonaceous spent shale will be disposed of within the near future, the problems of the impact from organic matter injected into the environment by this process will be with us and will have to be investigated rather thoroughly in a cooperative manner both by the respective industry as well as by other independent organizations.

REFERENCES

1. Graf, W. and H. Diehl. "The Natural Normal Levels of Carcinogenic Polycyclic Aromatic Hydrocarbons and the Reasons Thereof," *Arch. Hyg. Bakteriol.* **150**, 49 (1966).
2. Andelman, J. B. and M. J. Suess. "The Photodecomposition of 3,4-Benzopyrene Sorbed on Calcium Carbonate," in *Organic Compounds in Aquatic Environments*, S. D. Fouston and J. V. Hunter, Ed. (New York: Marcel Dekker, 1971), p. 439.
3. Stenbing, L. *Angew. Bot.* **45**, 1 (1971).
4. Borneff, J. and R. Fischer. "Carcinogenic Substances in Water and Soil. X. The Determination of Polycyclic Aromatic Hydrocarbons in the Phytoplankton of a Lake," *Arch. Hyg. Bakteriol.* **146**, 334 (1962).
5. Kelus, J. *Gaz. Woda Tech. Sanit.* **37**(2), 61 (1963).
6. Schmidt-Collerus, J. J. Personal communications, Professor Borneff, July 1973.
7. Jones, R. E. and D. T. A. Townend. "The Oxidation of Coal," *J. Soc. Chem. Ind. (London)* **68**, 197 (1949).
8. Garner, W. E. and D. McKie. "The Heat of Adsorption of Oxygen on Charcoal," *J. Chem. Soc. (London)*, 2451 (1927).
9. Nevens, T. D., W. J. Culbertson, Jr. and R. D. Hollingshead. "Disposal and Use of Oil Shale Ash," Final Report, *U. S. Bureau of Mines, Project No. SWD-8* (April 1970).
10. Kunte, von H. "Carcinogic Substances in Water and Soil. XVIII," *Arch. Hyg.* **151**, 13 (1970).
11. Evans, W. D. "The Organic Solubilization of Minerals in Sediments," in *Advances in Organic Geochemistry*, Colombo and Hobson, Ed. (New York: Pergamon Press, 1964), p. 263.
12. Klimisch, H. T. "Determination of Polycyclic Aromatic Hydrocarbons," *Anal. Chem.* **45**, 1960 (1973).
13. Ward, J. D., G. A. Margheim, and G. O. G. Lof. "Water Pollution Potential of Spent Oil Shale Residues," *Amer. Chem. Soc. Div Fuel Chem.* **15**(1), 47, Symp. on Shale Oil, Tarsands and Related Material, Los Angeles, California (1971). Report to Water Quality Office, EPA, Grant No. 14030 EDB (august 1971).
14. Striffler, W. D., I. F. Wymore, and W. A. Berg. "Characteristics of Spent Shale as Influencing Water Quality and Sedimentation and as a Plant Growth Medium," Interim Final Report; Phase 1-G, Colorado State Univ., Ft. Collins (December 1973).
15. Committee on Biological Effects of Atmospheric Pollutants. "Particulate Polycyclic Organic Matter," NAS, Div. Med. Sci., Natl. Res. Council, Washington, D.C. (1972). Also, *Chem. Eng. News* 17 (September 18 1972).

10

SULFUR RECOVERY BY DESULFOVIBRIO IN A BIOCHEMICAL METHOD OF OIL SHALE PRODUCTION

Kathleen E. Kim, Judith A. Higa and T. F. Yen

Department of Chemical Engineering
University of Southern California
Los Angeles, California

INTRODUCTION

Oil shale represents one of the largest undeveloped natural resources in the United States. The Green River formation alone is estimated to contain an equivalent of two trillion barrels. The amount currently recoverable constitutes 600 billion barrels. This is nearly twice the amount quoted for the Middle East petroleum deposits.

Kerogen, the organic component of the greatest potential, is trapped in a mineral matrix of dolomite (magnesium-calcium carbonate) and quartz. A portion of this mineral matrix can be dissolved through the action of sulfuric acid, a by-product of *Thiobacillus* spp. It has been shown that up to 40% of these minerals can be dissolved by sulfuric acid leaching.[1,2]

The sulfur-oxidizing bacteria, *Thiobacillus* spp., derive their energy from the oxidation of reduced inorganic sulfur compounds. This energy drives the metabolic process for synthesizing cell constituents with CO_2 as the sole carbon source.

It has been estimated that 133 kg of sulfuric acid is needed per ton of shale to give a weight loss of 12%.[3] This initial sulfur investment can be recovered utilizing sulfate-reducing bacteria, for example, *Desulfovibrio* sp., to regenerate sulfide from sulfate as in the Laseter process (Figure 10.1).[4,5] The sulfide can then be easily oxidized to elemental sulfur.

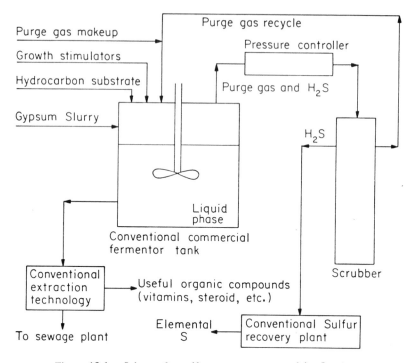

Figure 10.1 Scheme for sulfur recovery proposed by Laseter.

The present study was designed to demonstrate the recovery of sulfur in the form of sulfide. Future investigations will be done on direct application to industry.

MATERIALS AND METHODS

Cultures

Thiobacillus thiooxidans ATCC 8085 was obtained from the American Type Culture Collection. Stock cultures were maintained on Waksman's medium containing $(NH_4)_2 SO_4$ (0.2g); $KH_2 PO_4$ (3.0g); $MgSO_4 \cdot 7H_2 O$ (0.5g); $CaCl_2 \cdot 2H_2 O$ (0.25g); and distilled water (1 liter). The medium was adjusted to pH 3.5 with concentrated $H_3 PO_4$. The medium was first autoclaved and then surface-layered with elemental sulfur (see Plate 15, Chapter 1).

Desulfovibrio vulgaris, Hildenborough strain, NCIB 8303, was obtained from J. M. Akagi at the University of Kansas in Lawrence. This strain was cultured on Postgate's medium containing $(NH_4)_2 SO_4$ (1g); $KH_2 PO_4$ (0.5g); $Na_2 SO_4$ (2.6g); $MgSO_4 \cdot 7H_2 O$ (2.0g); $CaCl_2 \cdot 2H_2 O$ (0.06g);

yeast extract (1.0g); sodium lactate (6.0g); $Fe(NH_4)_2(SO_4)_2 \cdot 6H_2O$ (0.01g) and 1 liter of distilled water. Autoclaving plus membrane filtration were used as sterilization procedures. The final pH of the medium was adjusted to 7.2.

Oil Shale

The oil shale used was of the grade 40 gal/ton taken from Anvil Point of the Green River formation. The samples were supplied through the courtesy of G. U. Dinneen, Laramie Energy Research Center.

The shale samples were ground in a ball mill and sieved through a Tyler Standard Screen Scale No. 20 and retained by a No. 35.

Analytical Methods

Sulfate determinations were done gravimetrically with barium chloride (analytical grade).

Leaching

Fifty grams of shale were packed into a cylinder fitted with a cotton plug and filter paper. A 12-liter culture of *Thiobacillus thiooxidans* with a pH of 1.9 was percolated through the column at a rate of 1 l/day.

RESULTS

The feasibility of coupling a reductive process using *Desulfovibrio* sp. with an oxidative procedure of *Thiobacillus* sp., for cycling of sulfur, was demonstrated.

Thiobacillus thiooxidans was grown for 10 days in a series of flasks containing known amounts of shale. At the end of this time, oxidation was stopped and a portion of the flasks had lactate added as a growth substrate. These flasks were inoculated with *Desulfovibrio* sp. and sparged with nitrogen to establish anaerobiasis. Growth was demonstrated by the deep gray color indicative of FeS formation. The flasks that had the dead cell residuals of *Thiobacillus* as the sole energy source (*i.e.,* no lactate added) and the lactate of the transferred culture also showed a gray color indicating growth. At day 20, the flasks were re-aerated and re-inoculated with *Thiobacillus thiooxidans.* The oxidative action of *Thiobacillus thiooxidans* explained the disappearance of the gray color, thus confirming the feasibility of coupling the reductive process of *Desulfovibrio* sp. between two oxidative processes of the *Thiobacillus* sp. in an *in situ* leaching of shale.

The recovery of sulfur as sulfide was also investigated on continuous bioleaching of shale. Raw shale was continuously leached by gravity with a culture of *Thiobacillus thiooxidans*. The leachate was collected and supplemented with nutrients for growth of the sulfate reducer. The supplementary nutrients included NH_4Cl, KH_2PO_4, yeast extract, sodium lactate and $Fe(NH_4)_2(SO_4)_2$. The leachate medium was inoculated with *Desulfovibrio vulgaris*, and anaerobic conditions were initiated by a pyrogallic acid seal. Growth was detected by the grayish blackening of FeS formation, H_2S odor, and decrease in $SO_4^=$ concentration. The sulfate ion concentration was measured gravimetrically with $BaCl_2$. Figure 10.2 shows a definite decrease in sulfate ions in the medium demonstrative of the conversion of sulfate to sulfide by *Desulfovibrio* sp.

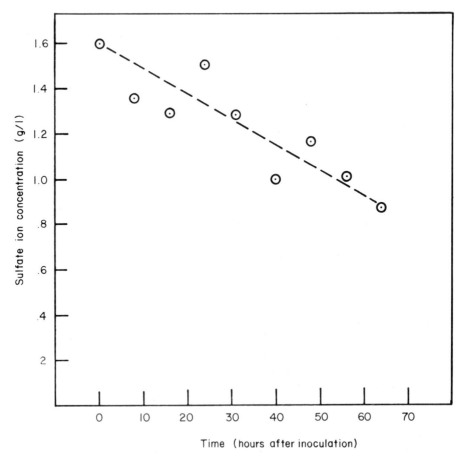

Figure 10.2 Decrease of sulfate ion due to conversion to sulfide by *Desulfovibrio vulgaris*.

DISCUSSION

The initial sulfur investment of approximately 200-335 lb/ton of oil shale in the biochemical leaching process for oil shale may be deemed reasonable by the sulfate-reducing bacterial species of the genus *Desulfovibrio*.

Desulfovibrio sp. reduces the sulfate produced by the oxidative procedure of *Thiobacillus* sp. to sulfide. The reduction of sulfate to sulfide is provided by the oxidation of a substrate such as lactate. Two molecules of lactate are needed to provide four electron pairs for the conversion of one molecule of sulfate to sulfide. The following scheme shows the heterotrophic sulfate reduction.[6]

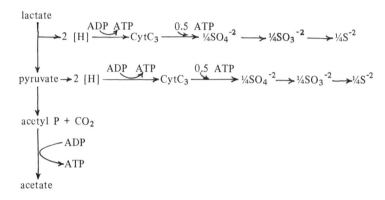

A suitable economical substrate substituted for lactate would make this sulfate reducer a feasible route to sulfur recovery.

Joel Wong of the consulting firm of J. L. Laseter and Associates[4,7] has adapted this bacteria to a practical scheme for sulfur recovery. His work involved the use of sewage, spent sulfite liquor, and brewery effluents as suitable substrates. He found, however, that selected petroleum substrates were more successful though more expensive.

Past studies in this laboratory have demonstrated that untreated bitumens, the soluble organics in the shale, cannot alone serve as an adequate carbon and energy source. Asphalt may be a practical substrate. It has been claimed that *Desulfovibrio desulfuricans* was found in the weather-damaged asphalt road in Australia.[8] The bacteria utilize the adhesive portion of the asphalt roads as food. This adhesive portion is probably composed of lower molecular weight hydrocarbons such as those found in oxidized products from oil shale.[9] Other future investigations are anticipated to deal with the feasibility of utilizing the soluble organic acids found in wastewater (*i.e.,* process water) from oil shale retorting plants as possible growth substrates.[10] Since this water contains almost 10% organic acids, if found successful this could provide an economical process for sulfur recovery, especially adaptable to the bioleaching process of oil shale.

ACKNOWLEDGMENT

This work is supported by NSF Grant No. GI 35683. The authors also thank Jay L. Stern for technical help.

REFERENCES

1. Findley, J. E., M. D. Appleman and T. F. Yen. Papers delivered at ACS, Div. Microbial Chemistry and Technology, Chicago, 1973.
2. Findley, J. E., M. D. Appleman, and T. F. Yen. "Degradation of Oil Shale by Sulfur-Oxidizing Bacteria," *J. Appl. Microbiol.* 28, 3 (1974).
3. Moussavi, M. "Engineering Feasibility Studies of an Ex-Situ Process for Bioleaching of Oil Shales," in *NSF Workshop on Possible Concepts for Biochemical Recovery of Oil Shales*, University of Southern California (December 2, 1974).
4. "Bug Process Removes Sulfur," *Chem. Eng. News*, 21 (March 20, 1967).
5. Yen, T. F. "Biodeterioration and Biodisintegration," in *Recycling and Disposal of Solid Wastes* (Ann Arbor, Michigan: Ann Arbor Science Publishers, Inc., 1974), pp. 1-41.
6. Doelle, H. W. *Bacterial Metabolism.* (New York: Academic Press, 1969).
7. Laseter, John L. personal communication, University of New Orleans January, 1975.
8. "Small Bugs Damage Australian Roads," *New York Times* (March 25, 1967).
9. Wen, C. S. and T. F. Yen. unpublished results.
10. Kim, K. E. "Alteration of the Environment for Sulfur-Oxidizing Bacteria and Sulfate-Reducing Bacteria," in *NSF Workshop on Possible Concepts for Biochemical Recovery of Oil Shales*, University of Southern California (December 2, 1974).

11

A COMPARISON OF SHALE GAS OIL DENITRIFICATION REACTIONS OVER Co-Mo AND Ni-W CATALYSTS

H. F. Silver and N. H. Wang

Department of Chemical Engineering
University of Wyoming
Laramie, Wyoming 82071

H. B. Jensen and R. E. Poulson

U.S. Energy Research and
Development Administration
Laramie Energy Research Center
Laramie, Wyoming 82071

INTRODUCTION

As the nation's needs for additional sources of petroleum products become ever more pressing, a role for oil shale in the synthetic fuels industry becomes more probable. One of the problems in converting shale oil to hydrocarbon liquid products is the elimination of nitrogen from the shale oil. Nitrogen compounds not only impart undesirable properties to the finished products but their basic nature makes them effective poisons for the acidic catalysts used in petroleum refining.

An efficient means of eliminating nitrogen from shale oil is hydro-denitrification of the oil in the presence of a dual function catalyst. In a study of the denitrification of model nitrogen compounds over an Ni-W on Al_2O_3 catalyst, Flinn[1] reported that amines and anilines reacted readily to form ammonia, but indole was much less active and quinoline was the most difficult to denitrify. Unfortunately, most of the nitrogen in shale oil has been found to be of the quinoline and indole types.[2]

163

In a previous study in this laboratory, the relative rates of disappearance of the types of nitrogen compounds present in shale gas oil were studied using a Co-Mo on Al_2O_3 catalyst. The present paper uses those Co-Mo results and results from experiments using Ni-W on Al_2O_3 and Ni-W on $SiO_2 \cdot Al_2O_3$ to compare the selectivity of these catalysts in denitrifying the types of nitrogen compounds in shale gas oil. These comparisons should afford insight into the role of the catalyst during denitrification reactions.

EXPERIMENTAL

A gas combustion retort shale gas oil was hydrogenated in a 2-liter externally heated, stirred reactor for one-half hour at 600°F and for three hours at 700°, 750°, and 825°F. Properties of this gas oil are listed in Table 11.1. The initial hydrogen pressure was 3,000 psig and, at operating temperatures, pressures varied from 3,500 to 5,500 psig. Details of the operating procedure have been reported previously.[3]

Table 11.1   Properties of Shale Gas Oil Feed Stock

Gravity, °API	21.5
Nitrogen, wt %	2.00
Sulfur, wt %	0.60
Boiling range, °F	515 to 900

Three different catalysts were used—Co-Mo on Al_2O_3 (Nalco, Nalcomo 471), Ni-W on Al_2O_3 (Nalco, NT 550), and Ni-W on $SiO_2 \cdot Al_2O_3$ (Harshaw, Ni-4301). The source and composition of these catalysts are presented in Table 11.2, and selected properties of the catalysts are presented in Table 11.3. Although it was recognized that different catalysts require unique pretreatment before use to maximize their individual activities, all three catalysts were given the same pretreatment to reduce the number of experimental variables. On the basis of work reported by Richardson[4] who indicated that the desulfurization activity of the Co-Mo catalyst could be optimized by preheating at 1,000°F, it was assumed that the same pretreatment would optimize denitrification activity, and all catalysts were preheated at 1,000°F for two hours and allowed to cool in a dessicator. The catalysts were then added to the reactor in the oxidized state where they were partially sulfided by the gas-oil desulfurization reactions occurring while the reactor was heated at a rate of 4°F per minute to reaction temperature.

Table 11.2   Source and Composition of Catalysts

Catalyst	Co-Mo on Al_2O_3	Ni-W on Al_2O_3	Ni-W on $SiO_2 \cdot Al_2O_3$
Supplier	Nalco Chemical	Nalco Chemical	Harshaw Chemical
Trade Name	Nalcomo 471	NT 550	Ni-4301
Composition, wt %	3.5 CoO	4 Ni	6 Ni
	12.5 MoO_3	16 W	19 W
	84.0 Al_2O_3	80 Al_2O_3	20 SiO_2
			55 Al_2O_3

Table 11.3   Selected Catalyst Properties

Catalyst	Co-Mo on Al_2O_3	Ni-W on Al_2O_3	Ni-W on $SiO_2 \cdot Al_2O_3$
Trade name	(Nalcomo 471)	(NT 550)	(Ni-4301)
Pore volume, cc/g	0.40	0.35.	0.20
Average pore radius, Å	35.1	35.7	19.5
BET area, m^2/g	226.4	195.7	208.5

Pore-Size Distribution

Pore Radius, Å	Vol %		
300-250	1.3	1.0	1.2
250-200	2.4	1.8	0.7
200-150	4.0	3.0	1.1
150-100	8.5	7.6	2.3
100-90	2.7	2.8	0.8
90-80	4.0	4.7	1.1
80-70	5.0	6.9	1.4
70-60	7.0	8.3	1.8
60-50	8.8	10.0	2.0
50-45	6.1	6.9	1.5
45-40	6.6	7.0	1.9
40-35	7.6	7.5	2.4
35-30	8.0	7.5	6.0
30-25	9.1	7.9	9.7
25-20	3.9	6.8	17.5
20-15	11.6	6.1	25.6
15-10	3.6	4.1	22.9
10-7	0.0	0.0	0.0

Samples of the product oil from the reactor were analyzed for total nitrogen using the Kjeldahl method[5] and, for nitrogen types, using nonaqueous, potentiometric titrations and infrared analyses as suggested by Okuno[6] and modified by Koros.[7] When the titration data were combined with the data from the infrared determination of indole-type compounds, it was possible to classify the nitrogen compounds into the following types: *Quinolines* (including pyridines, quinolines, acridines, and tertiary amines); *arylamines* (including 1,2,3,4-tetrahydroquinolines, 2,3-dihydroindoles, and anilines); *indoles* (including pyrroles, indoles, and carbazoles); *primary and secondary amines; amides* (including quinolones and oxindoles); and *unidentified compounds.* A complete discussion of the details of this classification procedure has been reported.[8]

RESULTS AND DISCUSSION

Table 11.4 lists catalysts, temperatures, times, percent of the total nitrogen removed, and nitrogen types expressed as their weight percent of the total nitrogen remaining in the product oil. The data in Table 11.4 show that the denitrification reactions were studied over the range of 0-80% nitrogen removal and, with the exception of one instance, 90 or more percent of the total nitrogen was classified into one of the five nitrogen types.

The selectivity of each of the three catalysts toward converting each of these five types of nitrogen to either ammonia or to another nitrogen type was determined by plotting the nitrogen type in the product oil as a function of the total nitrogen removed in the denitrification reaction. If the slope of the resulting plot is positive, that nitrogen type is being converted at a slower rate than the rate at which total nitrogen is removed. If the slope is negative, the relative rate is faster.

Figure 11.1 is the resulting plot for the quinoline-type nitrogen using the three catalysts. The positive slope of the Co-Mo curve shows that the conversion of quinoline when Co-Mo is the catalyst proceeds at a slower rate than the rate at which total nitrogen is removed. The negative slope of the Ni-W curve shows that the quinoline is being converted at a faster relative rate. Only one curve has been drawn through the two sets of Ni-W data because regression analyses of the Ni-W data showed very little difference when the four Ni-W on $SiO_2 \cdot Al_2O_3$ data points were added to the eight Ni-W on Al_2O_3 data points. This was true for the conversion of all five nitrogen types; hence, the Ni-W data were treated as one curve in all five cases.

Table 11.4   Nitrogen Types in Product Oils

Temp. ($^\circ$F)	Time (hr)	Total Nitrogen Removed (wt %)	Quinoline Type	Indole Type	Aryl-amine Type	Primary and Secondary amine Type	Amide Type	Unidentified
				Nitrogen Type, wt % of Total Nitrogen Remaining in Liquid Product				
				Feed Gas Oil				
–	–	–	52	16	1	2	20	9
				Co-Mo on Al$_2$O$_3$				
600	1/2	3	53	19	5	7	11	5
	3	6	51	16	9	15	8	2
700	1/2	12	52	16	10	14	6	2
	3	32	54	14	13	12	4	3
750	1/2	26	53	13	12	14	4	4
	3	70	61	14	19	3	2	1
825	1/2	65	55	13	20	7	2	3
	3	95[a]	–	–	–	–	–	–
				Ni-W on Al$_2$O$_3$				
600	1/2	0	51	18	4	2	15	10
	3	0	50	18	5	3	14	10
700	1/2	3	48	17	5	10	13	7
	3	12	46	13	7	16	11	7
750	1/2	16	48	14	7	15	13	3
	3	51	46	15	16	13	3	7
825	1/2	59	44	16	18	11	1	10
	3	79	41	17	25	6	1	10
				Ni-W on SiO$_2$·Al$_2$O$_3$				
700	1/2	2	49	18	4	7	16	6
	3	8	46	15	6	15	16	2
825	1/2	43	47	15	15	10	6	7
	3	75	37	15	29	3	4	12

[a]Not sufficient concentration to analyze product oil.

Figure 11.2 is the resulting plot for the indole-type nitrogen. Indole-type nitrogen accounts for 15% of the feedstock nitrogen and, at a nitrogen removal of 3% when using the Co-Mo catalyst, it accounts for 19% of the nitrogen remaining in the liquid product. When the two Ni-W catalysts are used, indole nitrogen accounts for 18% of the remaining nitrogen even

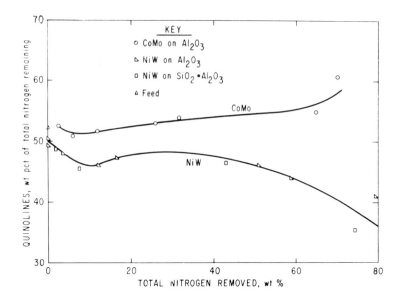

Figure 11.1

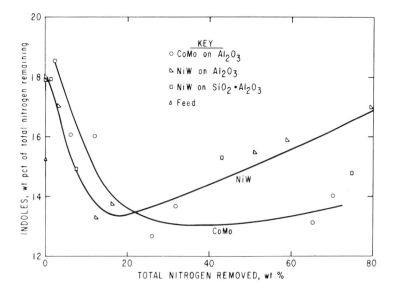

Figure 11.2

though there was not distinguishable removal of nitrogen from the liquid. These increased levels of indole-type nitrogen can only be accounted for by the conversion of other types of nitrogen to indole type. In a previous paper that reported Co-Mo results, we suggested that the amide type and unidentified type were the most likely sources of this increase in indole nitrogen. We now see the same selectivity when the two Ni-W catalysts are used.

Figure 11.2 also shows that once the initial buildup of indole is over, its conversion to ammonia or to other nitrogen types is much faster than the average conversion until about 25% of the denitrification reaction is completed. At this point indoles are converted more slowly when the Ni-W catalysts are used than when Co-Mo is used and, in both cases, the rates are slower than that for total nitrogen removal.

A conclusion that can be reached from the results shown in Figures 11.1 and 11.2 is, despite the compositional differences in the two Ni-W catalysts, there is little difference in their selectivity for the conversion of quinoline types and of indole types. These results do show that the selectivity of the two Ni-W catalysts is different than the selectivity of the Co-Mo catalyst for these two classes of compounds. The Ni-W catalysts convert quinolines faster than do the Co-Mo and, above 20% nitrogen removal, the Co-Mo converts the indoles faster than do the Ni-W catalysts.

These selectivity results might be explained on the basis of differences in the adsorption characteristics of the catalysts due to differences in the acidity of the catalyst supports. Haensel[9] reports that the ability of a catalyst to adsorb nitrogen compounds is largely influenced by the acidity of the catalyst. However, the Ni-W on Al_2O_3 catalyst and the Ni-W on $SiO_2 \cdot Al_2O_3$ catalyst show the same selectivity but the chemical compositions of their supports, as shown in Table 11.2 are different. Further, as shown in Table 11.3, the Co-Mo on Al_2O_3 catalyst and the Ni-W on Al_2O_3 catalyst are similar in their pore distribution patterns, yet their selectivities differ. Thus, it seems more likely that in this case the observed differences in selectivity should be attributed to the differences in the active-metal components, Co-Mo and Ni-W, rather than to the differences in the catalyst supports.

Figure 11.3 shows the relative percentage of the unconverted nitrogen compounds which have been classified as arylamine-type compounds (including hydrogenated quinolines, hydrogenated indoles, and anilines) as a function of the extent of the denitrification reaction. Arylamines can be formed by means of hydrogenation of quinoline-type and indole-type compounds and disappear by means of hydrocracking to form ammonia. These results show that at the high hydrogen pressures used in this study,

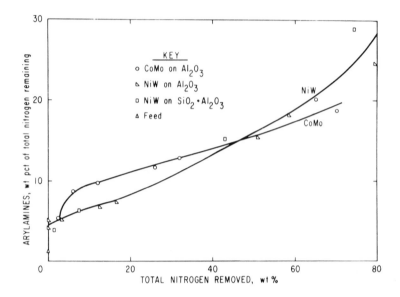

Figure 11.3

there is little difference in the three catalysts in their selectivity for converting arylamines. Also, the rate at which arylamines are formed by
hydrogenation of quinolines and indoles over all three catalysts is more
rapid than the rate at which the arylamines are converted by hydrocracking. This finding is substantiated by the work of Brown,[10] who reported
that anilines comprised about one-third of the tar bases in a shale-oil
naphtha produced by recycle hydrocracking of a crude shale oil. Even
though the results presented in Figure 11.1 show that the rate of
hydrogenation of quinoline-type nitrogen compounds is slower than the
rate at which total nitrogen is removed over the Co-Mo catalyst, the
results shown in Figure 11.3 suggest that the hydrogenation reaction
does not completely limit the overall rate of denitrification over this
catalyst even at $800°F$ as Koros[7] reported and as we have reported in
an earlier paper.[3]

    Figure 11.4 shows the relative percentages of the unconverted nitrogen
compounds which have been classified as primary and secondary amines
as a function of the removal of total nitrogen. Although we have shown
two curves in this figure, a regression analysis showed that there is little
difference in the Ni-W and Co-Mo data. Hence, there is little difference

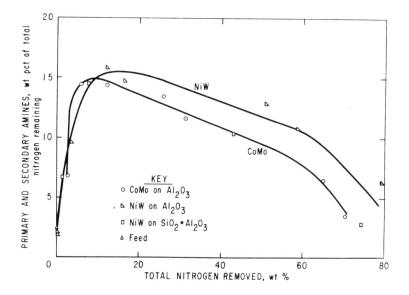

Figure 11.4

in the selectivity of these three catalysts in their ability to effect a conversion of the primary and secondary amines. Figure 11.4 shows that,
at nitrogen removals up to about 20%, the relative percentages of primary
and secondary amines increase significantly, but at higher nitrogen removals these compounds are rapidly converted to ammonia.

Figure 11.5 is a plot of the data for amide-type nitrogen. As shown
here, the relative percentage of amide nitrogen decreases rapidly at low
nitrogen removal. The Co-Mo catalyst exerts a stronger influence than
do the Ni-W catalysts in the conversion of amides at low nitrogen removals, but all three catalysts are quite effective in converting amide-type
nitrogen to other forms.

SUMMARY

The selectivity of three catalysts (Co-Mo on Al_2O_3, Ni-W on Al_2O_3,
and Ni-W on $SiO_2 \cdot Al_2O_3$) on influencing the conversion of five identifiable types of nitrogen compounds has been demonstrated. The two
Ni-W catalysts are somewhat more selective in converting quinoline-type
compounds than is the Co-Mo catalyst. Because there is no difference

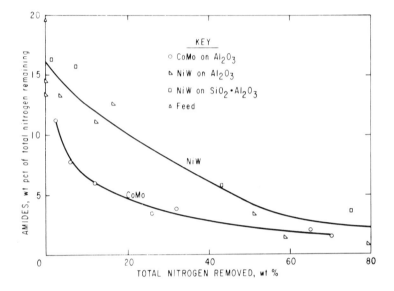

Figure 11.5

in the selectivity of the two Ni-W catalysts that differ from each other in the composition of their supports, it seems likely that the active-metal component of the catalyst is the determining factor in the selectivity of quinoline conversion. At low denitrification levels all three catalysts are effective in rapidly converting indole-type nitrogen, but above 20% nitrogen removal, the Co-Mo catalyst is more effective than the Ni-W catalysts. All three catalysts show that they are less effective in converting arylamines than in removing nitrogen; and they show approximately the same selectivity toward primary and secondary amines. The Co-Mo catalyst converts amide-type nitrogen much faster at low levels than do the two Ni-W catalysts; but all three catalysts are highly selective in promoting conversion of amide-type nitrogen.

The results also show that the relative percentages of different nitrogen compounds change as shale gas oil is denitrified. At low and intermediate levels of nitrogen removal, all five types of nitrogen compounds are present in the liquid product. However, at higher levels of nitrogen removal the identifiable nitrogen compounds remaining in the liquid product consist primarily of quinolines, indoles and arylamines. Primary and secondary amines and amides are practically missing from the product at levels approaching 80% removal of nitrogen.

ACKNOWLEDGMENTS

Reference to specific trade names or manufacturers does not imply endorsement by the Bureau of Mines. The work upon which this report is based was done under a cooperative agreement between the Bureau of Mines, U.S. Department of the Interior, the University of Wyoming, and the U.S. ERDA.

REFERENCES

1. Flinn, R. A., O. A. Larson, and H. Beuther. *Petrol. Refiner.* **42**, 129 (1963).
2. Dinneen, G. U., G. L. Cook, and H. B. Jensen. *Anal. Chem.* **30**, 2026 (1958).
3. Silver, H. F., N. H. Wang, H. B. Jensen, and R. E. Poulson. *ACS Div. Petrol. Chem. Preprints* **17**(4) G74 (1972).
4. Richardson, J. T. *Ind. Eng. Chem.* (fund.) **3**, 154 (1964).
5. Lake, G. R., P. McCutchan, R. A. Van Meter, and J. C. Neel. *Anal. Chem.* **23**, 1634 (1951).
6. Okuno, I., D. R. Latham, and W. E. Haines. *Anal. Chem.* **37**, 54 (1965).
7. Koros, R. M., S. Banic, J. E. Hofmann, and M. I. Kay. *ACS Div. Petrol. Chem. Preprints* **12**(4), B165 (1967).
8. Wang, N. H. "Hydrodenitrification Reactions in Shale Gas Oil," Master's Thesis, University of Wyoming (1973).
9. Haensel, V., E. L. Pollitzer, and C. H. Watkins. *Proc. Sixth World Petrol. Cong., Sec. III,* **Paper 17**, Frankfurt/Main, Germany (1963).
10. Brown, D., D. G. Earnshaw, F. R. McDonald, and H. B. Jensen. *Anal. Chem.* **42**, 146 (1970).

12

MICROBIAL DEGRADATION OF OIL SHALE

J. E. Findley, M. D. Appleman, and T. F. Yen

Department of Chemical Engineering
University of Southern California
Los Angeles, California 90007

Early efforts toward the utilization of oil shale as an energy source have relied almost completely on physical methods of recovering this form of energy from the geological formations known as oil shale. Release of the energy-yielding organic fraction from oil shale has been brought about by retorting the oil shale at temperatures above 500°C and distillating the organic material. The shale oil so produced is then available to be burned or otherwise processed into desired products. This approach has become the primary manner in which the problem of energy production from oil shale has been approached.

The technology of energy recovery from oil shale is varied and ranges from mining and retorting above ground to the *in situ* combustion method in which shale is burned beneath the ground. These methods depend on the destructive distillation of the organic portion of the oil shale and subsequent condensation of the reformed organic material. In the above-ground process, the shale must be mined. The result of this method is a deposit of large amounts of spent shale as a waste product, which causes environmental problems. The alternative method, *in situ* mining, obviates some of the objectionable features of the process, *i.e.,* it is not necessary to mine by conventional means or to strip-mine the shale and transport it to the refinery site. The *in situ* method utilizes holes bored into the shale formation into which air is pumped, and the shale is burned in place. The products, heat or vaporized organic material, can be utilized.

Heat can be used for the generation of useful clean energy, or organic materials can be pumped out, condensed and refined.

SEPARATION OF SHALE ORGANIC MATERIAL

Chemically, kerogen can be separated from the inorganic matrix in which it is trapped in the native shale. Separation and purification can be accomplished on a laboratory scale by dissolving the inorganic constituents in strong hydrofluoric-hydrochloric acid. Hydrochloric acid removes the carbonate portion of the shale and hydrofluoric acid removes the silicates and silica present in the material. This method is used to obtain relatively pure kerogen unbound from the inorganic matrix. Although useful for laboratory studies, it has not been commercially feasible. Organic solvents are unable to dissolve out the kerogen but are able to solubilize a small amount of organic material in the form of asphaltenes and bitumens. The kerogen fraction is untouched by these organic solvents.

Research on the release of useful energy-containing constituents from shale using biological methods has been directed toward two aspects of the problem: (1) solubilization of the inorganic fraction of the shale with the release of kerogen or breakdown productivity, and (2) breakdown of inorganic material with the release of usable degradation products.

SOLUBILIZATION OF INORGANIC MATRIX

Solubilization of the inorganic matrix of shale has been investigated using microorganisms which are able to produce large amounts of sulfuric acid.[1] The microorganisms used are able to oxidize elemental sulfur aerobically and produce large amounts of sulfuric acid. Sulfur is oxidized aerobically in a simple medium using carbon dioxide and ammonia in the medium as building blocks for cellular material. The energy released by the oxidation of elemental sulfur to sulfate is the energy utilized for their growth. These bacteria are able to decrease the pH of the medium from an initial value near neutrality to a value of one or less. Although the cells are relatively slow growing, the drop in pH is rapid for 8-10 days, then continues at a slow rate for several weeks (Tables 12.1 and 12.2).

Microorganisms usable for sulfuric acid production include species of *Thiobacillus* and *Ferrobacillus*. The former can oxidize sulfur to sulfuric acid and the latter can oxidize pyrite, marcasite or other sulfur compounds with production of sulfuric acid.[2] The effect upon native shale is two-fold. In addition to dissolving out the soluble inorganic components of the shale (Figure 12.1), the iron from the pyrite and marcasite

Table 12.1   pH of Inoculated Inorganic Sulfur Medium

Organism	Incubation Days								
	0	2	4	8	10	14	18	24	28
T. concretivorous	3.5	3.2	2.2	2.0	1.9	1.9	1.8	1.7	1.7
T. thiooxidans	3.5	3.2	2.1	2.0	1.7	1.8	1.7	1.7	1.7
T. thiooxidans + shale	3.5	3.2	2.2	2.5	2.8	3.3	3.4	3.5	3.5

Table 12.2   Sulfate Production in Inorganic Sulfur Medium

Organism	Incubation Days								
	0	2	4	8	10	14	18	24	28
T. concretivorous	3.4	10.5	17.5	25.6	35.7	39.2	47.3	47.0	50.2
T. thiooxidans	3.7	14.1	19.2	26.3	30.6	36.7	41.9	46.9	51.7
T. thiooxidans + shale	3.2	12.7	16.5	24.9	35.2	37.4	42.7	45.2	52.4

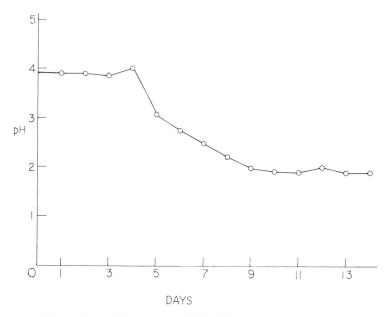

Figure 12.1   Effluent from *Thiobacillus* leaching of oil shale.

present in shale is dissolved (Figure 12.2). Thus the inorganic matrix in which the kerogen is bound can be dissolved partially by the acid. Experimentally it has been found that a 40% weight loss is obtained from ground shale leached with sufficient quantities of the acid-containing bacterial culture. (Table 12.3). About 98% of the dolomite and calcite present in the shale is dissolved by leaching. Leaching of minerals by bacterial cultures is a widely studied process.[3]

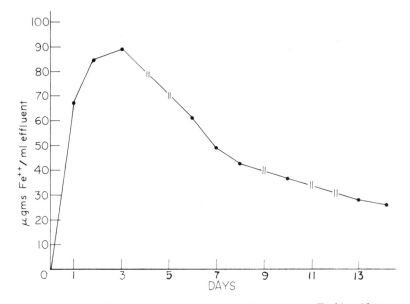

Figure 12.2 Fe^{++} release during leaching of 50 g shale by *T. thiooxidans.*

Another beneficial aspect of this type of bacterial leaching is that the organic disulfide- and polysulfide-bonded linkages, which are likely to be present in shales, also can be cleaved and utilized by *Thiobacillus.*[4] Thus, the possibility exists of desulfurization of the organic sulfur compound in oil shale by this method.

Although the extent of release of material is small, some additional loss of weight of shale leached with cultural solution of *Thiobacillus,* etc. can be attributed to the chelating agents present in the culture solution. Weathering of rocks and minerals in nature is known to be brought about by such things as citric acid and gluconic acid produced by microorganisms and released into the environment.[5]

Table 12.3　Continuous Bioleaching[a]

No.	Conditions[b]	No. Days Leached	% Wt. Loss
1	T. thiooxidans	12	36.00
2	T. thiooxidans	14	40.40
3	T. thiooxidans	14	38.20
4	T. thiooxidans	3	30.00
5	T. concretivorous	14	32.8
6	T. thiooxidans (10L) F. ferrooxidans (4L)	14	34.25
7	0.1 N H_2SO_4	14	38.46
8	1.0 N H_2SO_4	14	39.12
9	0.1 N Oxalic acid	14	23.34
10	0.1 N Citric acid	14	28.78
11	0.1 N H_2SO_4 + 0.001% EDTA[c]	14	35.14
12	T. thiooxidans heat treated	14	37.77

[a]The normality of all experiments is 0.1 N of acid; the flow rate is 1000 ml/day.
[b]The age of all cultures is 6 weeks.
[c]EDTA, Ethylenediaminetetraacetic acid.

BREAKDOWN OF KEROGEN MOLECULES

The second method attempted to release useful energy from shale involved the release of organic material from the kerogen molecule as a result of degradation by biological agents. Microorganisms capable of degrading hydrocarbons were used to look at this possibility. Cultures of *Alternaria* sp., *Aspergillum* sp., *Cladosporum* sp., and *Mycobacterium* sp. were grown in cultures in which partially purified kerogen was the exclusive energy source. Lack of significant growth in these kerogen-containing cultures but growth in media-containing hydrocarbons signifies the inability of the microorganisms to break down and use kerogen.

Cultures of microorganisms grown in hydrocarbon-containing medium were also used to leach shale in case the enzymes released into the medium would degrade the kerogen molecules in the shale.

In these experiments the shale was previously bioleached so that carbonates would be removed and the hydrocarbon-containing microorganisms would have better access to the kerogen molecule. Infrared spectrometric analysis of the organic portion of the shale indicates that no significant chemical changes were obtained by leaching with hydrocarbon-utilizing microorganisms.

In the studies with selected microorganisms not capable of utilizing hydrocarbons, there was no evidence they could be used as an energy source for growth, although detectable growth was observed in the case of three random microorganisms (Table 12.4). In the case of these three

Table 12.4   Growth +, No Growth -

Microorganism	Inorganic Medium + Shale	Inorganic Medium + Leached Shale	Inorganic Medium + Kerogen
Aspergillus clavatus	−	−	−
A. sulphureus	−	−	−
A. amstelodari	−	−	−
A. flavus	−	−	−
A. oryzae	−	−	−
A. sp.	−	−	−
A. sp.	−	−	−
A. sp. (fuel +)	−	−	±
Penicillium brevi compactum	−	−	−
P. ochro-chloron	−	−	−
P. fellutanum	−	−	−
P. sp.	−	−	−
P. sp.	−	−	−
Syncephalastrum sp.	−	−	−
Mucor sp.	−	−	−
Kernia sp.	−	−	−
Mortierella sp.	−	−	−
Gliocladium sp.	−	−	−
Phialophora sp.	−	−	−
Stachybotrys sp.	−	−	−
Stachybotrys sp.	−	−	−
Helmenthosporium sp.	−	−	−
Alternaria sp. (fuel +)	−	−	+
Curvalaria sp.	−	−	−
Monosporium sp.	−	−	−
Fusarium sp.	−	−	−
Sporotrichum sp.	−	−	−
Chrysosporium sp.	−	−	−
Cladosporium resinae (UD42)(hydrocarbon +)	−	−	−
Cladosporium resinae (UD43)(hydrocarbon +)	−	−	−
Mycobacterium vaccae (hydrocarbon +)	−	−	±
Unidentified fungus sp. (fuel +)	−	−	−

organisms, the kerogen recovered was analyzed by gas liquid chromatography and by infrared analysis for evidence of structural chemical changes, but no evidence was found. Further growth tests with these organisms failed to indicate the ability to use kerogen as an energy source.

The statement made by Davis[6] that kerogen is an organic molecule which is refractory to attack by microorganisms seems valid with respect to the microorganisms used in these studies.

CONCLUSIONS

It is indeed unlikely that kerogen molecules as such can be easily biodegraded by microorganisms. Basic structural research[7] has shown that kerogen is a complex, cross-linked, multifunctional, large, three-dimensional network (see Plate No. 16, Chapter 1). This molecule appears inaccessible to organisms without modification and fragmentation by other means. It is hopeful that a multidisciplinary, totally integrated system will aim toward the recovery of energy and resources from oil shales.[8]

ACKNOWLEDGMENT

This work was supported by NSF Grant No. GI-35683, AER-74-23797 and A. G. A. BR-48-12.

REFERENCES

1. Findley, J., M. D. Appleman and T. F. Yen. "Degradation of Oil Shale by Sulfur-Oxidizing Bacteria," *Appl. Microbiol.* 28(3), 360 (1974).
2. Leathen, W. W., S. A. Braley and L. O. McIntyre. "Acid from Certain Sulfuritic Constituents Associated with Bituminous Cell. II. Ferrous Iron Oxidizing Bacteria," *J. Appl. Microbiol.* 1, 65 (1953).
3. Karavaiko, G. I., S. I. Kruznetsov and A. I. Golomzik. "The Role of Microorganisms in Leaching Metals from Ores," *Nauk.* (Moscow) (1972).
4. Davis, A. J. and T. F. Yen. "Feasibility of a Biochemical Desulfurization Method," *Shale Oil, Tar Sands, and Related Fuel Sources,* ACS Symposium Series (Washington, D.C., American Chemical Society, 1976).
5. Duff, R. B., D. M. Webley and R. O. Scott. "Solubilizes of Minerals and Related Materials by 2-keto-gluconic Acid Producing Bacteria," *Soil Ser.* 95, 105 (1962).
6. Davis, J. B. *Petroleum Microbiology.* (Amsterdam: Elsevier, 1967).
7. Yen, T. F. "Structural Aspects of Organic Components in Oil Shale," in *Oil Shale* (Amsterdam: Elsevier, 1975), pp. 129-147.
8. Yen, T. F. "Current Status of Microbial Shale Oil Recovery," presented at Engineering Foundation on the Role of Microorganism in the Recovery of Oil, Easton, Maryland, November 1975.

13

INVESTIGATIONS OF THE HYDROCARBON STRUCTURE OF KEROGEN FROM OIL SHALE OF THE GREEN RIVER FORMATION

J. J. Schmidt-Collérus and C. H. Prien

University of Denver
Denver Research Institute
Denver, Colorado 80210

INTRODUCTION

Colorado Oil Shale of the Green River Formation contains about 16% kerogen—the insoluble organic matter. This represents about 80% of the total organic matter present. The remaining 20% soluble organic matter represents the soluble bitumen.

The problem of the nature and constitution of both kerogen and soluble bitumen and their relationship to each other is of considerable interest, both with respect to the question of the origin, genesis and geochemistry of oil shale and the problem of degradation mechanisms during pyrolysis.

This chapter discusses investigations on the structure of kerogen conducted at the Center for Fundamental Oil Shale Research of the University of Denver. Among several approaches for the structural elucidation of oil shale kerogen investigated to date, the MPGM-method developed at the Center proved most effective.

By using the combination of micro-pyrochromatography and mass spectrometry it could be shown that kerogen consists of a three-dimensional organic matrix of high molecular weight. The hydrocarbon portion of the matrix itself appears to consist of polycyclic "protokerogen" subunits or nuclei (of tetralin, terpenoid, phenanthrenoid and steroid type

183

structure) interconnected by long-chain alkanes and isoprenoids to form the three-dimensional network of the kerogen matrix. Studies on synthetic model compounds of the protokerogen type support this concept.

However, the matrix of kerogen in the conventional term also contains a substantial amount of entrapped long-chain alkanes, normal and branched fatty acids, and other uncondensed protokerogen subunits not removed by the normal extraction process. The presence of these compounds, which appear to have been overlooked, may considerably influence the results of structural investigations reported in the literature.

Morphological and physicochemical studies also indicate that Green River Oil Shale contains at least two major types of kerogen: alpha-kerogen and beta-kerogen. These are probably of different origins.

The chemical structure of the protokerogen subunits identified by macropyrolysis, chemical cleavage, and by the MPGM-method used in conjunction with reaction chromatography are described. The possible relationship between kerogen structure, the soluble bitumen and the biogenesis and geochemical origin of oil shale are discussed.

MATERIALS AND METHODS

Oil Shale Samples

Samples were taken from freshly mined raw shale of the Green River Formation that were part of a 100-ton lot from the underground room-and-pillar mine of the Colony Development Corporation in the East Middle Fork of the Parachute Creek in Colorado. The material was crushed to 1/4-in. size and riffled. Samples used for the extraction, separation and analysis experiments were ground to 100 mesh.

Extraction of Soluble Bitumen

The ground raw shale was exhaustively extracted by percolation at 50°C with a number of organic solvents, with successively increasing polarity over a period of several weeks. This was followed by treatment with acetic acid to remove inorganic carbonates and liberate any weaker acids present. The acid leached material was again exhaustively extracted with the same solvent sequence.

Concentration of Kerogen

Two methods were used for the separation of kerogen from the inorganic matrix: (1) density gradient separation and (2) chemical separation by acid leaching. The density gradient method yielded a kerogen concentrate with about 3% ash content. However, the yield was rather low. The acid leaching method gave a concentrate with about 12% ash content. This material was used during most of the preliminary investigations.

Analytical Methods

A number of different approaches were investigated for the degradation of kerogen to larger but tractable and identifiable fragments. Among these the most promising one was a combination of micropyrolysis with pyrochromatography and mass spectrometry, designated as the MPGM method. A schematic outline of this method is shown in Figure 13.1.

This controlled pyrolysis method combined with reaction chromatography and mass spectrometry was used successfully for the separation and identification of predominantly primary pyrolysis fragments. Such fragments can be identified and yield useful information for the evaluation of the structure of kerogen subunits and that of kerogen itself.

PROCEDURE

A modified "Fischer Technik" Induction Micropyrolysis instrument was used. This unit could be operated either in conjunction with a condenser unit or with a GC-MS unit consisting of a Beckman GC-4 unit and a AEI Model MS 12 mass spectrometer. The kerogen concentrate was applied to the pyrolysis needles in the form of a very thin coating. The needle was paced into a micropyrolysis chamber equipped with an injection syringe tip that was inserted into the injection port of the GC instrument or into a microcondenser unit. After ignition, the volatile material was analyzed directly by the GC-MS unit or collected in the condenser for preseparation of major fractions. To obtain sufficient material for the latter procedures, *i.e.,* GPC or microcolumn chromatography, up to 200 individual pyrolysis reactions had to be carried out. The prefractionation scheme used is shown in Figure 13.2. Some of these fractions (particularly the neutral hydrocarbon fractions) were subsequently analyzed by the GC-MS method.

Similar pyrolytic fragmentation experiments were carried out in conjunction with reaction chromatography using either selenium dehydrogenation or hydrogenation reactions. In this way, one obtains either aromatized or completely saturated derivatives of the primary pyrolysis fragments; most of them representing protokerogen moieties.

Comparison of these derivative structures with the original primary fragments using this method allows a better structural evaluation of the subunits of the hydrocarbon matrix of oil shale kerogen.

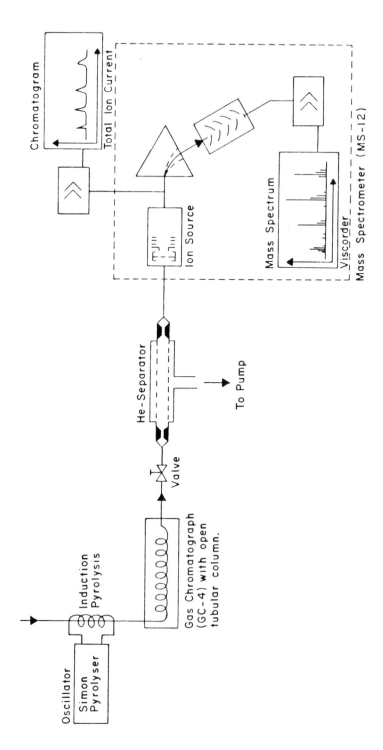

Figure 13.1 Schematic of the PGM system.

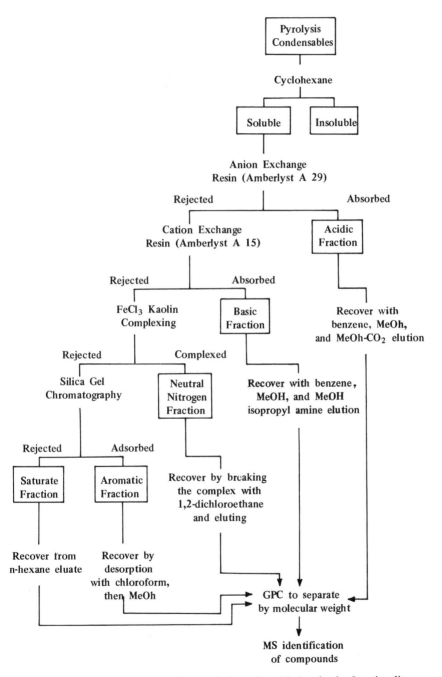

Figure 13.2 Separation procedure for pyrolysis condensable fraction by functionality.

The pyrolysis fragmentation pattern of major subunits obtained by the MPGM method and the mass spectral fragmentation patterns of a number of such subunits could be corroborated using identical or closely related synthetic reference compounds.

DISCUSSION

The results of these studies carried out over a period of several years led to the following conclusions:

1. Microscopic analysis and microspectrophotometric analysis of isolated kerogen particles indicates the presence of at least two types of kerogen components in the oil shale of the Green River Formation: the major component (designated as alpha-kerogen), represents an alginite-like material of low aromatic content; the second component is present in the form of darker reddish-brown particles (beta-kerogen) with a much higher content of aromatic (probably polycondensed) material. The latter represents about 5% of the total kerogen present.

2. Under controlled micropyrolysis alpha-kerogen yields several types of subunits: (a) normal and branched alkanes, (b) alkyl derivatives of decalins and tetralins (mostly o-substituted), and (c) alkyl substituted tricyclic terpenoid or phenanthrenoid type derivatives.

In addition, there are present a smaller number of higher molecular weight ring compounds of probably steroid origin. Some of the major subunits obtained by the MPGM method are summarized in Table 13.1.

3. From these subunits and others obtained by micropyrolysis from kerogen, one can rationalize a number of possible aspects concerning the structure of alpha-kerogen: (a) the hydrocarbon part of the kerogen appears to be relatively uniformly structured, i.e., consisting of nuclei of subunits (representing built-in protokerogen units), interlinked by normal or branched alkane bridges or long-chain ether bridges. The major part of the subunits consists of alkyl-substituted decalins or tetralins. A smaller proportion of these subunits may consist of ring systems containing heteroatoms, (b) the bulk of the skeleton is hetero-structural, i.e., several hundred different types of subunits form a three-dimensional organic matrix. However, there are repeatedly occurring predominant subunits of two- and three-membered ring-systems. These have characteristic structural features that might be very informative about the origin of the protokerogen subunits. Thus, the kerogen of the Green River Formation does not represent material of randomly connected carbon atoms (scrambled eggs) but appears to be structured, and (c) one can

Table 13.1   Principal Fragmentation Products of Kerogen Concentrate

No.	Name	Formula	Identified in Fraction
1	Aliphatic Hydrocarbons	$n\text{-}C_{10}$ to $n\text{-}C_{34}$	85-7
		$b\text{-}C_{10}$ to $b\text{-}C_{36}$	122-1
2	Alicyclic Hydrocarbons		
	Cyclohexane	$C_{10\text{-}13}\ H_{21\text{-}27}$	123-1
	Decalins	$C_{5\text{-}8}\ H_{11\text{-}17}$	123-1
3	Hydroaromatic Hydrocarbons		
	Dialkyltetralins	$C_{2\text{-}5}\ H_{5\text{-}11}$	122-1 123-1
		$C_{8\text{-}12}\ H_{17\text{-}25}$	122-1
	Hexahydro-phenanthrenes	$C_{1\text{-}3}\ H_{3\text{-}7}$ +6H	123-1
4	Dialkylbenzenes	$C_{8\text{-}13}\ H_{17\text{-}27}$	123-1
5	Dialkylnaphthalenes	$C_{3\text{-}4}\ H_{7\text{-}9}$	123-1 123-4
6	Alkylphenanthrenes	$C_{1\text{-}3}\ H_{3\text{-}7}$	121-4 123-2

make an attempt to put the principal subunits together and thus arrive at some reasonable reconstructed original structure of the kerogen molecule. From the structure of the subunits obtained, it appears that they were interlinked by di- and tri-substituted subunits. The structure of the hydrocarbon skeleton of kerogen could, therefore, be visualized by a generalized structure (Figure 13.3).

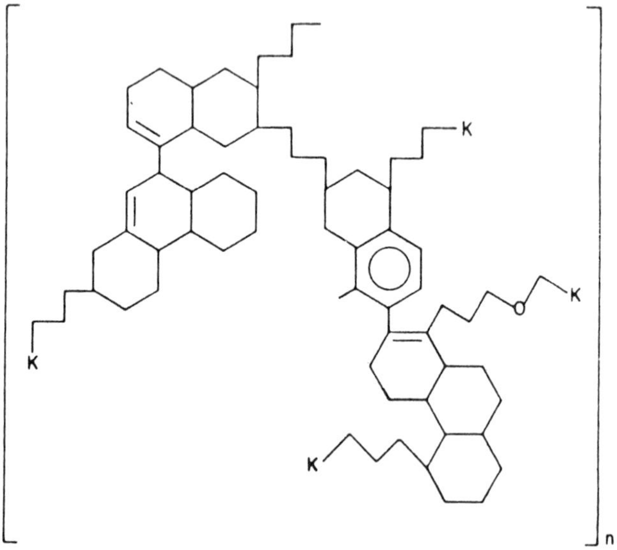

Figure 13.3 Generalized structure of kerogen of the Green River Formation.

4. A somewhat anomalous phenomenon observed in isolated kerogen concentrates provided additional information on the possible structure of kerogen. Exhaustively extracted kerogen stored under nitrogen for two years yielded, upon re-extraction with n-hexane, 5-6% of material which, upon analysis, proved to be a mixture of normal and branched saturated hydrocarbons from C_{10} to C_{25}. Since the material was stored at ambient temperature ($25°C$), it must be assumed that these hydrocarbons have diffused to the surface of the kerogen particle from the interior of the kerogen matrix. Subsequent investigations not only corroborated this assumption but also indicated that, in addition to these hydrocarbons, there are entrapped within the organic matrix a number of other residual protokerogen components such as normal and branched fatty acids, alkylcyclic acids and/or their alkyl derivatives, cyclic subunits such as alkyl derivatives of decalins and tetralins, and terpenoids. These compounds

can be extracted from the matrix if one "swells" the kerogen particle by treatment with alkaline alcoholic solutions or by heat. The entrapped fatty acids present in the matrix might explain their presence in the pyrolysate obtained under inert gas, *e.g.,* helium.

5. These experiments might indicate that these compounds could be the residual subunits from which the kerogen was formed by hetero-condensation. It can be assumed that this condensation process is still progressing, although at a very slow rate, as part of the diagenetic process; however, because of the high viscosity of the substrate and the reduced diffusion rate, the condensation reaction is strongly reduced. Thus, a more complete structure of the isolated kerogen material could be visualized as shown schematically in Figure 13.4.

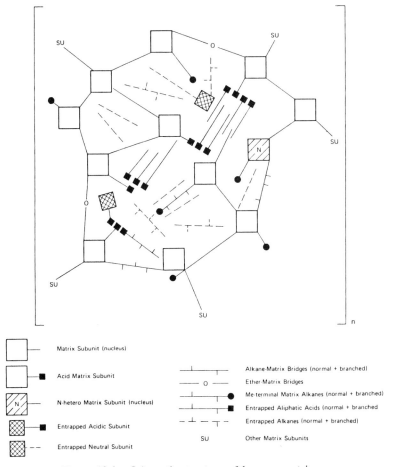

Figure 13.4 Schematic structure of kerogen matrix.

6. The entrapped material is very similar in composition to that of the soluble bitumen. The latter is diffusely distributed in the oil shale between the kerogen particles and the inorganic mineral matrix. This portion of the organic matter in the oil shale of the Green River Formation might, therefore, also represent protokerogen, containing material as yet not condensed to kerogen. Since the Green River Formation is a relatively young geologic formation, it may explain the presence of the relatively high percentage (20%) of still soluble lower molecular weight compounds in the organic matter of the oil shale.

•

14

STRUCTURAL INVESTIGATIONS ON
GREEN RIVER OIL SHALE KEROGEN

T. F. Yen

Departments of Medicine (Biochemistry),
   Chemical Engineering, and Environmental Engineering
University of Southern California
Los Angeles, California 90007

Kerogen is usually defined as the insoluble fraction of organic components of oil shale in contrast to the soluble fraction which is called bitumen.[1] Structural elucidation of kerogen is difficult due to the following: (a) kerogen is a large complex molecule belonging to the multipolymer class,[2] (b) the insoluble nature of the kerogen is closely related to the nonuniform three-dimensional gel nature of a giant cross-link network, and (c) inhomogeneity due to diagenesis. All of these have challenged a number of researchers;[3-5] so far the molecular structure of kerogen remains unsolved.

For a number of years, the writer and his associates have been engaged in the structural elucidation of bitumens. A summary of the findings has appeared in a recent review.[6] Recently he and his associates began to tackle the more complex and difficult structural problem—the structure of kerogen. The objective of this investigation is several-fold. Not only will it contribute to the genesis and origin of fossil fuels but will also provide valuable information for the production and refining of them. Elucidation of kerogen structure at the University of Southern California includes such procedures as thermal analysis,[7] stagewise oxidative cleavage,[8,9] electrolytic reaction (see Chapter 7), gas chromatography-mass spectrometry and NMR,[10] and biological consideration.[11]

EXPERIMENTAL •

A method has been developed for the structural elucidation of amorphous and mesomorphic carbonaceous organic materials.[12] It is possible to obtain a number of structural parameters from X-ray diffraction.[13]

The kerogen concentrate of Green River oil shale was obtained from W. E. Robinson of the Laramie Energy Research Laboratory. The bitumen-free sample was subjected to the usual acid leaching procedure to remove the carbonate and silicate minerals with about 10% of the ash content remaining.

The powdered sample of kerogen concentrate was packed in an aluminum holder and mounted in a goniometer. A Norelco diffractometer was used to measure the intensities ranging angularly from $2\Theta = 8$ to $100°$ (Figure 14.1).

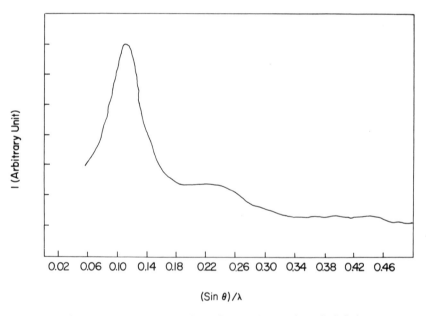

Figure 14.1 Raw data of X-ray diffraction for Green River oil shale kerogen. The intensity is in arbitrary units, but has been adjusted for polarization.

1. Adjusting the data for polarization by $(1 + \cos^2 2\Theta)/2$.
2. Fitting the data to electronic units, A, by normalization of the amplitude to the region of $0.40 \leqslant (\sin \Theta)/\lambda \leqslant 0.50$.
3. Subtracting tabulated values of incoherent scattering, C.
4. Dividing each value by the proper value (for isolated carbon atoms) of the independent coherent scattering, E.

This reduced intensity, (A-C)/E of the Green River oil shale kerogen concentrate over the angular range of (sin θ)/λ of 0.02 to 0.50 is shown in Figure 14.2.

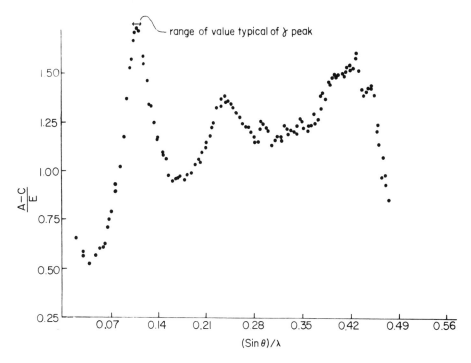

Figure 14.2 X-Ray pattern of Green River oil shale expressed in reduced intensity. The points are individual experimental comments.

RESULTS BASED ON X-RAY DIFFRACTION

For the data of kerogen in Figure 14.2 the first band in the low angle region does not appear as a doublet. The distance of the single peak centers at (sin θ)/λ = 0.11 A^{-1} definitely corresponds to a γ-band [(sin θ)/λ = 0.10 A^{-1}]. There is no peak or shoulder of the (002)-band at (sin θ)/λ = 0.14 A^{-1}. Based on this information alone, it is concluded that there are few or no aromatic carbon skeletons in the kerogen matrix. This is further substantiated by the fact that the controlled oxidation-derived products from oil shale contain no aromatic protons.[8] The low angle peak in the X-ray scan of Figure 14.2 is shifted slightly to the high-angle side (from 0.10 to 0.11 A^{-1}). This fact may indicate that in the saturated structure there may be some isolated double bonds.

The next two strong bands which center around $(\sin \theta)/\lambda = 0.25$ and 0.42 A^{-1} are generally classified as (10)- and (11)-reflections, respectively. These two bands correspond to the first and second nearest neighbors (2.1 and 1.2 A) in cyclic compounds for both aromatics and naphthenics. Because these fall in the two-dimensional reflection region, a number of theoretical calculations have been made and were available.[14,15]

The simplest procedure for comparison will be that of the profile matching. From calculated patterns of (10)- and (11)-regions, only the contour of (11)-band of the kerogen fits the saturated-ring (naphthenic) structure. The dash-dotted line (Figure 14.3) is perhydro-(a,g,h,i)-dibenzoperylene and the dash line (Figure 14.4) is perhydroanthracene (both structures are indicated). The maxima of the patterns of both saturated-ring compounds check quite well with the maximum of the pattern of the kerogen. If there is an aromatic-ring structure in the kerogen, a two- or three-unit shift in $(\sin \theta)/\lambda$ to the high-angle region would be expected. Examples are provided by the solid line in Figure 14.4, which corresponds to a polycyclic aromatic compound, anthracene and the solid line in Figure 14.3, which is also a polycyclic aromatic compound, dibenzo-(a,g,h,i)-perylene. Evidently, the pattern of aromatic compounds does not match that of the oil shale kerogen.

Another important feature for these two-dimensional patterns is the bandwidth. As the ring number increases, usually the bandwidth decreases.[12] The profile for both (10)- and (11)-bands of the kerogen do indeed correspond to a 3-ring naphthenic (dash line, Figure 14.3) better than a 7-ring naphthenic (dash-dotted line, Figure 14.4). In this instance, matching should be emphasized on the band shape (x-axis), not on the vertical y-direction since the intensities are relative. From this alone, it is plausible to conclude that the saturated clusters within oil shale kerogen are small, in the 3- or 4-ring range.

In the γ- and (002)-band region, we have failed so far to locate the sharp doublet of (110)- and (200)-bands, as these are prerequisites for wax-like long-chain alkane-containing compounds.[16] Usually these two peaks, 4.15 and 3.74 A, occur close to the γ-band in polymethylene chain-like-containing materials. These crystalline reflections exist in all pure samples of long-chain paraffins. The absence of these two bands suggests there is no free end or flexible long-chain polymethylene in the kerogen of Green River oil shale. This is supported by the fact that we have not observed any 725 cm^{-1} band, which is so characteristic of the -(CH$_2$)^n, (n > 4) structure in our infrared work, even at a lower temperature. However, one cannot rule out the possibility of condensed or isolated cycloparaffin in which the flexibility has been inhibited. Also one cannot eliminate the situation of an entrapped paraffin molecule

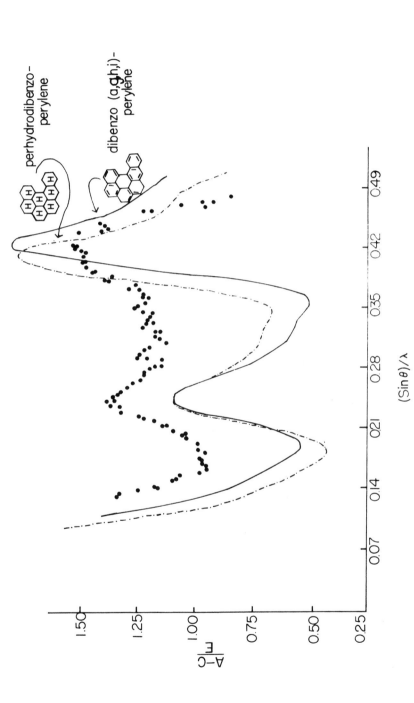

Figure 14.3 Computed two-dimensional X-ray profile of large-ring polycyclic hydrocarbons. The solid line represents the intensities of dibenzo(a,g,h,i)-perylene; the dot-dashed line represents perhydrodibenzoperylene. Experimental intensities of Green River oil shale kerogen are superimposed as dots.

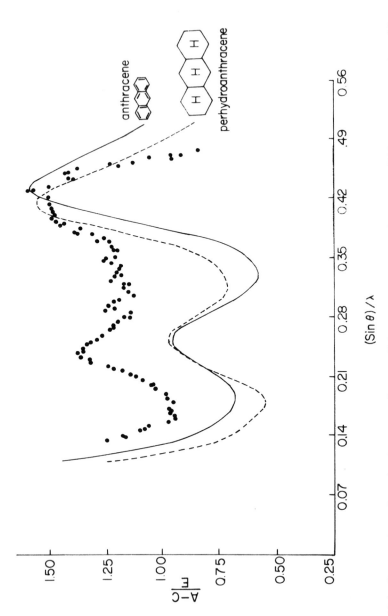

Figure 14.4 Computed two-dimensional X-ray profile of small-ring polycyclic hydrocarbons. The solid line represents the intensities of anthracene; the dashed line represents perhydroanthracene. Experimental intensities of Green River oil shale kerogen are superimposed as dots.

whose freedom is inhibited by twisting and entanglement within other saturated molecules such as a snake-cage model of polyelectrolyte.

Finally, the multiple weak peaks between the $(\sin \theta)/\lambda = 0.28$-$0.35$ A^{-1} range in Figure 14.2 of the kerogen could suggest the presence of diamond-like cross-link structures. One such example is the (102)-band of hexagonal diamond crystallite. Of course, there are also possibilities of other contaminations.

DISCUSSION AND CONCLUSION

The present X-ray diffraction method strongly supports the following features for Green River oil shale kerogen:

1. There are few aromatic carbon skeletons in kerogen. Aromaticity for this kerogen is extremely low (approaches zero). There is a possibility of the presence of isolated double-bonded carbon structure.[17]

2. The bulk of the carbon structure is naphthenic containing 3-4 rings. It is possible that these are clusters and are linked by heterocyclic atoms and short-chain bridges.

3. No free-end and flexible long-chain linear polymethylene structures are present in this kerogen. This does not rule out the possibility of the presence of the cross-link structure of elaterite[2] which could be foreseen as polymantane-like,[1] since alkyl adamantanes are easily converted by Lewis acid from a great number of precursors including steroids and terpenoids.

4. The C/O atomic ratio of kerogen is 18. The distribution of oxygen functional groups in this kerogen is predominantly of ether type (53%) and ester type (25%).[18] The cross-link sites of the structure of (2) are anticipated to be largely oxygen.

5. The age of the Eocene formation of Green River oil shale kerogen is considered to be geochemically youthful.[19] The organic diagenesis is in an early stage. Actually, the difference of bitumen versus kerogen is of degree, not of kind. The analogy is similar to the difference between asphaltenes and the insoluble carbenes and carboids in source rocks. In this sense the structure of kerogen can be reflected from the structure of bitumens.

6. The structure of kerogen is a multipolymer consisting of monomers which are the molecules so far identified from bitumen origin. These molecules in bitumen are steranes, triterpanes and isoprenoids, such as squalene, lycopene, cyclic carotenoids of C_{40}, etc.[20-23] The monomers also can be inferred when the kerogen is subjected to oxidation by aqueous permanganate.[8] In this instance the products are mono- and di-carboxylic acid homologs.

7. There is as anticipated not only the primary bonding but secondary and tertiary bonding as well. The inter- and intramolecular hydrogen bondings as well as the charge-transfer bonding play an important role. Molecular entrapment of which the molecular force is in

the van der Waals range become important. This is especially true since the nature of kerogen is comparable to a molecular sieve and can retain small molecules present in bitumens.

A HYPOTHETICAL MODEL

Based on the above findings, a hypothetical model is proposed for the structure of kerogen and its relation with bitumen (Figure 14.4).   In this scheme, the components are held or cross-linked by bridges. Major components are isoprenoids, steroids, terpenoids and carotenoids (Figure 14.5). The common bridges consist of disulfide, ether, ester,

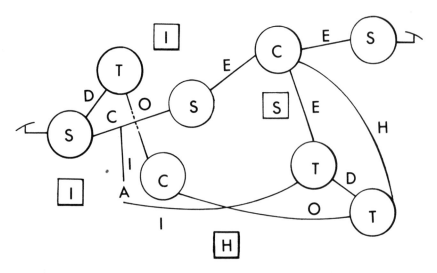

Figure 14.5   Hypothetical structural model of a multipolymer representing the organic component of Green River oil shale. The nomenclature of the components are in Figure 14.4. The circles represent essential components of kerogen. The cross-links are indicated by bridges linked among components. The squares represent molecules trapped in the kerogen network which are bitumens.

heterocyclic and alkadiene   (Figures 14.5, 14.6). The reason for inclusion of melanin as a bridge is that nitrogen-containing humic acid can be formed biochemically from oxidation of tyrosine or di-hydroxyphenyla-lanine during biostratinomy process.[24]   The inclusion of cyclo-alkadiene type of linkages is due to the identification of algal lipids, botryococcene and isobotryococcene, which have been found in torbanite.[25]   Tentative scheme of the organic shale is shown in Figure 14.3. A framework

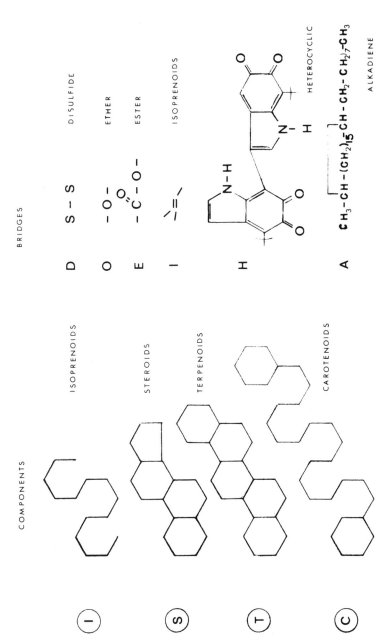

Figure 14.6 Abbreviations for the common components and bridges in the organic portions of shales.

molecular model was constructed which approximates 39 x 27 x 25 A^3. The total organics has a H/C ratio of 1.50, which compares with actual experiment value of 1.53. From the structure, kerogen is approximately $CH_{330}O_{13}N_2S_4$, which yields %C, 79.42 and %H, 9.81. The experimental analysis indicates %C, 80.5 and %H, 10.4. In this model, the bitumen is 27% of the total organic which compares with an actual case of 25%. This conceptual model is by no means the final structure of kerogen. However, it does serve as a guide of a working hypothesis toward future refinement and modification. (See Plate 16, Chapter 1, for framework model.)

ACKNOWLEDGMENT

This work is supported by NSF GI-35683 and AER-74-23797.

REFERENCES

1. Yen, T. F. "Terrestrial and Extraterrestrial Stable Organic Molecules," in *Chemistry in Space Research*, R. F. Landel and A. Rembaum, Eds. (New York: American Elsevier, 1972), pp. 105-153.
2. Yen, T. F. *Energy Sources* 1, 117 (1973).
3. Djuricic, M., R. C. Murphy, D. Vitorovic and K. Biemann. *Geochim. Cosmochim. Acta* 35, 1201 (1971).
4. Burlingame, A. L., P. A. Haug, H. K. Schnoes, and B. R. Simoneit. *Adv. Org. Geochem. Proc. 4th Int. Congr.* (Oxford: Pergamon Press, 1969), pp. 85-129.
5. Schmidt-Collerus, J. J. and C. H. Prien. *ACS, Div. Fuel Chem. Preprints* 19(2), 100 (1974).
6. Yen, T. F. *Energy Sources* 1, 447 (1974).
7. Scrima, D. A., T. F. Yen, and P. L. Warren. *Energy Sources* 1, 321 (1974).
8. Young, D. K., S. Shih, and T. F. Yen. *ACS, Div. Fuel Chem. Preprints* 19(2), 169 (1974).
9. Young, D. K. and T. F. Yen, unpublished work.
10. Young, D. K. and T. F. Yen. *Cosmochim. Geochim. Acta* in press.
11. Yen, T. F. "Structural Aspects of Organic Components in Oil Shales," in *Development in Future Energy Sources*, Vol. 1, *Oil Shale* (New York: American Elsevier, 1975), Chapter 7.
12. Yen, T. F., J. G. Erdman, and S. S. Pollack. *Anal. Chem.* 33, 1587 (1961).
13. Yen, T. F. *ACS, Div. Petrol. Chem. Preprints* 17, F102 (1972).
14. Ergun, S., W. Donaldson, and R. W. Smith, Jr. "X-ray Diffraction Data for Aromatic, Hydroaromatic, and Tetrahedral Structures of Carbon," Bull. 620, U.S. Bureau of Mines (1965).
15. Diamond, R. *Acta Cryst.* 10, 359 (1957).
16. Yen, T. F. *Nature Phy. Sci.* 233, 9-13, 36 (1971).

17. Yen, T. F. and J. G. Erdman. "Asphaltenes (Petroleum) and Related Substances: X-ray Diffraction," in *Encyclopedia of X-rays and Gamma-rays*, G. L. Clark, Ed. (New York: Reinhold Pub. Corp., 1963), pp. 65-68.

18. Fester, J. I. and W. E. Robinson. "Oxygen Functional Groups in Green River Oil Shale Kerogen and Trona Acids," in *Coal Science* (ACS, 1966), pp. 22-31.

19. Yen, T. F. and S. R. Silverman. *ACS, Div. Petrol. Chem. Preprints* **14**(3), E32 (1969).

20. Anders, D. E. and W. E. Robinson. *Geochim. Cosmochim. Acta* **35**, 661 (1971).

21. Gallegos, E. J. *Anal. Chem.* **43**, 1151 (1971).

22. Burlingame, A. L., P. Haug, T. Belsky and M. Calvin. *Proc. Nat. Acad. Sci.* **54**, 1406 (1965).

23. Ensminger, A., A. van Dorsselaer, C. H. Spyckerelle, P. Albrecht, and G. Ourisson: 6th International Meeting on Organic Geochemistry September 1973.

24. Manskaya, S. M. and T. V. Drozdova. *Geochemistry of Organic Substances.* (Oxford: Pergamon Press, 1968), p. 88.

25. Cane, R. F. "The Origin and Formation of Oil Shale," in *Development of Future Energy Sources*, Vol. 1 *Oil Shale* (New York: Elsevier Pub. Co., 1975), Chapter 3.

15

ENVIRONMENTAL IMPROVEMENTS
BY OIL SHALE LEACHING

Mohsen Moussavi and T. F. Yen

University of Southern California
Los Angeles, California 90007

GEOCHEMISTRY OF OIL SHALE

Oil shales are considered as sedimentary rocks (fine-grained) containing mineralized organics (both bitumen and kerogen) of varied composition, predominantly derived from algae, spores or pollen. The morphology of the common U.S. oil shales has been fully discussed and well illustrated by the color photomicrographs in Chapter 1 (see Plates 1-10, Chapter 1).

As the biomass such as algae and fungi becomes fossilized through biostratinomy and taphonomy process, the environment of deposition may be important in influencing the composition and structure of a particular deposition. The principal environments in which oil shale is formed are as follows: (a) large lake basins, (b) shallow seas on continental platforms and shelves, and (c) small lakes, bogs, lagoons, associated with coal-forming swamps. Each type of deposit is illustrated by particular types of shales (Table 15.1). Also the algal source may be different, due to the environment in which they originated. It is obvious that the organisms in marine deposits are different from those in lacustrine ones.

MINERALOGY OF OIL SHALES

The inorganic components of oil shales differ substantially from one to another. They may be as follows: (a) silicate-rich—quartz plus feldspar, clay opal or chert; (b) carbonate-rich—calcite or dolomite;

205

Table 15.1 Classification of Major Oil Shales

Location	Type	Age	Source
Large lake basins	Green River Formation Stanleyville Basin, Congo Albert Shale, New Brunswick	Eocene Triassic Mississippian Mississippian	Cyanophycea
Shallow seas on continental plat- form & shelves	Alaskan Tasmanite, Brooks Range Phosphoria Formation Monterey Formation Irati Shale, Brazil	Mississippian Permian Miocene Late Permian	Unknown— may be red algae
Small lakes, bogs, lagoons, associated with coal-forming swamps	NSW Torbanite Fusan, Manchuria	Devonian Tertiary	Xanthophyceae *Botryococcus* *braunii*

(c) saline-containing—saline minerals such as trona, dawsonite, halite are occasionally present; (d) sulfide containing—pyrite and other metallic sulfides and phosphatic minerals sometimes are present. Even in U.S. shales, there is quite a divergent value for the ash content (Table 15.2). Detailed analysis for a number of well-known shales of foreign origin are in Table 15.3.

Table 15.2 Ash Analysis of U.S. Oil Shales

Source	SiO_2	$Al_2O_3 + Fe_2O_3$	CaO	MgO
DeBeque, Colorado	44.7	25.6	17.7	5.3
Elko, Nevada	66.5	25.6	9.6	9.8
Uragen, Utah	45.8	16.4	33.9	7.9
Green River, Wyoming	38.9	12.4	38.3	4.9
Kentucky	52.0	19.1	12.5	8.2
Ione, California	41.0	38.1	8.7	2.5
Casmalia, California	75.8	19.1	1.4	0.9

Table 15.3 Mineralogy of Some Oil Shales (%)

Oil Shale	Ash	Mineral Matter	Amorphous Silica and Quartz	Feldspar	Clay Minerals	Gypsum CaSO$_4$	Pyrite (FeS$_2$)	Calcite (CaCO$_3$)	Magnesite (MgCO$_3$)	Siderite (FeCO$_3$)
Newness, N.S.W.	20.1	20.79	74.0	n.d.[a]	17.9	0.3	0.4	—	3.3	—
Kukersite, Estonia	36.3	47.87	9.0	6.75	13.9	1.1	4.25	56.1	—	—
Kimmeridge, Dorset	37.8	40.89	38.97	5.74	20.68	8.56	4.64	3.51	—	—
Amherst, Burma	43.9	46.78	34.33	5.63	27.45	5.49	0.19	trace	—	—
Ermeld, Transvaal	44.9	47.85	50.13	5.14	29.45	0.24	2.03	1.73	0.24	—
Boghead, Autun	65.0	79.2	32.4	n.d.	17.4	1.1	0.7	37.3	—	—
Cypris shale, Brazil	65.9	669.50	66.33	n.d.	17.13	0.78	1.24	5.25	0.62	—
Broxburn, Maine	67.4	76.15	16.55	11.30	45.85	0.43	1.76	2.91	2.63	11.24
Kohat, N.W.F.P. India	68.7	88.83	12.40	2.47	40.68	0.49	trace	22.68	8.34	3.76
Massive shale, Brazil	72.8	48.5	n.d.	37.2	37.2	0.4	1.4	2.6	1.1	—
Pumpherston I	75.0	83.45	24.6	n.d.	22.9	trace	2.35	5.8	4.15	2.15
Middle Dunnet	77.6	84.76	26.5	n.d.	54.65	0.3	0.55	4.25	3.65	—
Tasmanite, Tasmania	79.2	82.05	56.3	6.0	23.75	1.45	1.64	—	—	—

[a]n.d. = not determined

NATURE OF TRACE METALS IN OIL SHALE

Metal varies with different types of shales (Table 15.4). In aiding the study of genesis maker horizons may be set up by spectrographic analysis of the trace elements ratio mainly V/Ni, S/Ba, and Cu/Ni as a correlation of stratigraphic formation of the shale deposits.

Table 15.4   Shale Samples: Analysis by X-Ray

Element	Net Counts			
	Green River	Black	Chattanooga	Kentucky
K	2555	2346	2514	2044
Ca	23030	406	395	1124
Ti	948	3175	2999	2125
V	0	1032	218	193
Cr	0	3	0	13
Fe	83613	166500	264575	212160
Ni	0	209	0	0
Cu	692	1043	748	626
Zn	749	6703	1700	1129
Ga	0	88	126	72
Pb and As	1713	2041	2984	2920
Se	0	586	0	45
Pb L_β	301	711	391	830
Rb	5529	12472	6250	7485
Sr	54612	6877	3341	6311
Y and Rb $K\beta$	1620	5865	2829	4160
Zr and Sr $K\beta$	15713	16638	10348	12986
Mo	1264	17832	15546	14688
Al	8025	20699	14186	14936
Si	154844	248889	195071	224347
S	4165	12707	41193	33167

Trace metals in different oil shale samples of Green River Formation contain a number of heavy metals; those which influence health are summarized in Table 15.5.

NATURE OF SULFUR COMPOUNDS IN OIL SHALES

Besides a small fraction of sulfate sulfur and a more frequently distributed pyritic sulfur, the main body of sulfur in shale has organic structure. Organic sulfur is distributed among heterocyclic, aromatic and saturated hydrocarbons. The most abundant compounds in this family were

Table 15.5   Trace Metals in Oil Shale Samples (ppm)

Sample and Source	Cd	Fe	Hg	Pb
Fresh shale colony mine	1.1	13	0.1	0.04
Processed shale colony fresh pile	1.6	24	0.1	0.05
Fresh shale, 30 gal/ton Anvil Points	1.0	24	0.1	0.03
Fresh shale, high grade Anvil Points	1.8	20	0.1	0.04
Spent shale, Anvil Points	1.7	23	0.1	0.04
Mean	1.4	21	0.1	0.04
	±37	±4.7		

recently identified[1] as 2,2'-dithienyls, 2-phenylthiophenes, thionaphthenes, and thiophenes. When thiophenes in shale oil undergo hydrogenation, normal alkanes or monomethyl alkanes are obtained, which are frequently formed in shale oil. This fact suggests a reverse phenomenon of dehydrogenation to have taken place in shale oil throughout diagenetic processes. When dehydrogenation is subsequently followed by cyclization around the sulfur atom thiophenes are formed.

$$-CH_2-\underset{R}{CH}-S-\underset{CH_3}{CH}-CH_2- \xrightarrow{-2H} -CH=\underset{R}{C}-S-\underset{CH_3}{CH}-CH_2-$$

$$\downarrow -4H$$

Thiophenes can also be formed through reversible reactions with their pyrrolic and furanic analogs.[2]

$$\text{furan} + H_2S \rightleftharpoons \text{thiophene} + H_2O$$

$$\text{pyrrole} + H_2S \rightleftharpoons \text{thiophene} + NH_3$$

A good fraction of sulfur compounds is decomposed to hydrogen sulfide and removed simply by retorting processes. However, certain thiols and thiophenols resist heat treatment. Being polar they can react with basic solutions to form ionizable salts. Methylation-hydrogenation of unsubstituted thiophenes at 2-position by Raney nickel[3] can open the thiophenic rings to yield corresponding alkanes, which can be separated by catalytic cracking. Other methods, such as distillation,[4] have also been practiced to isolate the sulfur compound accompanying the shale. Generally, a combination of several of the above processes should be applied for removal of sulfur compounds from shale oil.

NATURE OF NITROGEN COMPOUNDS IN OIL SHALE

Most of the nitrogen compounds in shale oil are accumulated in the kerogen portion. This portion contains, generally, from 0.3 to 2% nitrogen.[5] The nitrogen compounds have been classified into three types: weak base, very weak base, and others, each comprising the following percentage

base nitrogen	63%
weak-base nitrogen	29%
nontitratable	8%

This classification is based on the type of ion exchange resin which retains each particular type.[6] The basic nitrogen compounds are mainly quinoline-type or as tertiary alkylamine. The weakly basic nitrogen compounds are mainly indole-type or primary and secondary alkyl amines.

Other types of nitrogen compounds that do not contain mobile hydroxyl groups such as pyrroles, tetrahydrocarbazoles, and some indoles can be identified to a lesser extent.[7]

New nitrogenous compounds are produced through isomerization, methylation and also through rearrangement by heat treatment. It was recently reported that quinolines can be produced when alkyl indoles are heated around $600°C$.[8,9] Pyrocoll, diazines, amides, nitriles and ammonia were found to be produced when kerogen porphyrins were pyrolyzed.[10] Due to formation of nitrogen oxides while burning, nitrogen oxide compounds are considered to be pollutants. Their removal can be practiced by application of a strong acid in aqueous solution. The basic nitrogen reacts with acid and remains in aqueous phase. This method was applied by using the amino salt of a strong nonvolatile inorganic acid and the separated nitrogen base was replaced by NH_4^+. Acid is released from its NH_4^+ salt and recycled.[11]

Catalytic conversion of nitrogen to ammonia in the presence of hydrogen gas has also been practiced to reduce the nitrogen content of shale oil.[12-14]

ENVIRONMENTAL ASPECTS IN FUEL UTILIZATION

The main impeditive factor in the route of shale utilization as a source of fuel is the environmental consideration regarding the problems associated with the processes of combustion. Here, emissions of sulfur dioxide and nitrogen oxides are more severe than any other types of fossil fuel. Nitrogen oxides are produced more due to their higher content of bound nitrogen.

Atmospheric nitrogen combines with air oxygen in a series of reversible reactions to form NO_x. The formation of NO_x obtains a significant rate when temperature is approximately 1500°C. However, oxidation of bound nitrogen takes place at lower temperatures. Nitrogen dioxide has not been proved to be harmful to the health of human beings if its concentration is kept below 0.1 ppm. However, its side effects are of more significance. Nitrogen dioxide is very absorptive of ultraviolet energy, which, through a photolysis process, decomposes to yieldrreactive free radicals.

The cyclic sequence of these chain reactions enable NO_2 in the atmosphere to become fairly stable and a continuous source of production of other oxidants such as ozone and atomic oxygen.

$$NO_2 \longrightarrow NO^\circ + O^\circ$$
$$\uparrow NO^\circ \qquad \downarrow O_2$$
$$O + NO_2{}^\circ \longleftarrow O_2{}^\circ + NO$$
$$\downarrow \qquad + O^\circ$$
$$O_3$$

The atmospheric analysis of O_3 and nitrogen oxides accords with the above scheme (Figure 15.1).[15] A nitrogen dioxide radical is also postulated to be responsible for formation of other oxidants such as peroxyacetylnitrate (PAN),

$$CH_3-CH{=}CH_2 + O^\circ \rightarrow CH_3-\overset{\overset{\text{O}}{\|}}{C}-O-O^\circ$$

$$CH_3-\overset{\overset{\text{O}}{\|}}{C}-O-O^\circ + NO_2{}^\circ \rightarrow CH_3-\overset{\overset{\text{O}}{\|}}{C}-O-O-NO_2$$

a larger extension of the diagenetic process in these materials. Mono-, di- and polysulfide bonding can generally be found in the organic portion of the

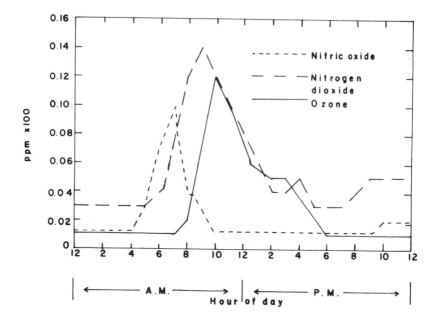

Figure 15.1   Correlation of nitrogen oxides and ozone in atmosphere.

shale;[16]   also, pyritic sulfur is in the shale mass.   Regardless of its chemical nature in oil shale, it seems that sulfur content is more in the organic extract of shale than in equivalent coal.[17]   Thus, the sulfur problem is more severe in shale oil than that in coal, if this oil is considered as a fuel.

ENVIRONMENTAL PROBLEMS WITH OIL RECOVERY

The morphological structure of the oil shales is the result of deposition of minerals generated when equilibrium in the chemical environment of an aquatic system was disturbed.   The deposits are intersticed by biotic metabolites that have undergone an extensive series of diagenetic reactions.   The whole network has gained an anisotropic appearance which is severely directional.   This feature facilitates the formation of microscopic fractures in the minerals'phase.   The interstitial organic phase can expectedly absorb the forces applied by the fractured layers through movement processes that they make.   This phenomenon is responsible for the migration of an organic layer, which is still under the above forces, through the fractured planes to adjoint the close organic layer.   Consequently, an equilibrated distribution of forces is achieved with a mortar-like continuum of the organic phase.

The tendency of minerals to fracture and their ability to generate such a continuum as mentioned above, depends on the magnitude of the pressures coming from the upper layers and, different types of lateral forces, which may be generated through geologic processes. These elements cover a wide range of magnitudes and as a result leave behind an absolutely non-uniform structure so that both cases of a dispersing inorganic phase in a dispersant mineral matrix and a dispersing inorganic phase in a dispersant organic mortar appear to be equally common.

Because of this particular structure, any model representing internal flow patterns of fluids will be heavily pore size-dependent. The methods used thus far are unanimously based on destructive distillation principles where the pressure generated by formation of hot gaseous mixtures in the organic phase causes fractures in the minerals network, which in turn facilitates the outflow of liquefied organic compounds. Obviously, the required temperature for the achievement of these reactions is controlled by the physical constants of average thermal conductivity of the rock, and magnitude of pressure drop inserted against the flow through the formation. A close linear proportionality exists between the pressure drop and the porosity of the formation.

The extent of exposure of organic compounds to high temperature is also another factor which depends on the above physical constants. The high temperature and long duration of exposure to high temperatures can both be detrimental to the organic content of the shale. This shortcoming not only downgrades the quality of the oil, but also causes the formation of a series of compounds that might be harmful to human health.

The volatile fraction of a shale oil, which has been produced by dry distillation at 932°F, causes damage to the respiratory system in the concentration of 0.5 mg/l. Chronic inhalation of a 10 mg/l dilution causes damage in the other regulatory organs, such as spleen and supra-renal glands. When nonvolatile compounds of oil shale undergo further heat treatment processes in lower temperatures, volatile compounds are produced that present no noticeable abnormalities under identical conditions.[18]

There are indications that there is a correlation between the 3,4-benzopyrene concentration in the oil shale soot and the temperature at which shale oil was initially recovered.[19,20] The carcinogenic as well as mutagenic effects of this chemical on the bronchial mucosa and lung respiratory tissue are well known. It seems that phenolic compounds in the shale oil is another factor responsible for the generation of irregularities in certain parts of respiratory system. Dominant lethal mutation has also been observed by the carboxylic acids content in the vapors of the shale oil. The concentration of 3,4-benzopyrene can increase by three orders of magnitude in retorting conditions.[21]

ENVIRONMENTAL PROBLEMS WITH
WASTES DISPOSAL

The liquid and solid wastes produced in a shale oil recovery process must be completely stabilized prior to disposal. Incomplete stabilization of wastes can cause contamination of underground waters and translocation of waste components by the plants growing in the area and the animals and birds that live on those plants. It has been proven that the root and epigeal parts of plants absorb titanium, strontium, lead, barium and nickel from soil mixed with spent shale.[22]

Dolomitic calcium and magnesium in spent shale are dissolved away by rainwater saturated with carbon dioxide to mix with underground waters. Other minerals and elements can leach away by processes such as dissolution, dispersion, and chelation. Any calculation applied to formulate the underground formation is associated with an unavoidable degree of failure risk. This type of failure is also as damaging as other types. An unpredicted permeable formation at the bottom of an oil-producing sand caused salt water springs to suddenly spout in a nearby surface.[23]

In a series of experiments, a shale sample was treated with chelants.[24] It was found that a 0.57% aqueous solution of ethylenediaminetetracetic acid (EDTA) sodium salt dissolved 100 times more iron from the sample than pure water under identical conditions. The above agent leached also between 10 and 30 times more Ca, Mg, and Na. Even water-insoluble polycyclic aromatic hydrocarbons have been shown to get into the water systems by forming stable emulsions. These effects can drastically change the quality of such waters.

The unremoved organic compounds left in the spent shale provide a source of contamination to the soil and atmosphere. The carbonized char formed through retorting by an incomplete combustion process is an active site for adsorption of molecules of oxygen which, through slow processes, may produce SO_2 and other obnoxious compounds. Unless retorting is substituted by other processes that are less damaging environmentally, or is modified, advancement in industrial oil shale production will not be considerable.

If heat is designed to do the task of oil recovery, the two factors that can affect the process are thermal conductivity and the porosity and permeability of the rock, which could be manipulated to ease the task. Little can be done to increase the thermal conductivity of the rock; however, it has been demonstrated that an increase in permeability and porosity of the rock by several orders of magnitude is achievable through certain chemical reactions. If the process of increasing the permeability and porosity is properly done, not only a major decline in heat supply can be obtained but also the thermal degradation of oil will be considerably less extensive.

On the average, about 40% of the shales is composed of carbonaceous minerals such as dolomite and calcite.[25] This fraction can be attacked by any mineral acid in the pH range below 3. Experiments have shown that treatment of samples with sulfuric or hydrochloric acid solution can produce a weight loss of up to 15% of the raw shale within a few hours. This level of weight loss corresponds to an increase in permeability of approximately three orders of magnitude (Figure 15.2). Further experiments have proved that such treated shale produces the same yield when thermally treated about 50°C lower.

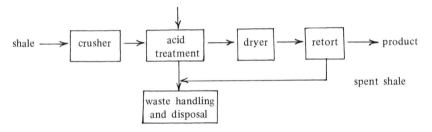

Figure 15.2 Treatment to increase the porosity.

Apparently this treatment generates a volume of liquid and solid wastes which, overall, is slightly more than that in untreated processes. However, the nature of these wastes is different. They can be expected to be more refractory. Being exposed to retorting temperature in a shorter period of time, the thermal degrading reactions such as thermocracking and aromatization-polymerization processes will develop to a lesser degree.

The following chemical reactions characterize the treatment

$$GaCO_3 + H_2SO_4 \rightarrow CaSO_4 + CO_2 + H_2O$$

$$MgCO_3 + H_2SO_4 \rightarrow MgSO_4 + CO_2 + H_2O$$

If the geometry and the design of the treatment vessel are selected properly so that stagnant zones are prevented and a minimum space velocity is maintained, calcium sulfate can be separated in a separate tank before it clogs up the pore sites of the shale (Figure 15.3).

$$CaSO_4 + 1/2\ H_2O \xrightarrow{k_1} CaSO_4 \cdot 1/2\ H_2O$$

$$CaSO_4 + 2\ H_2O \xrightarrow{k_2} CaSO_4 \cdot 2\ H_2O$$

In this tank, soluble magnesium sulfate is also precipitated out by addition of lime:

$$MgSO_4 + Ca(OH)_2 \rightarrow Mg(OH)_2 + CaSO_4 \cdot 2H_2O$$

Sulfuric or hydrochloric acid can be supplied by an outside source.

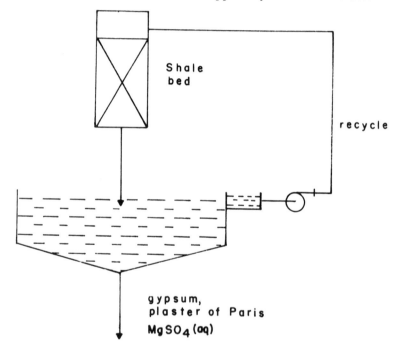

Figure 15.3   Separation of Ca and Mg.

In a series of simulated experiments,[15] raw shale was treated with a solution of sulfuric acid with the initial concentration of 0.25 molarity. The space velocity of the solution was maintained around 0.15 sec^{-1}. With the geometry of the column utilized in the experiments, the flow was entirely laminar (N_{Re} = 0.395). In spite of the great risk of formation of stagnant zones in the packed bed, no considerable precipitation of calcium sulfate was observed in pore sites.

The cumulative dissolution rate of calcium and magnesium ions generally follows the pattern in Figure 15.4. Considering the total amount of available calcium and magnesium in the original sample, it seems that

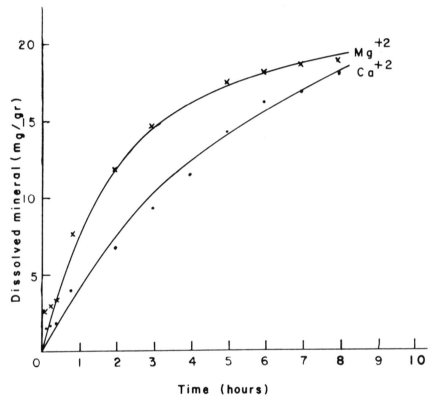

Figure 15.4   Dissolution of Ca.

dissolution of magnesium takes place in a faster and more complete way. However, when the temperature is raised for 25°C the rate of dissolution of calcium increases noticeably. The reaction also goes to a more complete degree (Figure 15.5). The slow flow of calcium sulfate out of the grain pore sites may be due to early nucleation of calcium sulfate precipitate, which generates a drag against the flow of nucleates in the bulk. If this hypothesis is true, the nucleates should redissolve when they enter the main recipient. However, such a process was not observed. Other unsupported speculations have been suggested, but further analysis of the collected data is yet to be done to establish a sound basis.

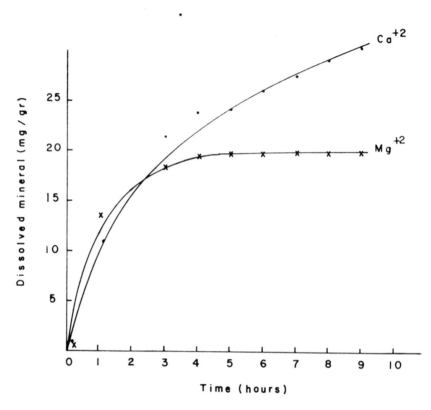

Figure 15.5   Dissolution of Ca and Mg in shale by H_2SO_4 at $t=50°C$.

If we assume that the carbonaceous minerals matrix is a continuous phase then a close linear correlation can be expected to exist between the degree of weight loss and the increase in porosity. This correlation has been proved to exist[26] when the carbonaceous minerals matrix is removed from organic-free oil shale by acid leaching.

The contribution of carbonaceous minerals in generation of porosity and permeability due to heat seems trivial at retorting temperature. According to Jukkola et al.,[27] the dolomite in oil shale begins to decompose somewhat below 1050°F while the calcite begins to decompose from 1150-1200°F. Generally, thermal treatment of oil shales for organics recovery takes place below 950°F.

CONCLUDING REMARKS

The effect of minerals leaching prior to retorting or any other processes utilized for recovery of organics from oil shales is multifunctional. A considerable decrease in required retorting temperature may be obtained by leaching. Formation of certain polycondensed aromatic compounds, which are known to be hazardous to health, will be retarded or totally eliminated.

The volume of liquid and solid wastes left behind by shale oil industries is considerably high. If the leaching step is also taken, it will become higher. However, since the nature of waste is environmentally more refractive, it is preferred.

The leaching of carbonaceous minerals matrix may be considered a conditioning step that introduces further capital investments and further operations costs. There are indications that higher yield and other advantages would make the process economically feasible. There seems to be no difficulty in adapting this conditioning step to any of the processes including *in situ* and *ex situ*, which exist today.

ACKNOWLEDGMENT

This work is supported by NSF GI-35683, AER-74-23797 and A.G.A. GR-48-12.

REFERENCES

1. Pailer, M. and H. Gruenhaus. *Monatsh. Chem.* **104**(1), 312 (1973).
2. Yur'ev, Yu. K. *Ber.* **69B**, 444 (1936).
3. Blicke, F. F. and D. G. Sheets. *J. Amer. Chem. Soc.* **71**, 4010 (1949).
4. Kinney, I. W., Jr., J. R. Smith, and J. S. Ball. *Anal. Chem.* **24**, 1749 (1952).
5. Mapstone, G. E. *J. Proc. Roy. N. S. Wales* **82**, 71 (1948).
6. Poulson, R. E., H. B. Jensen, and G. L. Cook. *ACS Preprints, Div. Fuel Chem.* (March 1971), p. A49.
7. Koros, R. M., *et al.* *ACS Preprints, Div. Petrol. Chem.* **12**(4), B165 (1967).
8. Jacobsen, I. A., Jr. *Bureau of Mines* **RI-7529** (1971).
9. Jacobsen, I. A., Jr. and H. B. Jensen. *Bureau of Mines* **RI-6720** (1966).
10. Mapstone, G. E. *J. Proc. Roy. Soc. N.S. Wales* **82**, 91 (1948).
11. McKinnis, A. C. U.S. 2,518,353 (August 8, 1950).
12. Benson, D. B. and L. Berg. *Chem. Eng. Prog.* **62**(8), 61 (1966).
13. Matu, D. *Chem. Eng. Prog. Symp. Ser.* **61**(54), 68 (1965).
14. Montgomery, D. P. *Ind. & Eng. Chem. Prod. Res. & Dev.* **7**(4), 272 (1968).

15. "Air Quality Criteria for Photochemical Oxidants," National Air Pollution Control Administration, Pub. No. AP-63.
16. Smith, J. W. *Anal. Chem.* **36**(3), 618 (1964).
17. Dinneen, G. U., *et al. Chem. Eng. Prog. Symp. Series* **64**, 15 (1968).
18. Key, M. M. "Statement in Oil Shale Technology Hearings," U.S. House of Representatives, HR 9693, May 1974.
19. Hueper, W. C. and H. J. Cahnmann. *AMA Arch. Path.* **65**, 608 (1958).
20. Hueper, W. C. *AMA Arch. Indust. Hyg. Occ. Med.* **8**, 307 (1953).
21. Schmidt-Collerus, J., F. Bonomo and C. H. Prien. 167th National Meeting, *ACS Div. Fuel Chem.* **19**(2), 115 (1974).
22. Alekseeva-Popova, N. V. *Bot. Zh. Leningrad.* **55**(9), 1304 (1970).
23. Evans, D. M. Presented at 135th Meeting of Am. Assoc. Adv. Sci., Dallas, Texas, 1968.
24. Moussavi, Mohsen, unpublished work.
25. Yen, T. F. and G. V. Chilingar. in "Oil Shale," *Development of Future Energy Sources* (New York: Elsevier, 1975), Chapter 1.
26. Tisot, P. R. *J. Chem. Eng. Data.* **12**(3), 405 (1967).
27. Ellis, C. *The Chemistry of Petroleum Derivatives.* (New York: Reynolds, 1937), p. 49.

INDEX